W9-BRZ-517

Garfield
POTBELLY OF GOLD

BY JIM DAVIS

ATTENTION PARTY ANIMALS!
Check out the
TOP 50 REASONS TO PARTY!
on page 48

Ballantine Books • New York

JESSAMINE COUNTY PUBLIC LIBRARY
600 South Main Street
Nicholasville, KY 40356

A Ballantine Books Trade Paperback Original

Copyright © 2010 by PAWS, Inc. All rights reserved.
"GARFIELD" and the GARFIELD characters are trademarks of PAWS, Inc.

Published in the United States by Ballantine Books, an imprint of The Random House Publishing Group,
a division of Random House, Inc., New York.

BALLANTINE and colophon are registered trademarks of Random House, Inc.

ISBN 978-0-345-52244-3

Printed in China

www.ballantinebooks.com

9 8 7 6 5 4 3 2

Watch. Read. Shop. Play.

DON'T FORGET THE SNACKS!

garfield.com

✳ **The Garfield Show**
An all-new animated TV show on Cartoon Network!
Watch FREE episodes online!

✳ **The Comic Strip**
Search & read thousands of GARFIELD® comic strips!

✳ **Garfield on Facebook & Twitter**
Read daily posts from Garfield. Share photos
and connect with other Garfield fans!

✳ **Shop all the Garfield stores!**
Original art & comic strips, books, apparel, personalized products, & more!

✳ **Play FREE Garfield games!**
Plus, buy Garfield apps & games for your iPhone or iPod touch.

the GARFIELD show

BURP
GARFIELD®
© 2007 PAWS, INC. All Rights Reserved.
JIM DAVIS 3-4
www.garfield.com
PLOP
Distributed by Universal Press Syndicate
Kitty Treats

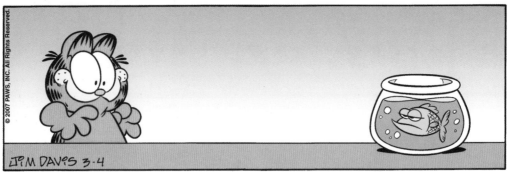

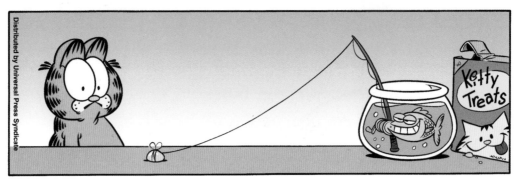

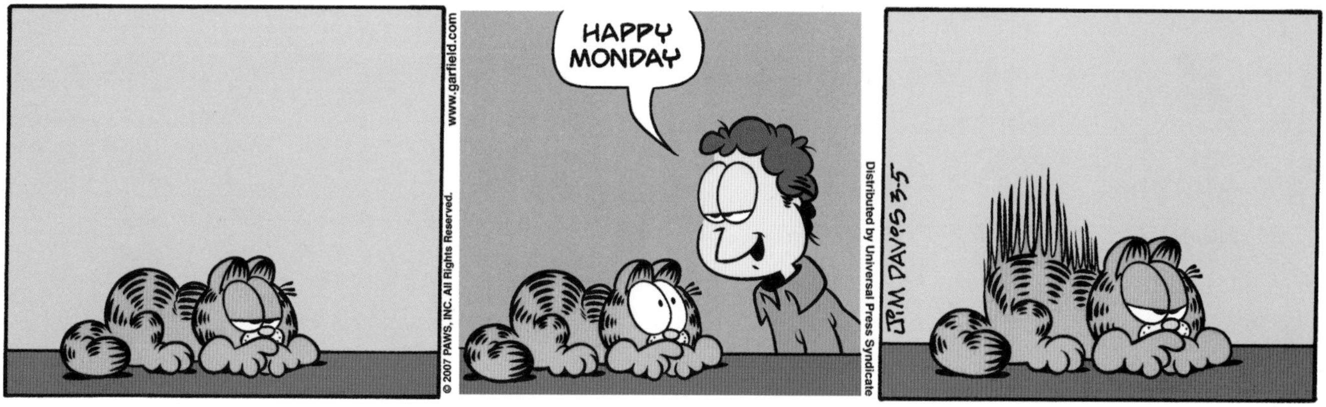
© 2007 PAWS, INC. All Rights Reserved. www.garfield.com
HAPPY MONDAY
Distributed by Universal Press Syndicate
JIM DAVIS 3-5

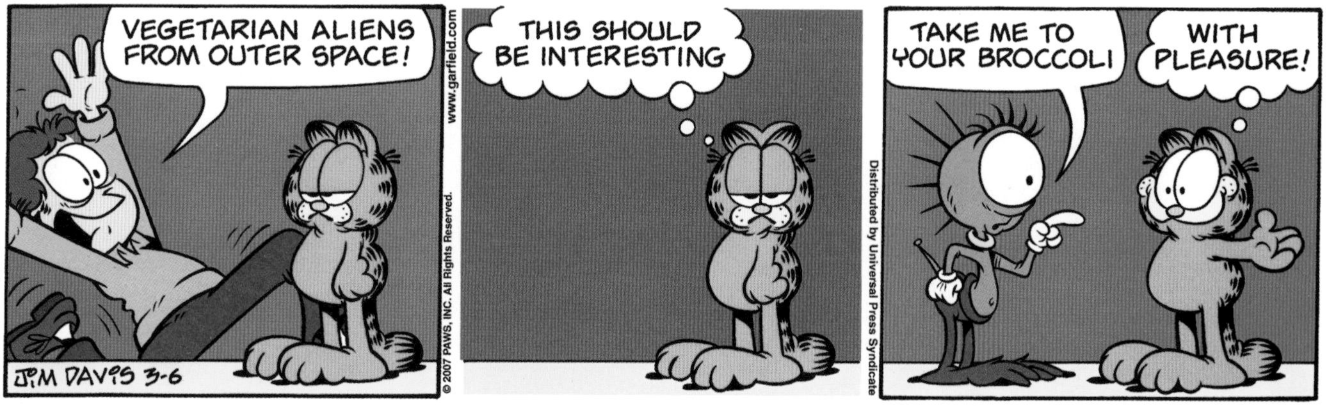
VEGETARIAN ALIENS FROM OUTER SPACE!
JIM DAVIS 3-6
© 2007 PAWS, INC. All Rights Reserved. www.garfield.com
THIS SHOULD BE INTERESTING
Distributed by Universal Press Syndicate
TAKE ME TO YOUR BROCCOLI
WITH PLEASURE!

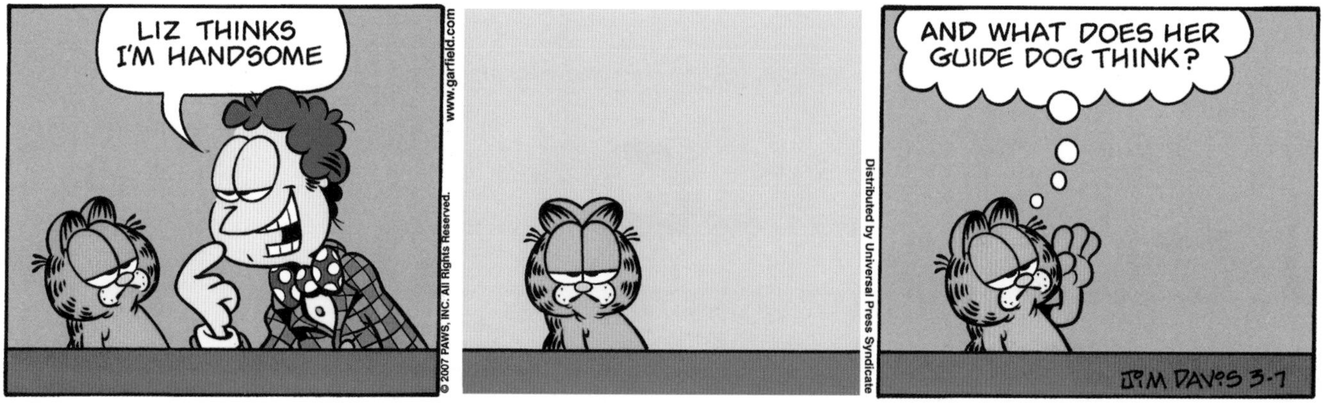
LIZ THINKS I'M HANDSOME
© 2007 PAWS, INC. All Rights Reserved. www.garfield.com
Distributed by Universal Press Syndicate
AND WHAT DOES HER GUIDE DOG THINK?
JIM DAVIS 3-7

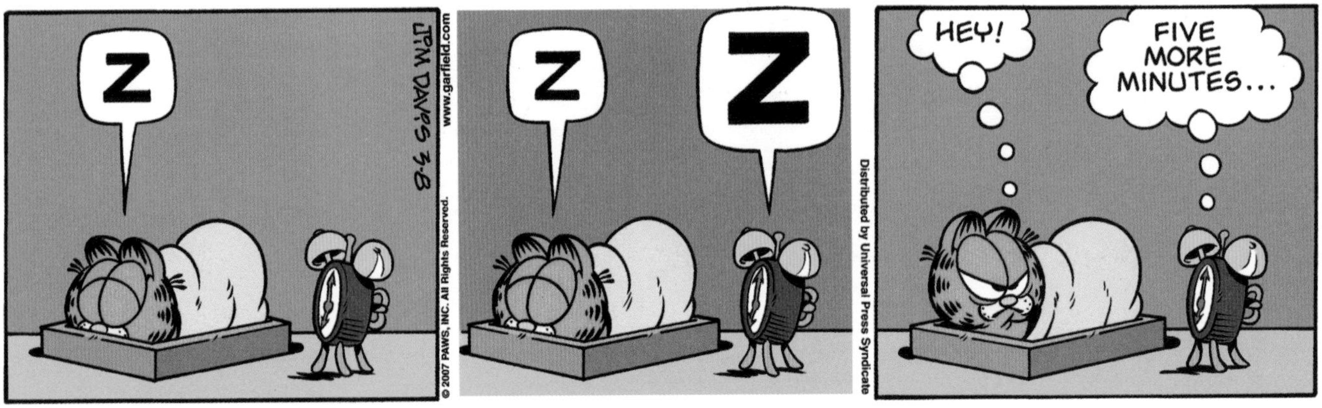
Z
Z
Z
HEY!
FIVE MORE MINUTES...
JIM DAVIS 3-8
www.garfield.com
© 2007 PAWS, INC. All Rights Reserved.
Distributed by Universal Press Syndicate

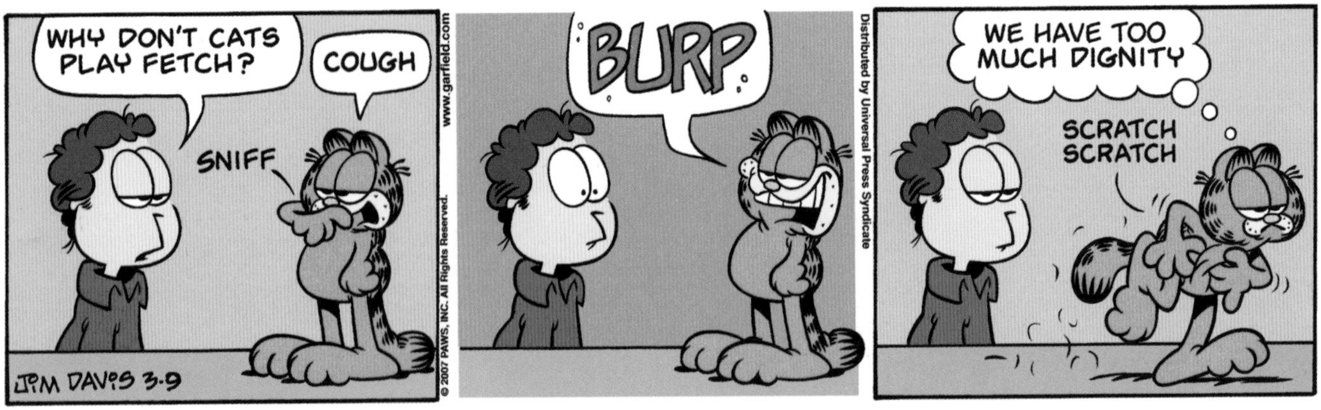
WHY DON'T CATS PLAY FETCH?
COUGH
SNIFF
BURP
WE HAVE TOO MUCH DIGNITY
SCRATCH SCRATCH
JIM DAVIS 3-9
www.garfield.com
© 2007 PAWS, INC. All Rights Reserved.
Distributed by Universal Press Syndicate

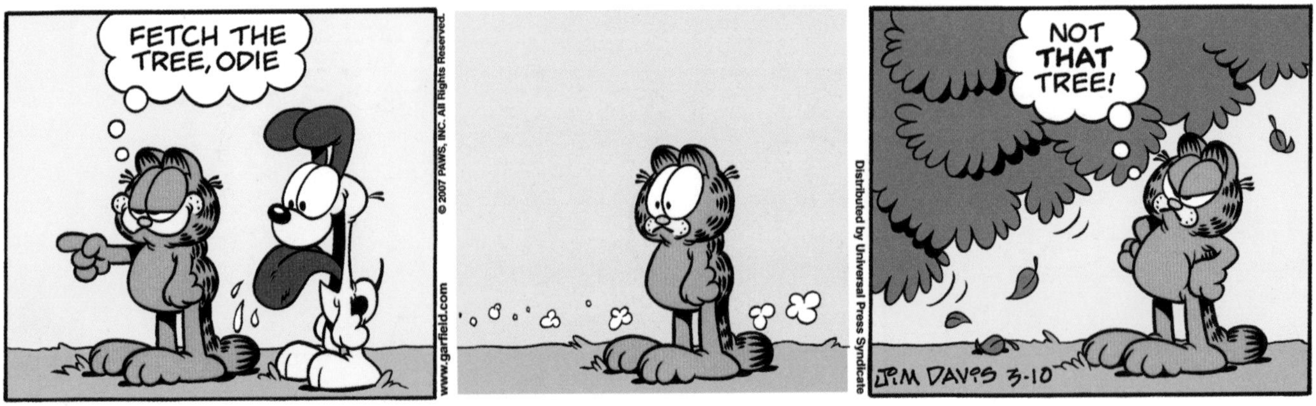
FETCH THE TREE, ODIE
NOT THAT TREE!
JIM DAVIS 3-10
www.garfield.com
© 2007 PAWS, INC. All Rights Reserved.
Distributed by Universal Press Syndicate

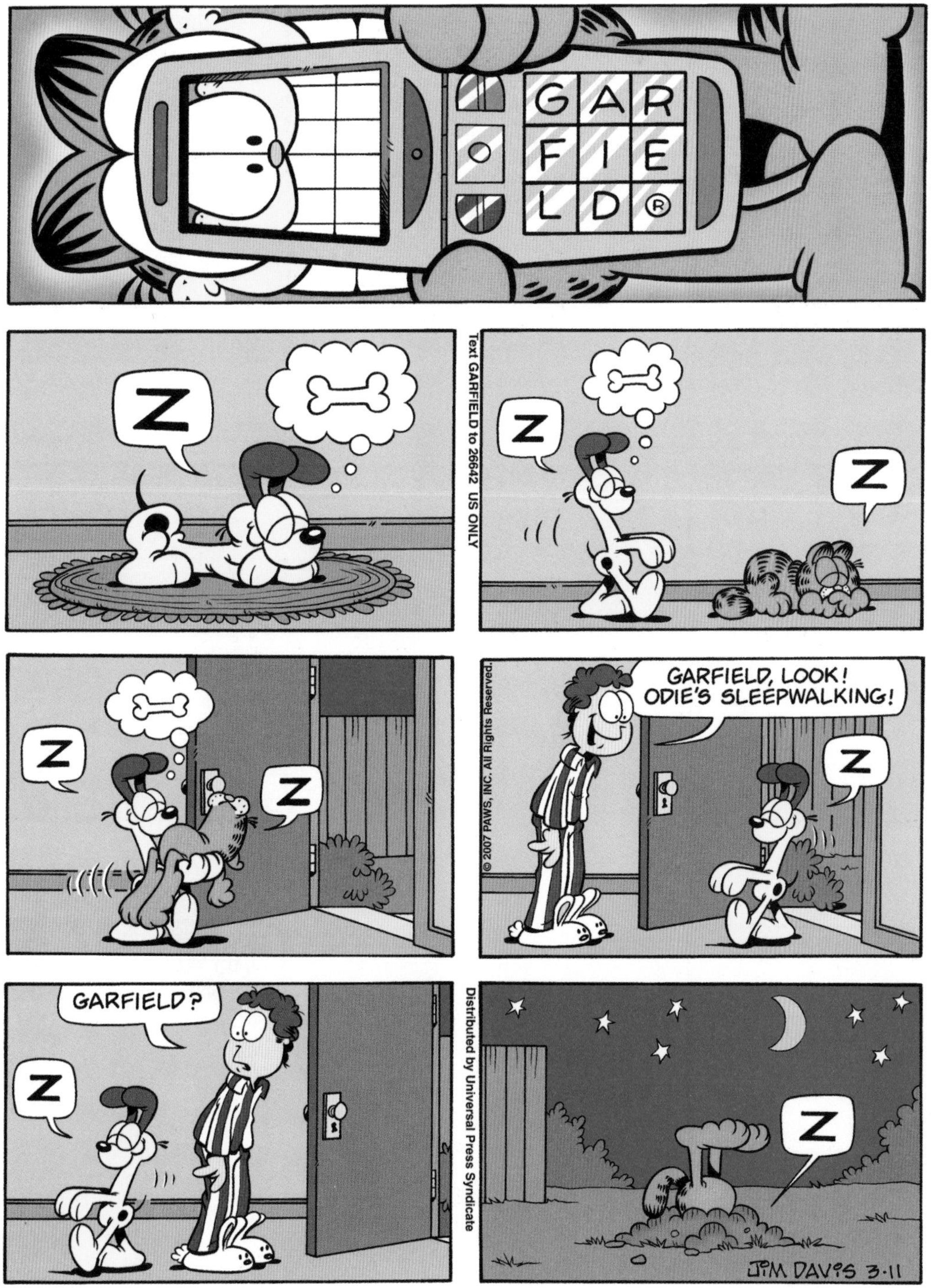
GARFIELD®
Text GARFIELD to 26642 US ONLY
Z
Z
Z
Z
Z
© 2007 PAWS, INC. All Rights Reserved.
GARFIELD, LOOK! ODIE'S SLEEPWALKING!
Z
GARFIELD?
Z
Distributed by Universal Press Syndicate
Z
JIM DAVIS 3·11

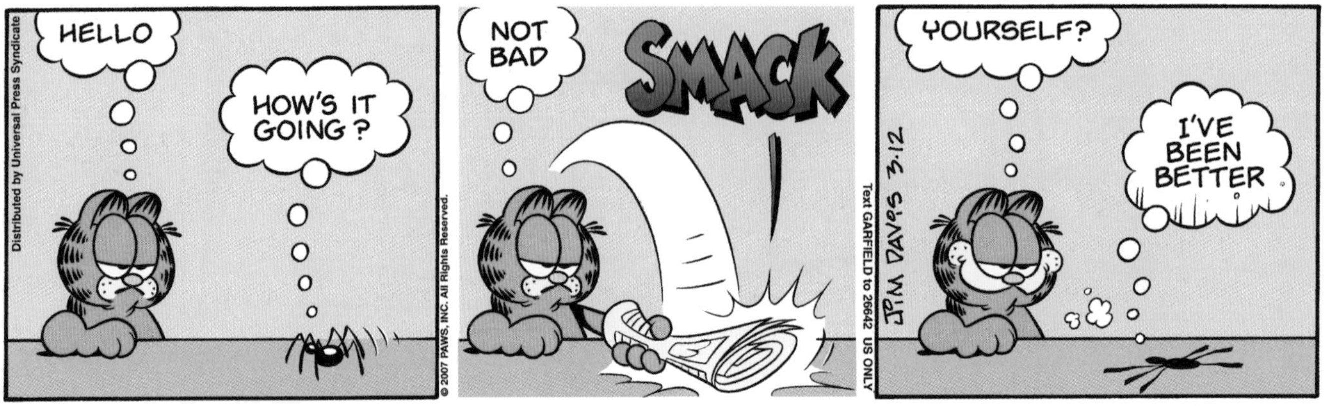
HELLO
HOW'S IT GOING?
NOT BAD
SMACK
YOURSELF?
I'VE BEEN BETTER
JIM DAVIS 3-12
Distributed by Universal Press Syndicate
© 2007 PAWS, INC. All Rights Reserved.
Text GARFIELD to 26642 US ONLY

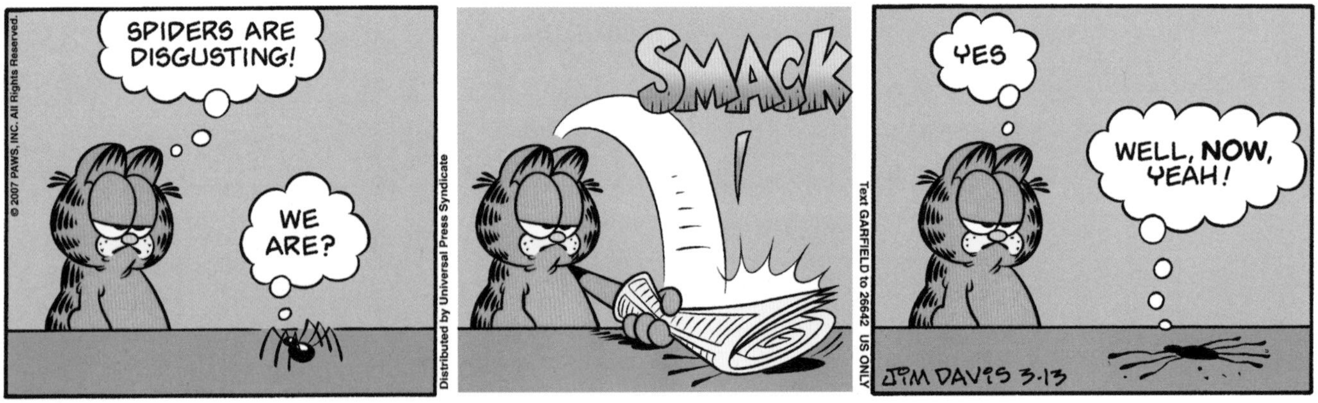
SPIDERS ARE DISGUSTING!
WE ARE?
SMACK
YES
WELL, NOW, YEAH!
JIM DAVIS 3-13
© 2007 PAWS, INC. All Rights Reserved.
Distributed by Universal Press Syndicate
Text GARFIELD to 26642 US ONLY

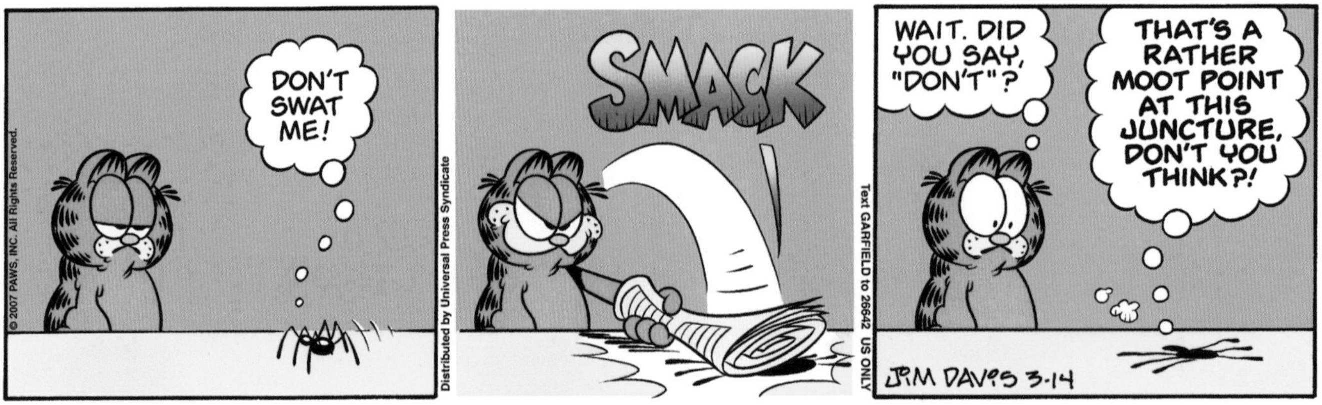
DON'T SWAT ME!
SMACK
WAIT. DID YOU SAY, "DON'T"?
THAT'S A RATHER MOOT POINT AT THIS JUNCTURE, DON'T YOU THINK?!
JIM DAVIS 3-14
© 2007 PAWS, INC. All Rights Reserved.
Distributed by Universal Press Syndicate
Text GARFIELD to 26642 US ONLY

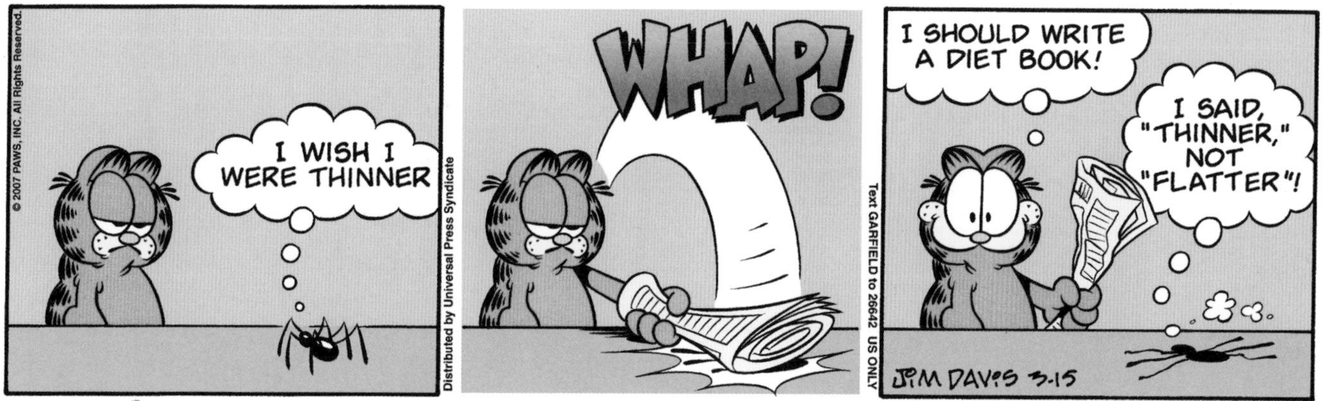

© 2007 PAWS, INC. All Rights Reserved.
I WISH I WERE THINNER
Distributed by Universal Press Syndicate
WHAP!
Text GARFIELD to 26642 US ONLY
I SHOULD WRITE A DIET BOOK!
I SAID, "THINNER," NOT "FLATTER"!
JIM DAVIS 3-15

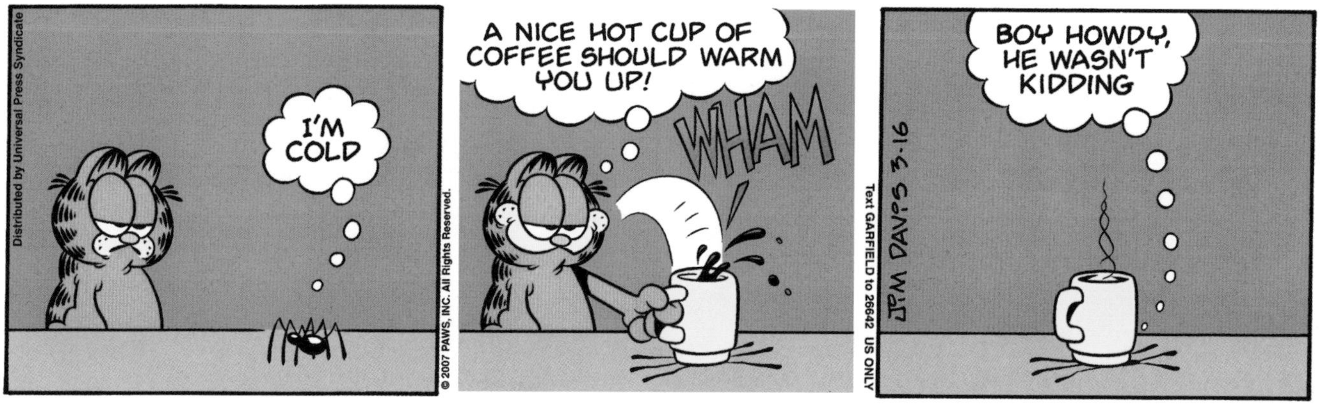

Distributed by Universal Press Syndicate
I'M COLD
© 2007 PAWS, INC. All Rights Reserved.
A NICE HOT CUP OF COFFEE SHOULD WARM YOU UP!
WHAM
Text GARFIELD to 26642 US ONLY
JIM DAVIS 3-16
BOY HOWDY, HE WASN'T KIDDING

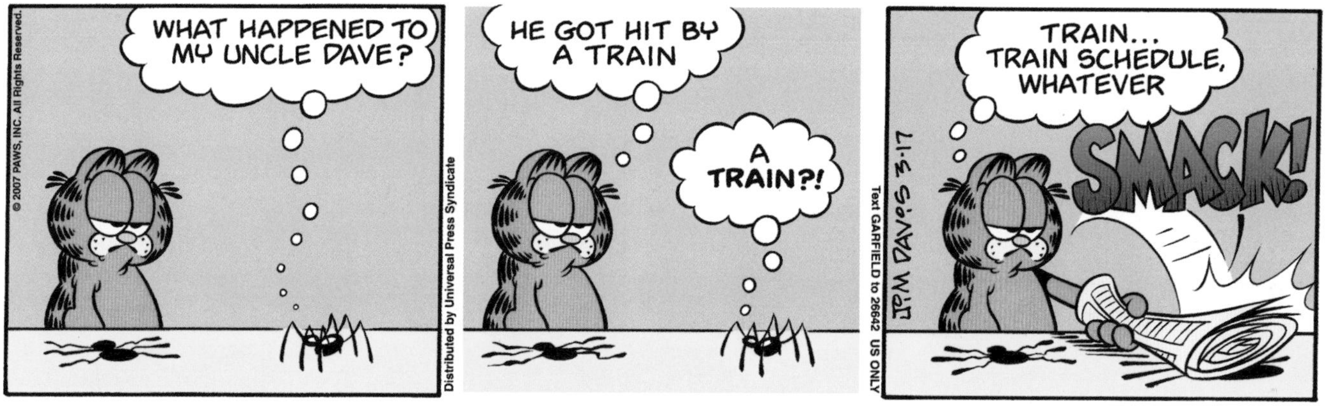

© 2007 PAWS, INC. All Rights Reserved.
WHAT HAPPENED TO MY UNCLE DAVE?
Distributed by Universal Press Syndicate
HE GOT HIT BY A TRAIN
A TRAIN?!
Text GARFIELD to 26642 US ONLY
JIM DAVIS 3-17
TRAIN... TRAIN SCHEDULE, WHATEVER
SMACK!

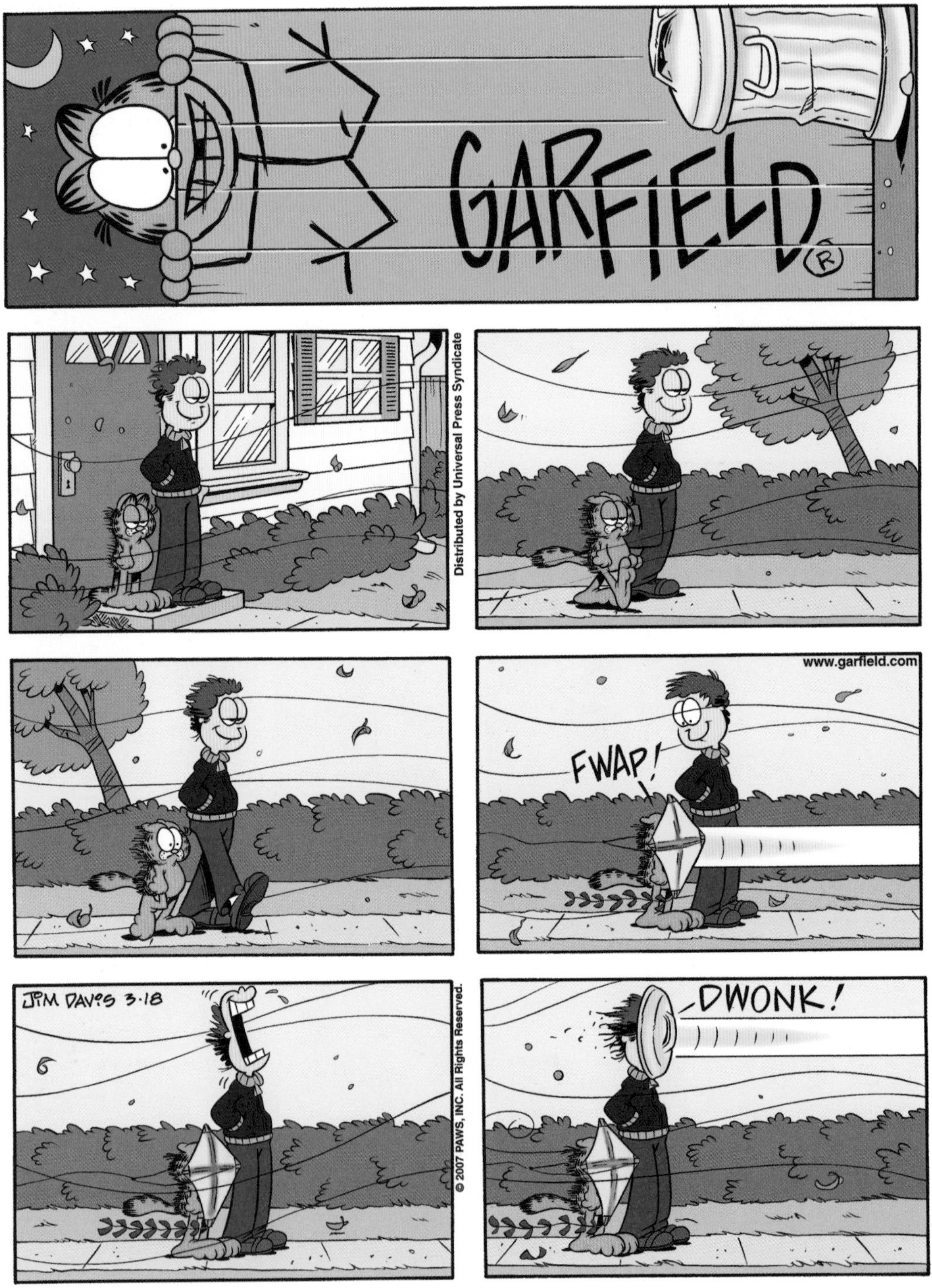
GARFIELD®
Distributed by Universal Press Syndicate
www.garfield.com
FWAP!
JIM DAVIS 3-18
© 2007 PAWS, INC. All Rights Reserved.
DWONK!

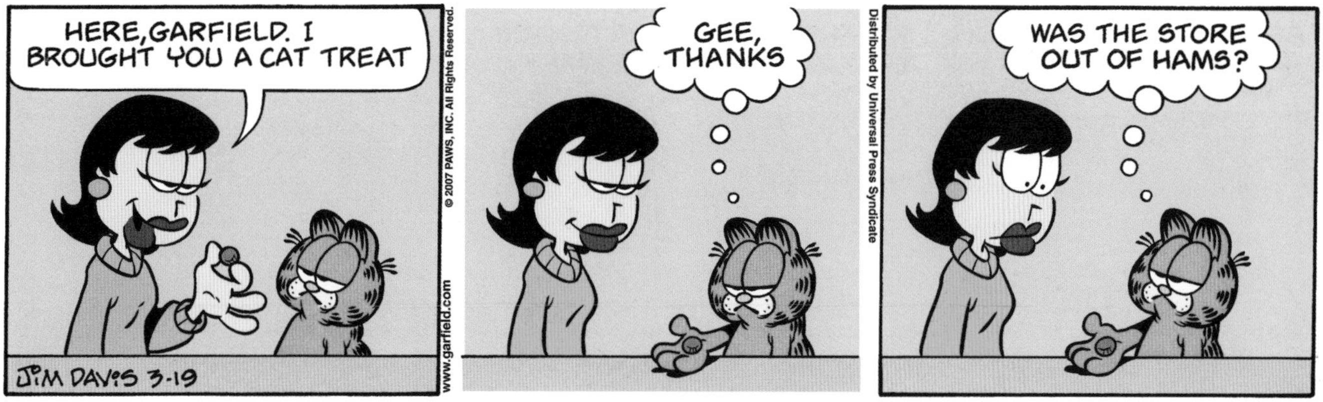
HERE, GARFIELD. I BROUGHT YOU A CAT TREAT
JIM DAVIS 3-19
© 2007 PAWS, INC. All Rights Reserved.
www.garfield.com
GEE, THANKS
Distributed by Universal Press Syndicate
WAS THE STORE OUT OF HAMS?

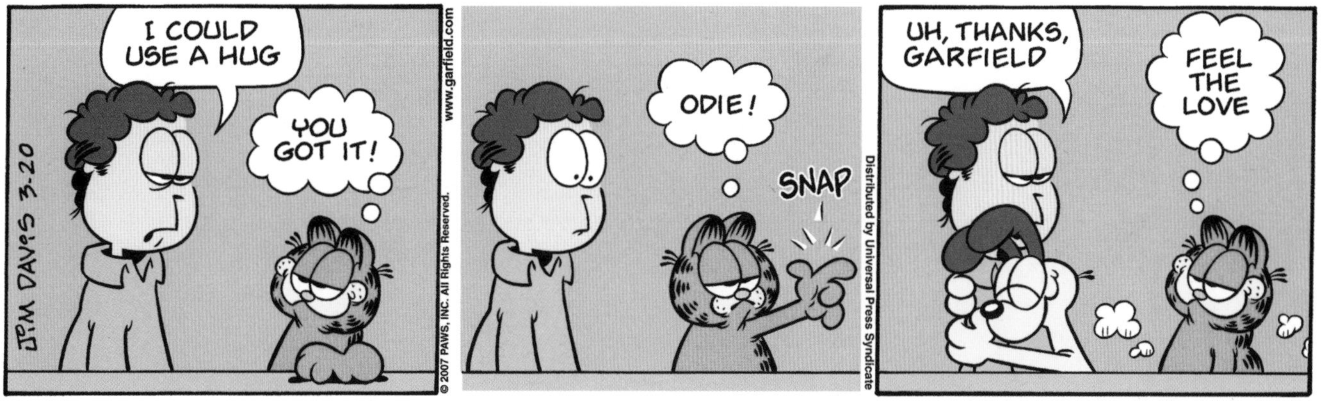
I COULD USE A HUG
YOU GOT IT!
JIM DAVIS 3-20
www.garfield.com
© 2007 PAWS, INC. All Rights Reserved.
ODIE!
SNAP
Distributed by Universal Press Syndicate
UH, THANKS, GARFIELD
FEEL THE LOVE

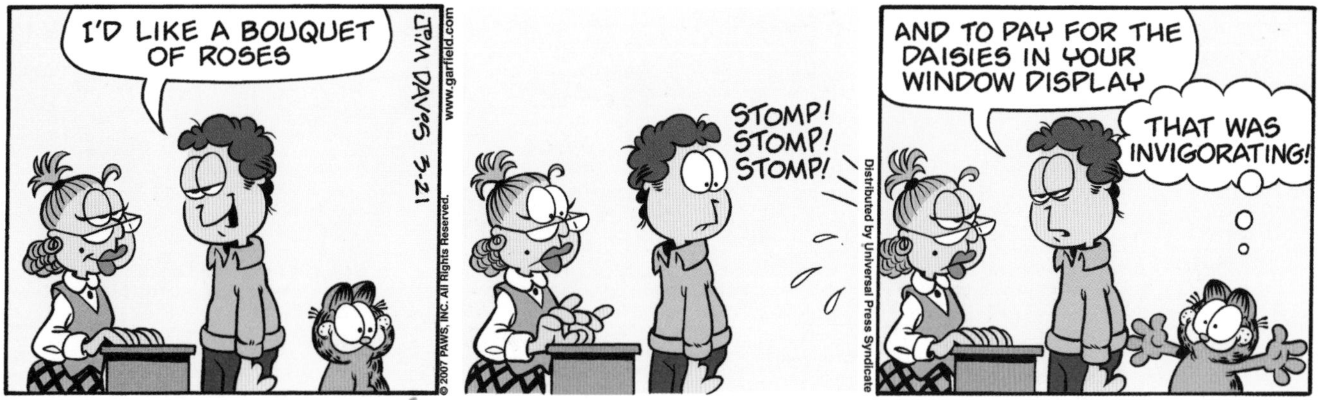
I'D LIKE A BOUQUET OF ROSES
JIM DAVIS 3-21
www.garfield.com
© 2007 PAWS, INC. All Rights Reserved.
STOMP! STOMP! STOMP!
Distributed by Universal Press Syndicate
AND TO PAY FOR THE DAISIES IN YOUR WINDOW DISPLAY
THAT WAS INVIGORATING!

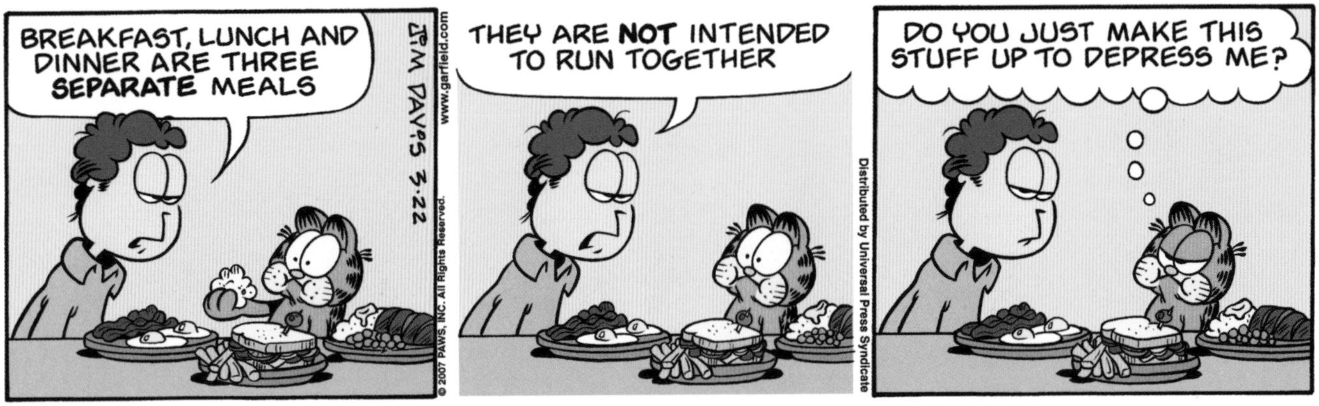
BREAKFAST, LUNCH AND DINNER ARE THREE SEPARATE MEALS
JIM DAVIS 3.22
www.garfield.com
© 2007 PAWS, INC. All Rights Reserved.
THEY ARE NOT INTENDED TO RUN TOGETHER
Distributed by Universal Press Syndicate
DO YOU JUST MAKE THIS STUFF UP TO DEPRESS ME?

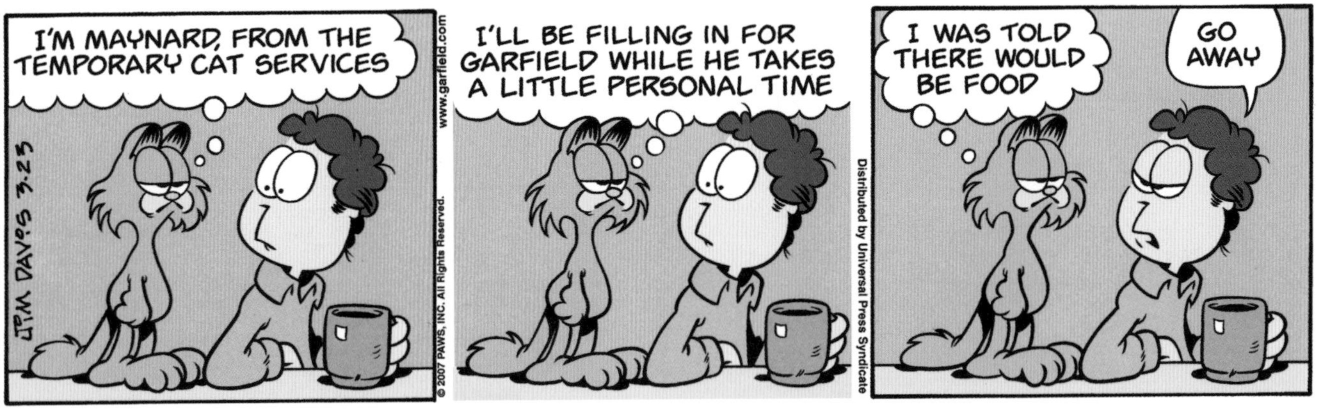
I'M MAYNARD, FROM THE TEMPORARY CAT SERVICES
JIM DAVIS 3.23
www.garfield.com
© 2007 PAWS, INC. All Rights Reserved.
I'LL BE FILLING IN FOR GARFIELD WHILE HE TAKES A LITTLE PERSONAL TIME
Distributed by Universal Press Syndicate
I WAS TOLD THERE WOULD BE FOOD
GO AWAY

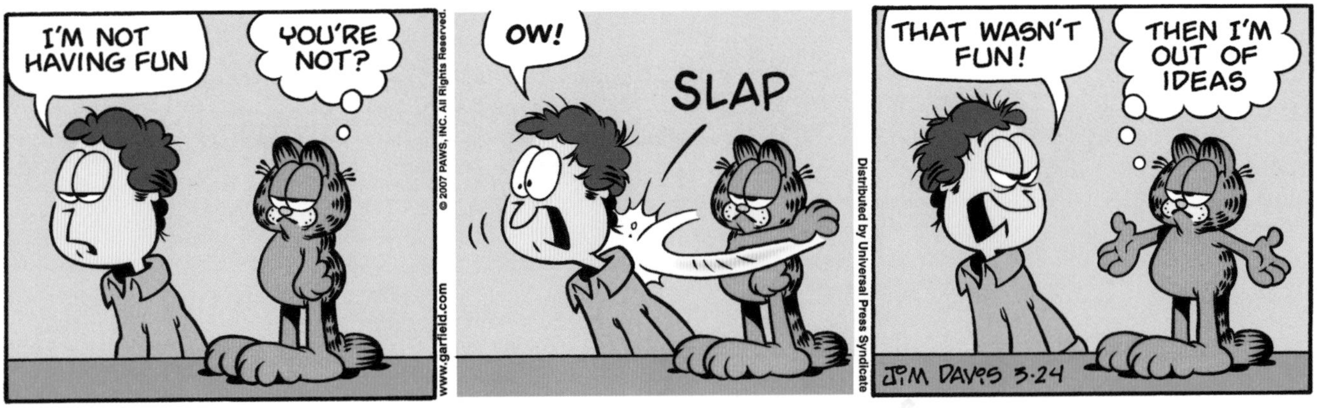
I'M NOT HAVING FUN
YOU'RE NOT?
© 2007 PAWS, INC. All Rights Reserved.
www.garfield.com
OW!
SLAP
Distributed by Universal Press Syndicate
THAT WASN'T FUN!
THEN I'M OUT OF IDEAS
JIM DAVIS 3.24

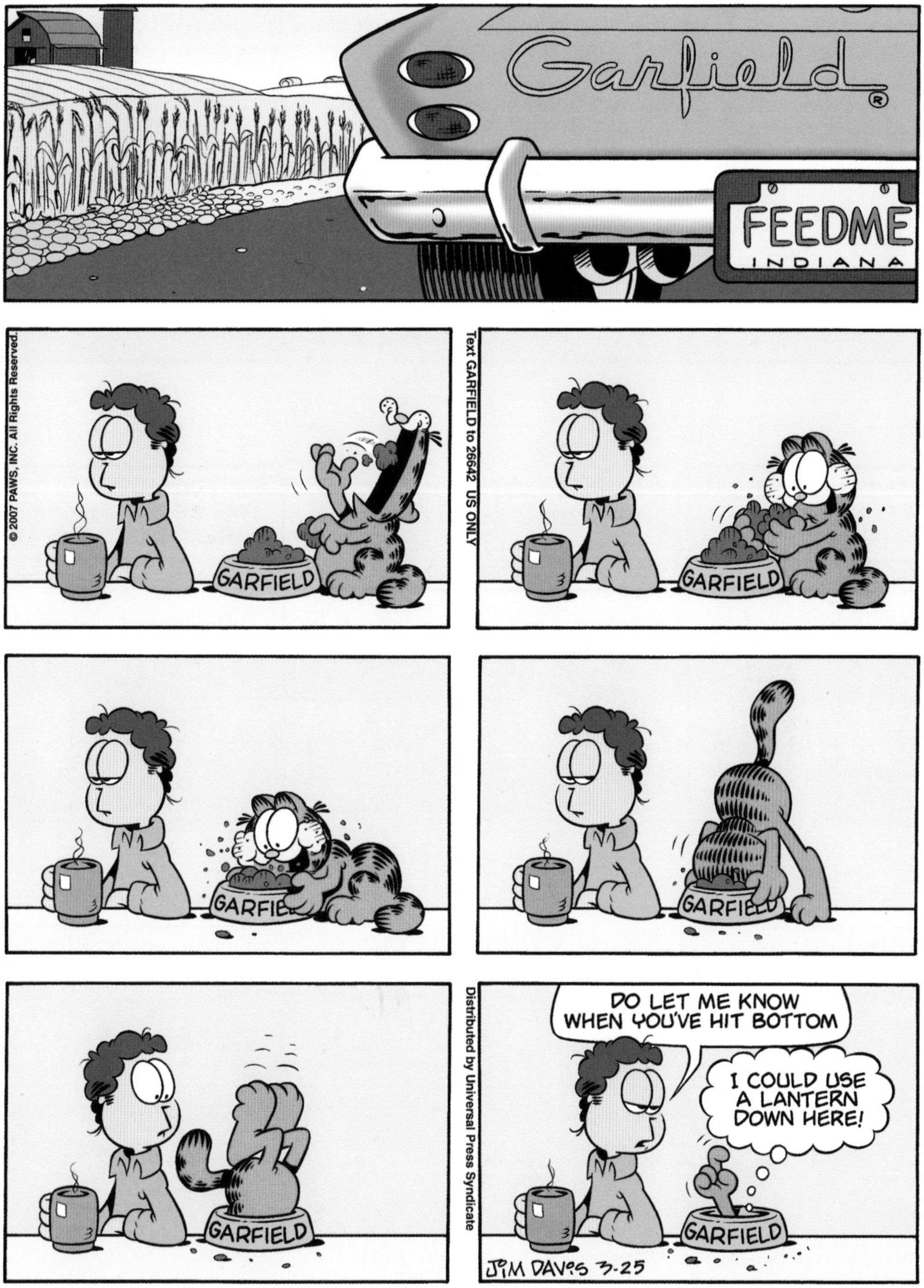
Garfield
FEEDME
INDIANA
© 2007 PAWS, INC. All Rights Reserved.
Text GARFIELD to 26642 US ONLY
GARFIELD
GARFIELD
GARFIE
GARFIEL
GARFIELD
Distributed by Universal Press Syndicate
DO LET ME KNOW WHEN YOU'VE HIT BOTTOM
I COULD USE A LANTERN DOWN HERE!
GARFIELD
JIM DAVIS 3-25

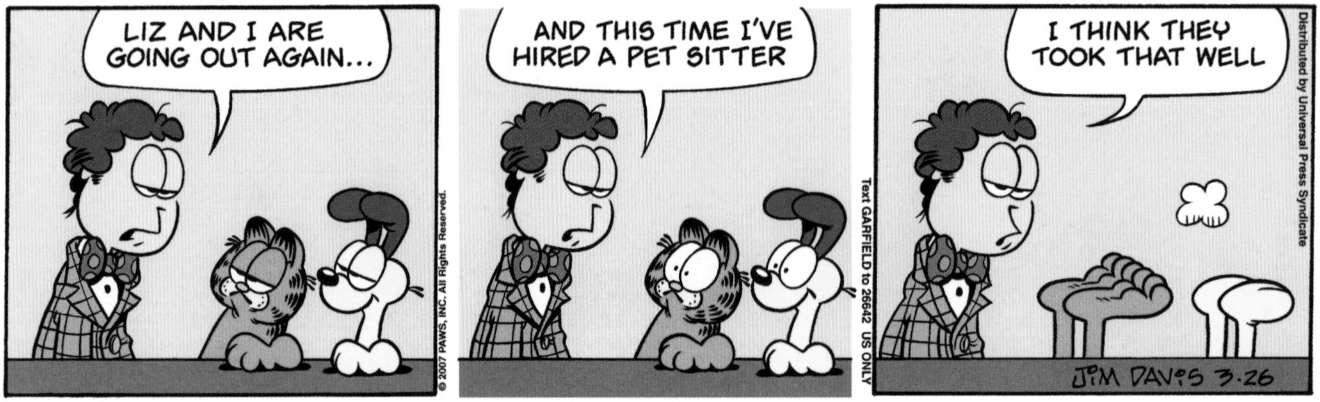
LIZ AND I ARE GOING OUT AGAIN...
AND THIS TIME I'VE HIRED A PET SITTER
I THINK THEY TOOK THAT WELL
JIM DAVIS 3-26
© 2007 PAWS, INC. All Rights Reserved.
Text GARFIELD to 26642 US ONLY
Distributed by Universal Press Syndicate

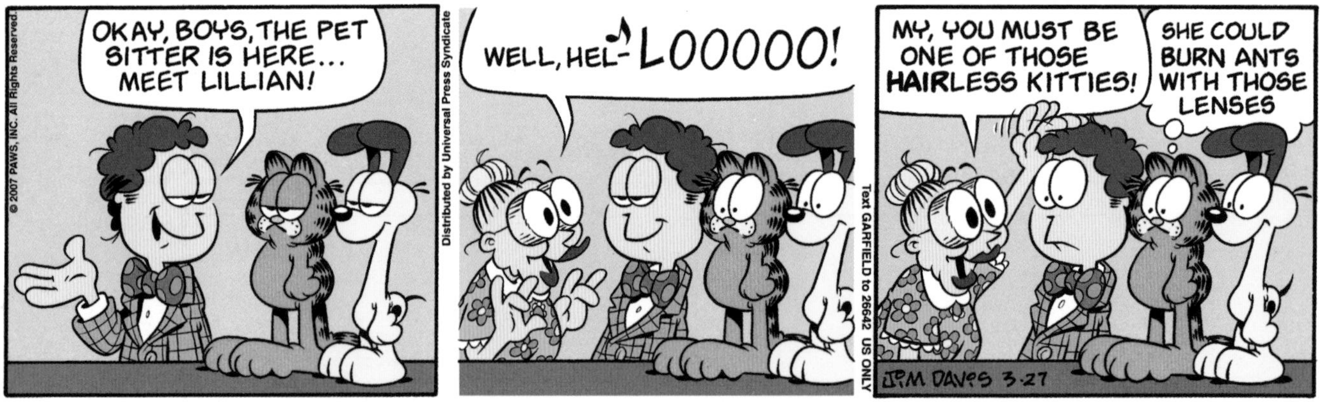
OKAY, BOYS, THE PET SITTER IS HERE... MEET LILLIAN!
WELL, HEL-LOOOOO!
MY, YOU MUST BE ONE OF THOSE **HAIR**LESS KITTIES!
SHE COULD BURN ANTS WITH THOSE LENSES
JIM DAVIS 3-27
© 2007 PAWS, INC. All Rights Reserved.
Distributed by Universal Press Syndicate
Text GARFIELD to 26642 US ONLY

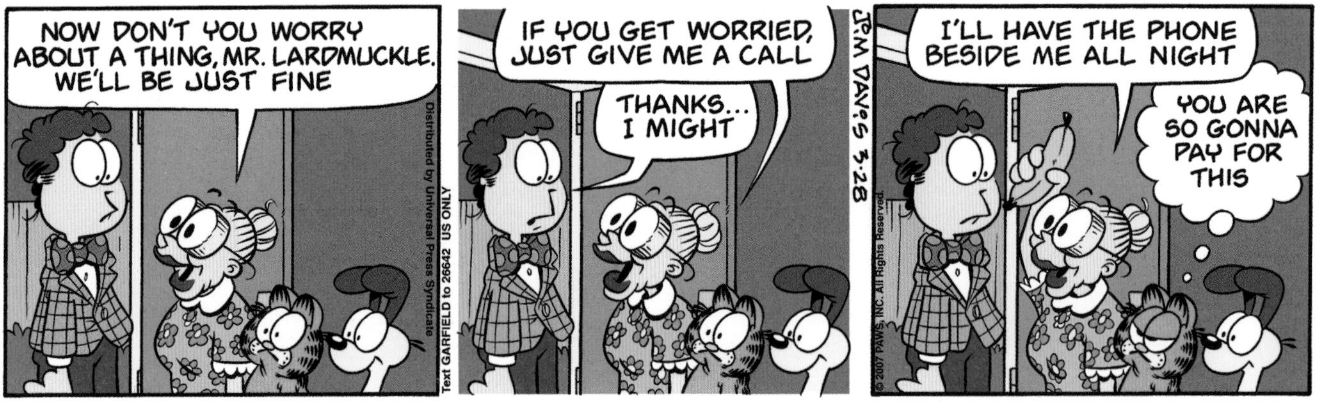
NOW DON'T YOU WORRY ABOUT A THING, MR. LARDMUCKLE. WE'LL BE JUST FINE
IF YOU GET WORRIED, JUST GIVE ME A CALL
THANKS... I MIGHT
I'LL HAVE THE PHONE BESIDE ME ALL NIGHT
YOU ARE SO GONNA PAY FOR THIS
JIM DAVIS 3-28
Distributed by Universal Press Syndicate
Text GARFIELD to 26642 US ONLY
© 2007 PAWS, INC. All Rights Reserved.

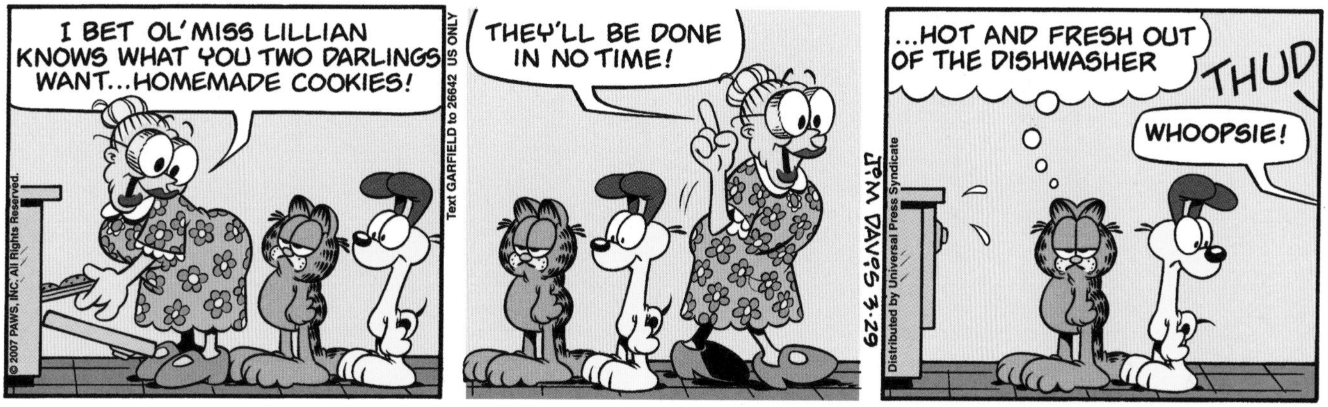
I BET OL' MISS LILLIAN KNOWS WHAT YOU TWO DARLINGS WANT...HOMEMADE COOKIES!
© 2007 PAWS, INC. All Rights Reserved.
Text GARFIELD to 26642 US ONLY
THEY'LL BE DONE IN NO TIME!
JIM DAVIS 3·29
Distributed by Universal Press Syndicate
...HOT AND FRESH OUT OF THE DISHWASHER
THUD
WHOOPSIE!

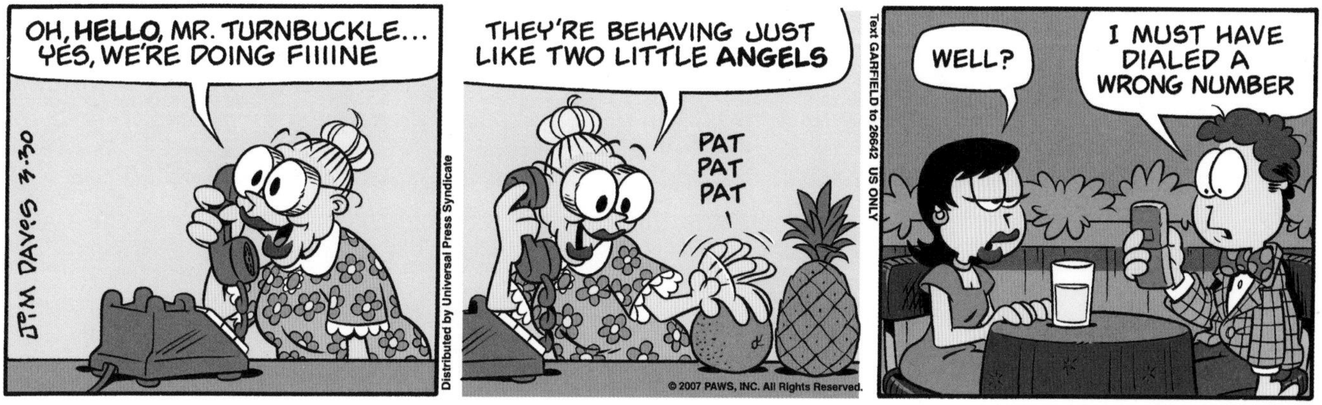
OH, HELLO, MR. TURNBUCKLE... YES, WE'RE DOING FIIIINE
JIM DAVIS 3·30
Distributed by Universal Press Syndicate
THEY'RE BEHAVING JUST LIKE TWO LITTLE ANGELS
PAT PAT PAT
© 2007 PAWS, INC. All Rights Reserved.
Text GARFIELD to 26642 US ONLY
WELL?
I MUST HAVE DIALED A WRONG NUMBER

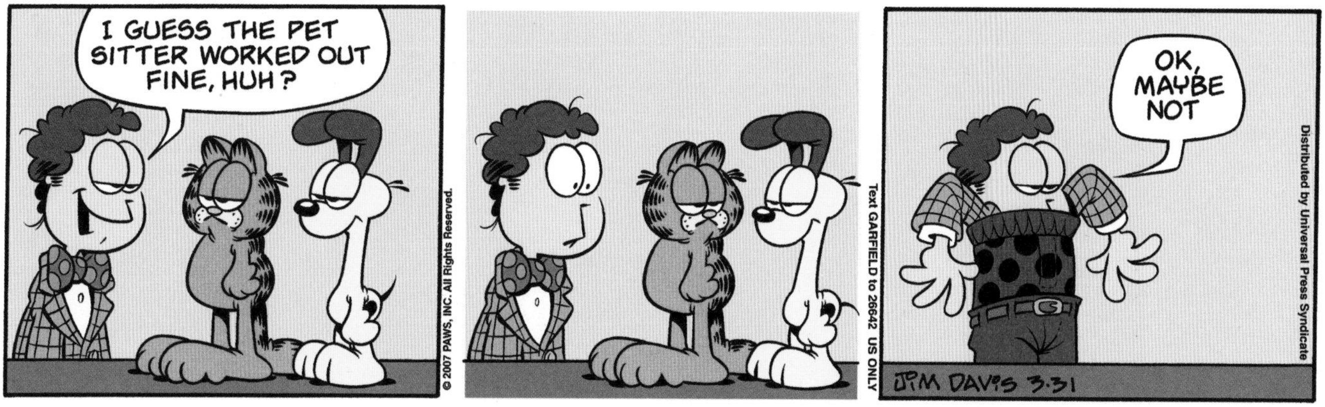
I GUESS THE PET SITTER WORKED OUT FINE, HUH?
© 2007 PAWS, INC. All Rights Reserved.
Text GARFIELD to 26642 US ONLY
OK, MAYBE NOT
JIM DAVIS 3·31
Distributed by Universal Press Syndicate

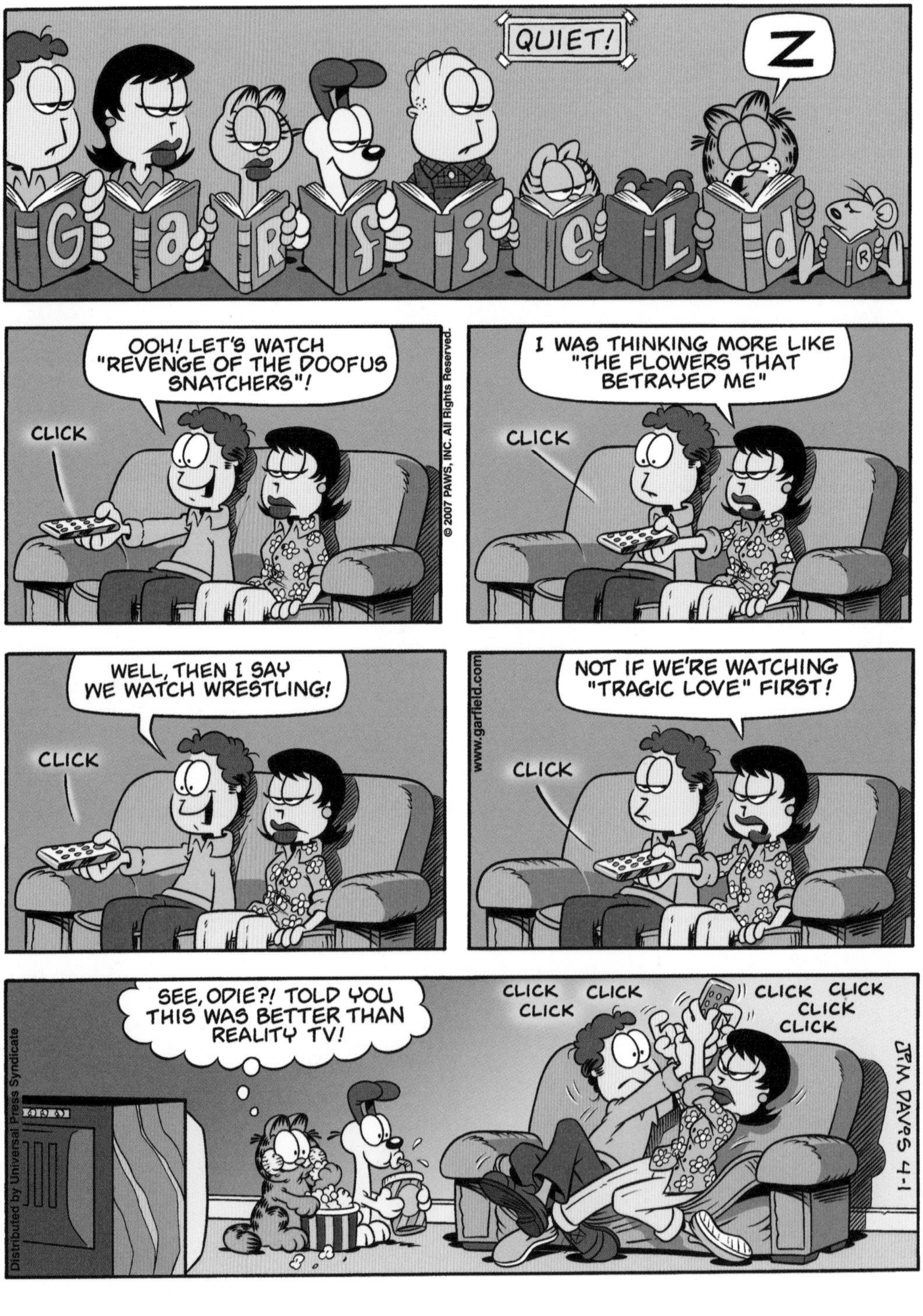
QUIET!
Z
GaRfieLd
OOH! LET'S WATCH "REVENGE OF THE DOOFUS SNATCHERS"!
CLICK
© 2007 PAWS, INC. All Rights Reserved.
I WAS THINKING MORE LIKE "THE FLOWERS THAT BETRAYED ME"
CLICK
WELL, THEN I SAY WE WATCH WRESTLING!
CLICK
www.garfield.com
NOT IF WE'RE WATCHING "TRAGIC LOVE" FIRST!
CLICK
Distributed by Universal Press Syndicate
SEE, ODIE?! TOLD YOU THIS WAS BETTER THAN REALITY TV!
CLICK CLICK CLICK
CLICK CLICK CLICK CLICK
JIM DAVIS 4-1

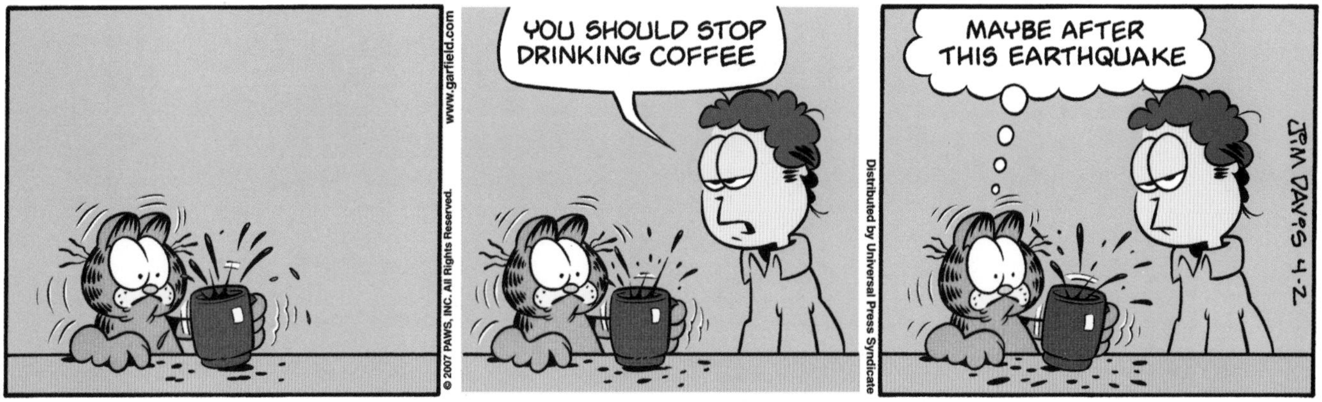
YOU SHOULD STOP DRINKING COFFEE
MAYBE AFTER THIS EARTHQUAKE
JIM DAVIS 4-2
© 2007 PAWS, INC. All Rights Reserved. www.garfield.com
Distributed by Universal Press Syndicate

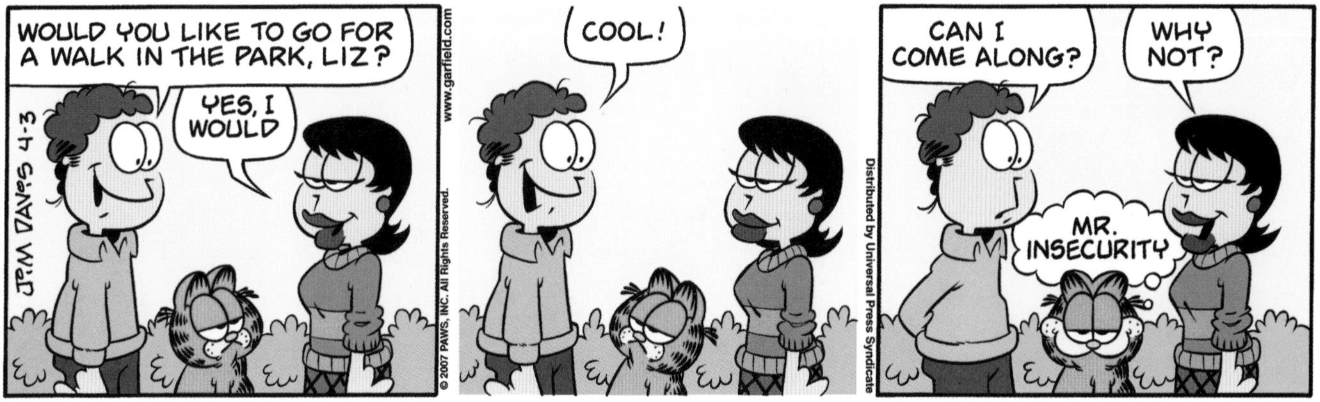
WOULD YOU LIKE TO GO FOR A WALK IN THE PARK, LIZ?
YES, I WOULD
JIM DAVIS 4-3
COOL!
CAN I COME ALONG?
WHY NOT?
MR. INSECURITY
© 2007 PAWS, INC. All Rights Reserved. www.garfield.com
Distributed by Universal Press Syndicate

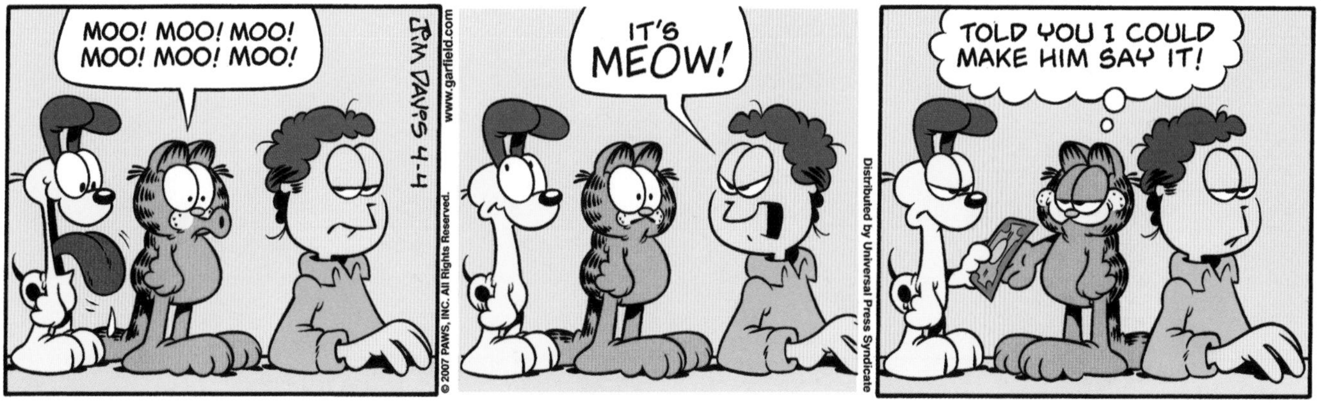
MOO! MOO! MOO! MOO! MOO! MOO!
JIM DAVIS 4-4
IT'S MEOW!
TOLD YOU I COULD MAKE HIM SAY IT!
© 2007 PAWS, INC. All Rights Reserved. www.garfield.com
Distributed by Universal Press Syndicate

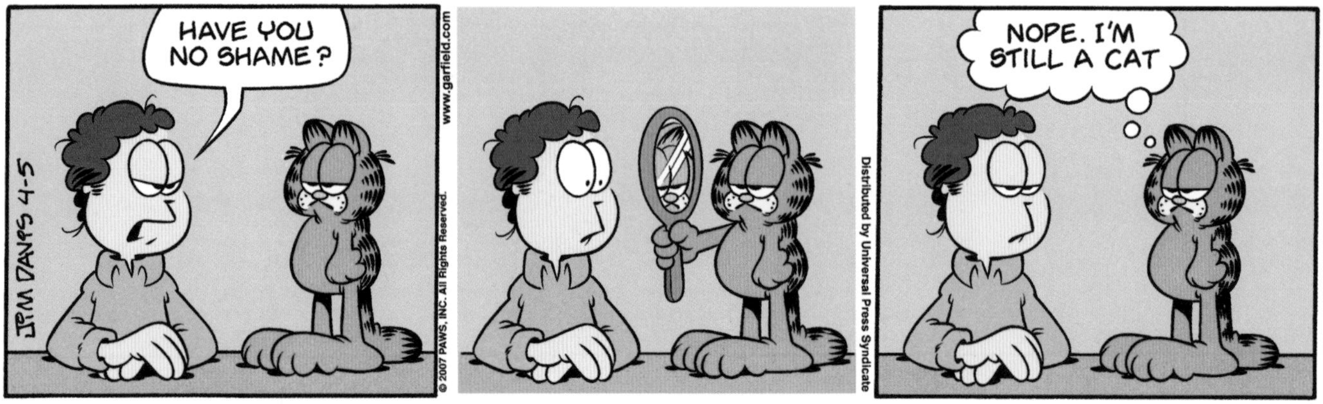
HAVE YOU NO SHAME?
NOPE. I'M STILL A CAT

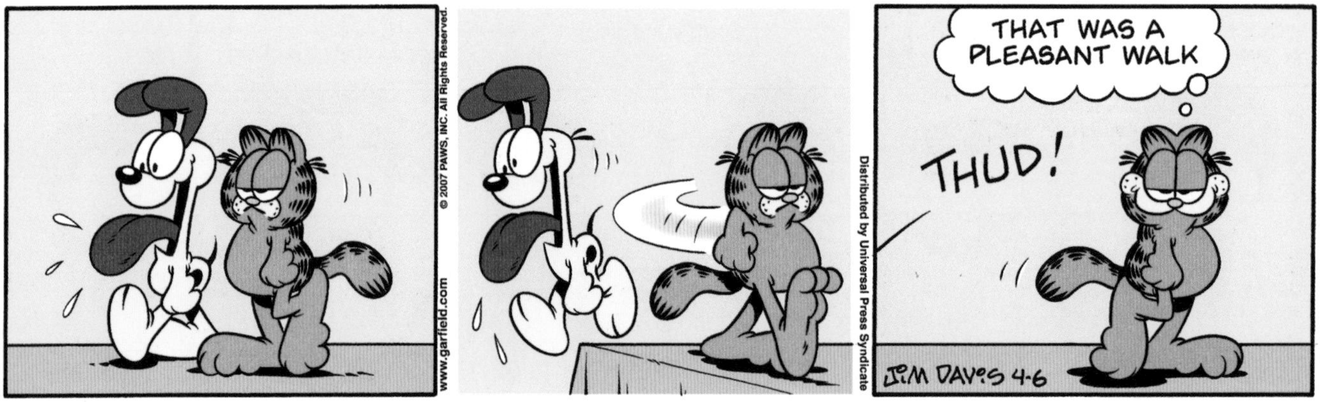
THUD!
THAT WAS A PLEASANT WALK

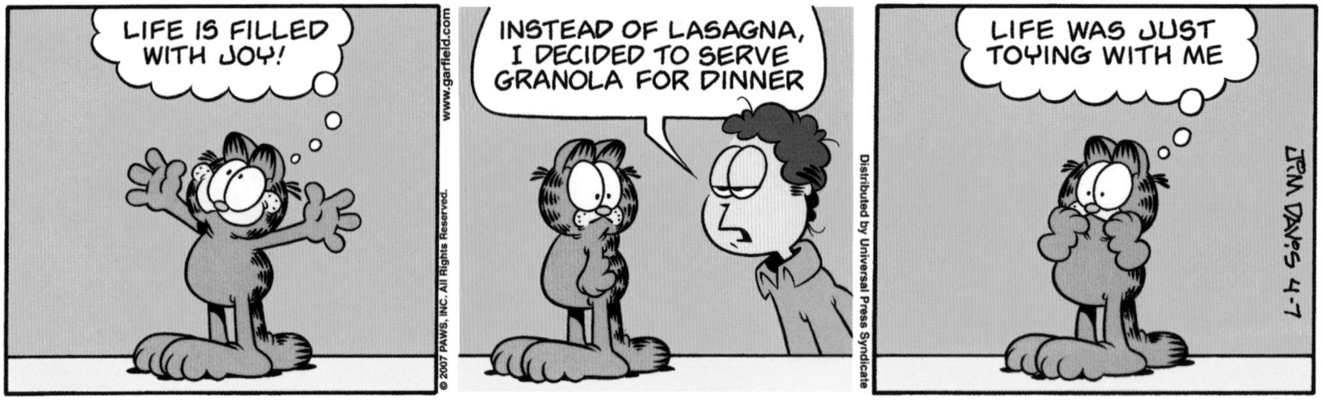
LIFE IS FILLED WITH JOY!
INSTEAD OF LASAGNA, I DECIDED TO SERVE GRANOLA FOR DINNER
LIFE WAS JUST TOYING WITH ME

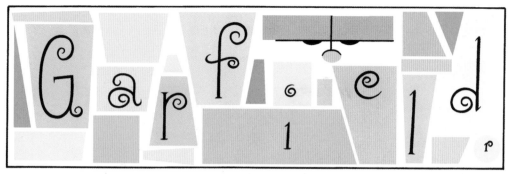

© 2007 PAWS, INC. All Rights Reserved.

RAINY SUNDAYS ARE ALWAYS THE SAME...THE STEADY PATTER OF RAIN ON THE ROOF...

THE COMFORTING THRUM OF THE FURNACE IN THE BASEMENT...

Distributed by Universal Press Syndicate

THE SOUND OF WATER RUSHING THROUGH THE GUTTERS AND DOWNSPOUTS...

JON SHRIEKING AT THE TOP OF HIS LUNGS...

CLICK

JIM DAVIS 4-8

Text GARFIELD to 26642 US ONLY

GARFIELD, UNLOCK THE DOOR THIS MINUTE !!!

AH, THERE IT IS...

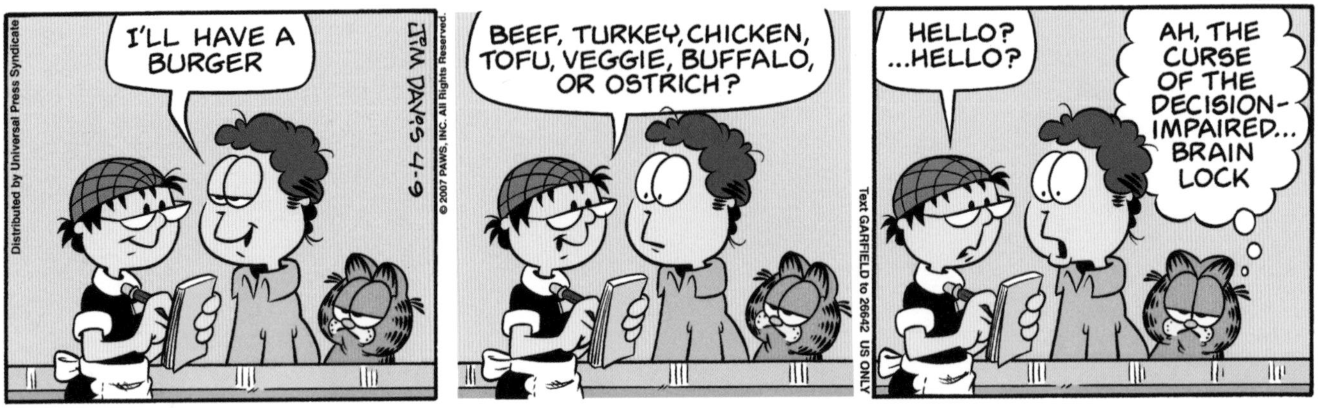
I'LL HAVE A BURGER
JIM DAVIS 4-9
Distributed by Universal Press Syndicate
© 2007 PAWS, INC. All Rights Reserved.
BEEF, TURKEY, CHICKEN, TOFU, VEGGIE, BUFFALO, OR OSTRICH?
Text GARFIELD to 26642 US ONLY
HELLO? ...HELLO?
AH, THE CURSE OF THE DECISION-IMPAIRED... BRAIN LOCK

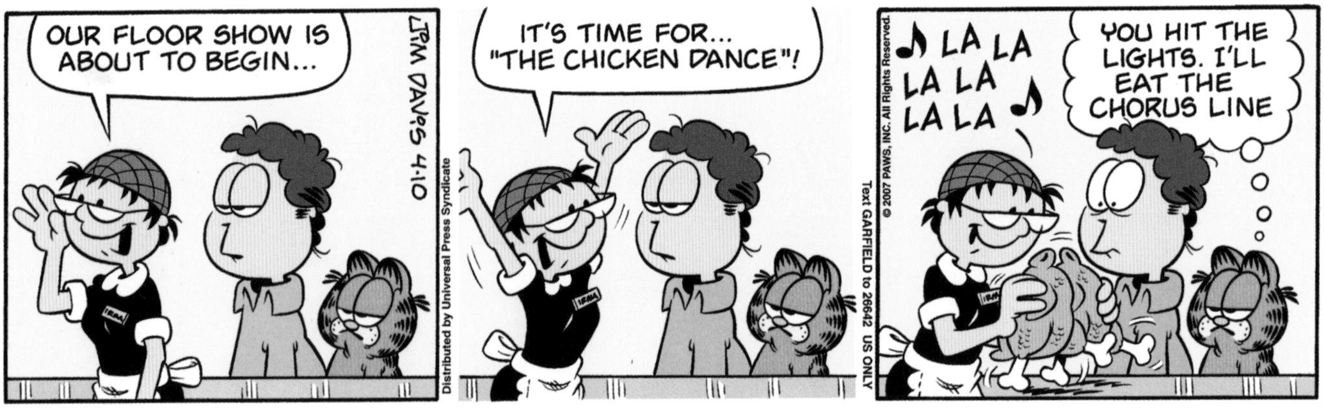
OUR FLOOR SHOW IS ABOUT TO BEGIN...
JIM DAVIS 4-10
IT'S TIME FOR... "THE CHICKEN DANCE"!
Distributed by Universal Press Syndicate
Text GARFIELD to 26642 US ONLY
© 2007 PAWS, INC. All Rights Reserved.
♪ LA LA LA LA LA LA LA ♪
YOU HIT THE LIGHTS. I'LL EAT THE CHORUS LINE

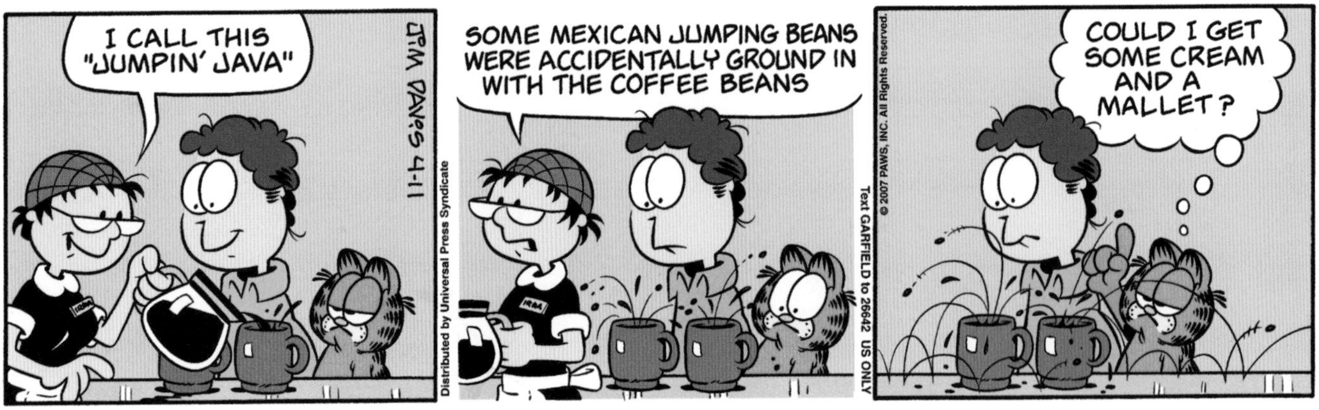
I CALL THIS "JUMPIN' JAVA"
JIM DAVIS 4-11
Distributed by Universal Press Syndicate
SOME MEXICAN JUMPING BEANS WERE ACCIDENTALLY GROUND IN WITH THE COFFEE BEANS
Text GARFIELD to 26642 US ONLY
© 2007 PAWS, INC. All Rights Reserved.
COULD I GET SOME CREAM AND A MALLET?

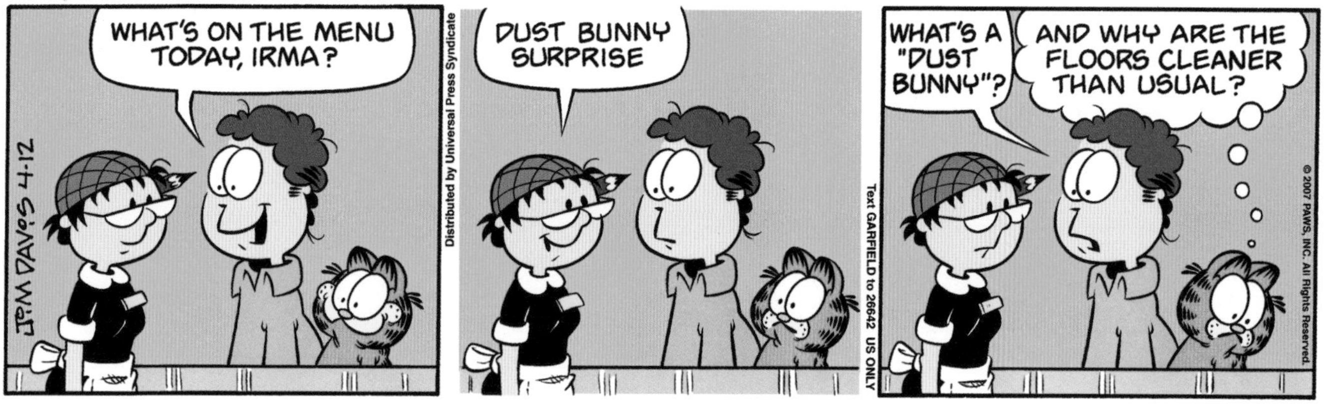
JPM DAVIS 4-12
WHAT'S ON THE MENU TODAY, IRMA?
Distributed by Universal Press Syndicate
DUST BUNNY SURPRISE
Text GARFIELD to 26642 US ONLY
WHAT'S A "DUST BUNNY"?
AND WHY ARE THE FLOORS CLEANER THAN USUAL?
© 2007 PAWS, INC. All Rights Reserved.

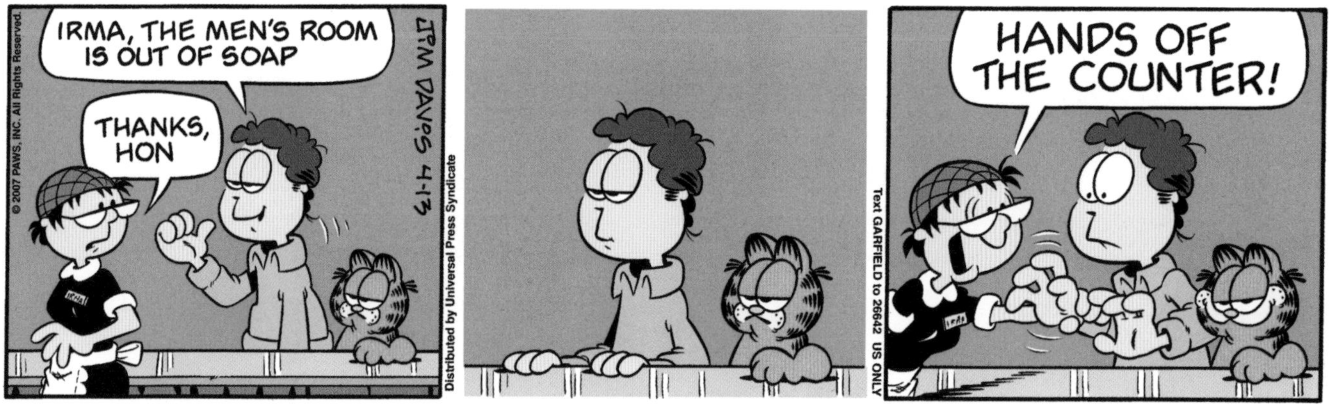
© 2007 PAWS, INC. All Rights Reserved.
IRMA, THE MEN'S ROOM IS OUT OF SOAP
JPM DAVIS 4-13
THANKS, HON
Distributed by Universal Press Syndicate
Text GARFIELD to 26642 US ONLY
HANDS OFF THE COUNTER!

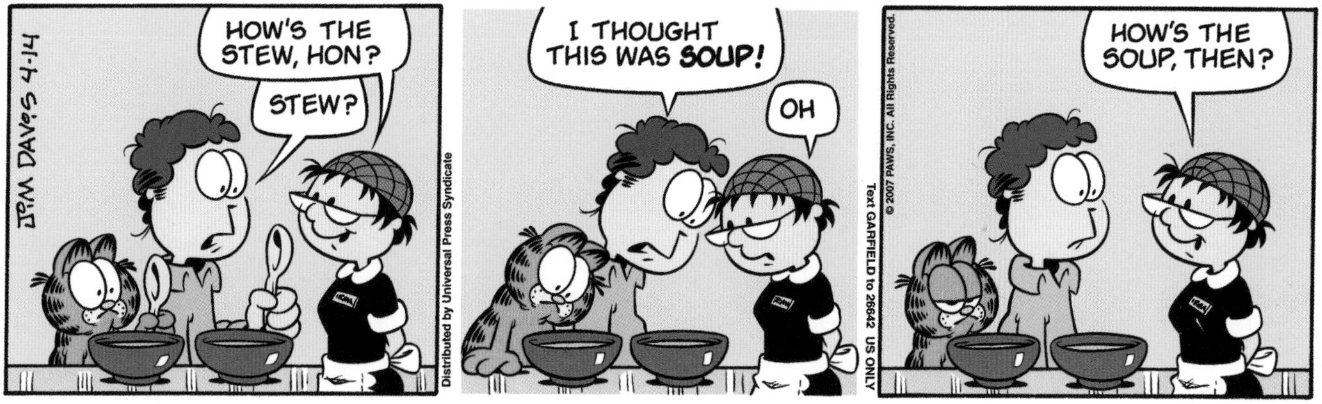
JPM DAVIS 4-14
HOW'S THE STEW, HON?
STEW?
Distributed by Universal Press Syndicate
I THOUGHT THIS WAS SOUP!
OH
Text GARFIELD to 26642 US ONLY
© 2007 PAWS, INC. All Rights Reserved.
HOW'S THE SOUP, THEN?

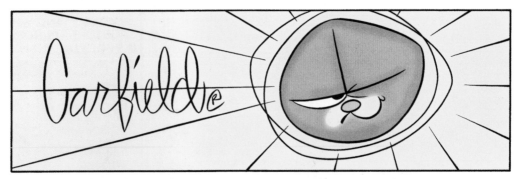

www.garfield.com

© 2007 PAWS, INC. All Rights Reserved.

EWWW!

THERE'S A **FLY** IN MY COFFEE!

JIM DAVIS 4-15

WHAT COULD BE MORE DISGUSTING THAN **THAT**?!

Distributed by Universal Press Syndicate

THAT

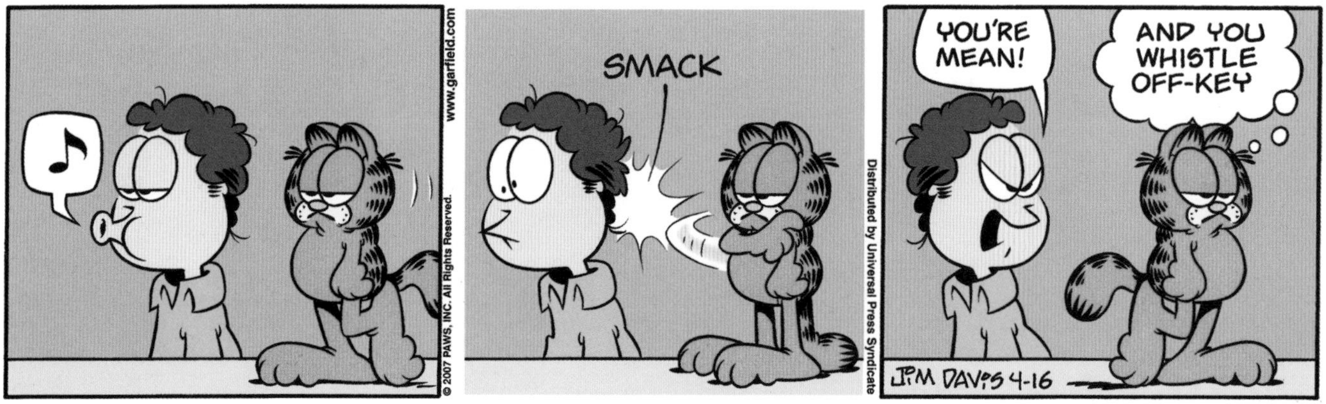
♪
SMACK
YOU'RE MEAN!
AND YOU WHISTLE OFF-KEY
JIM DAVIS 4-16

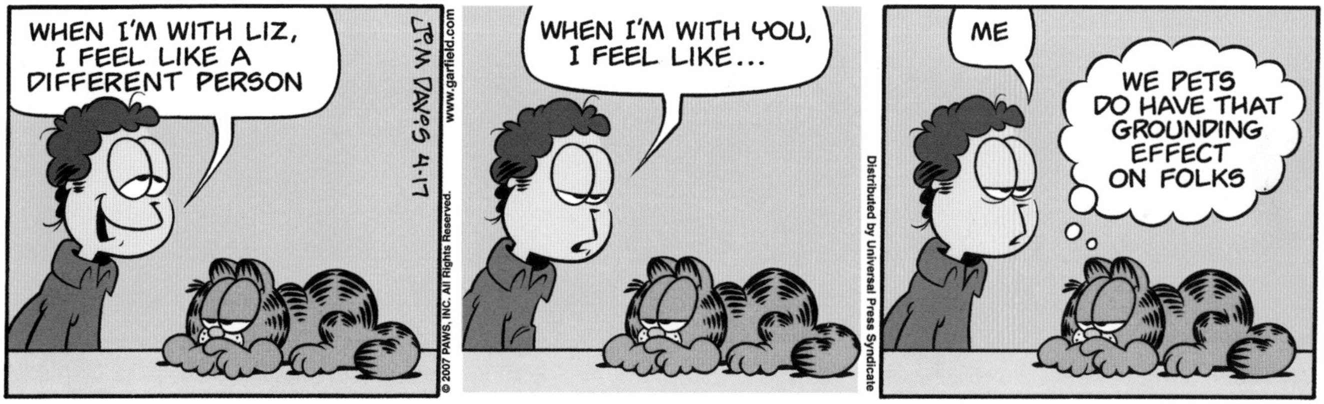
WHEN I'M WITH LIZ, I FEEL LIKE A DIFFERENT PERSON
WHEN I'M WITH YOU, I FEEL LIKE...
ME
WE PETS DO HAVE THAT GROUNDING EFFECT ON FOLKS
JIM DAVIS 4-17

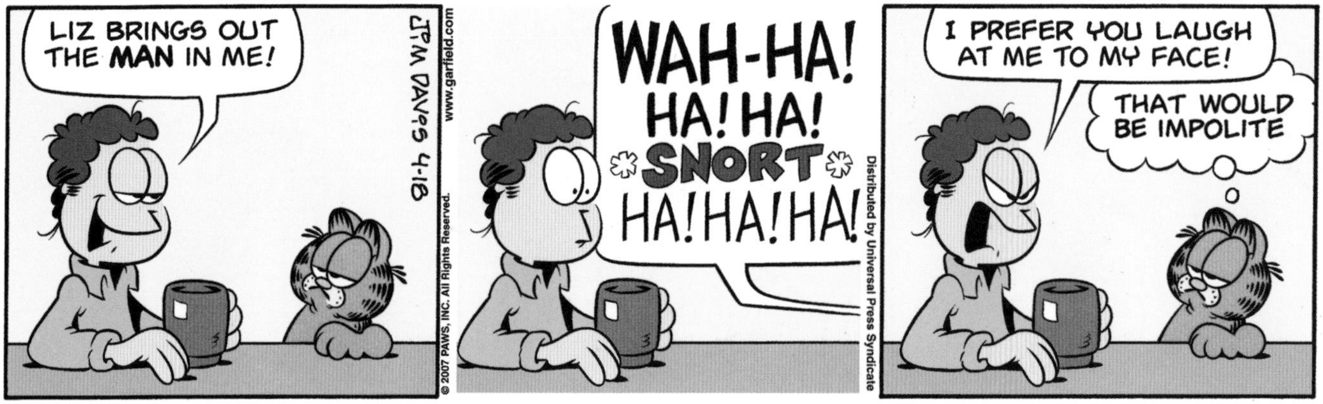
LIZ BRINGS OUT THE **MAN** IN ME!
WAH-HA! HA! HA! *SNORT* HA! HA! HA!
I PREFER YOU LAUGH AT ME TO MY FACE!
THAT WOULD BE IMPOLITE
JIM DAVIS 4-18

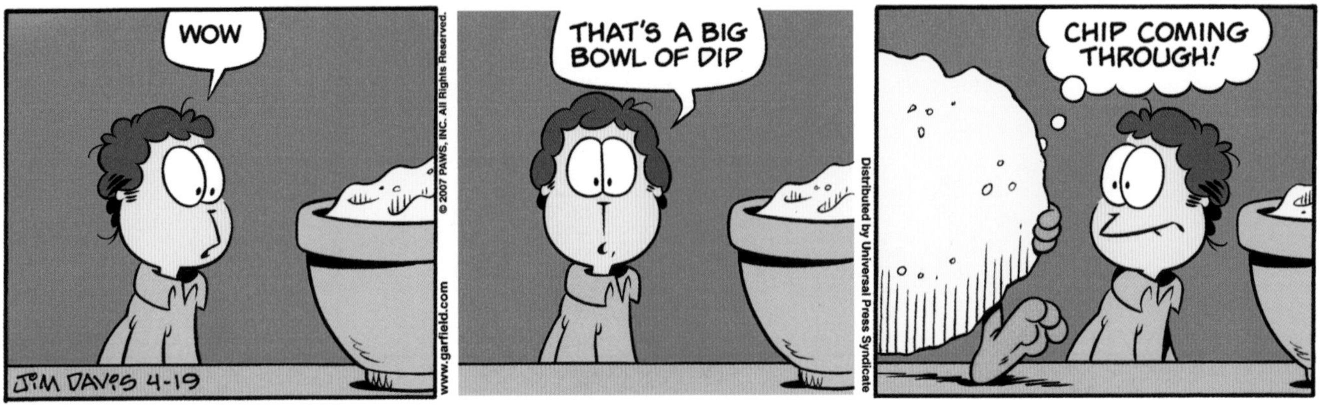
WOW
JIM DAVIS 4-19
© 2007 PAWS, INC. All Rights Reserved.
www.garfield.com
THAT'S A BIG BOWL OF DIP
Distributed by Universal Press Syndicate
CHIP COMING THROUGH!

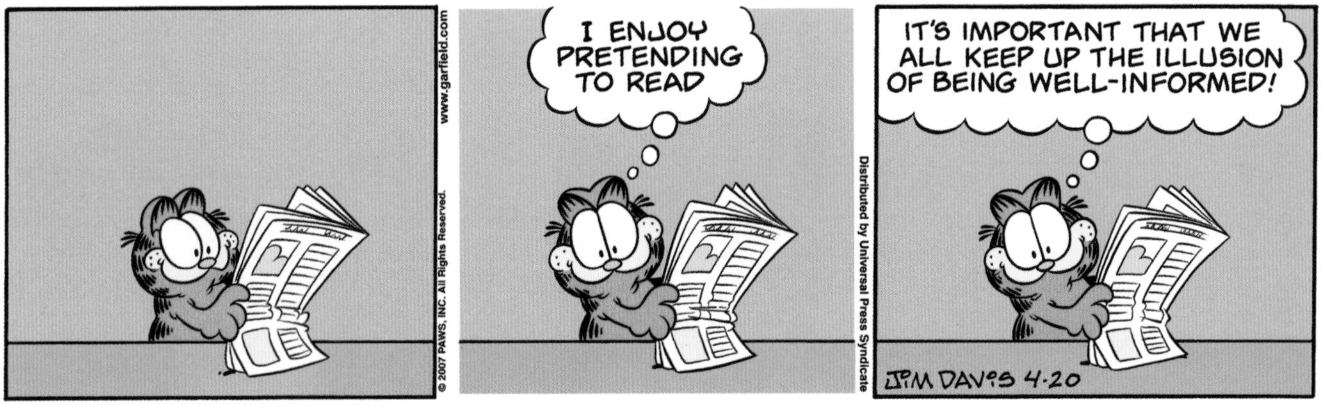
© 2007 PAWS, INC. All Rights Reserved.
www.garfield.com
I ENJOY PRETENDING TO READ
Distributed by Universal Press Syndicate
IT'S IMPORTANT THAT WE ALL KEEP UP THE ILLUSION OF BEING WELL-INFORMED!
JIM DAVIS 4-20

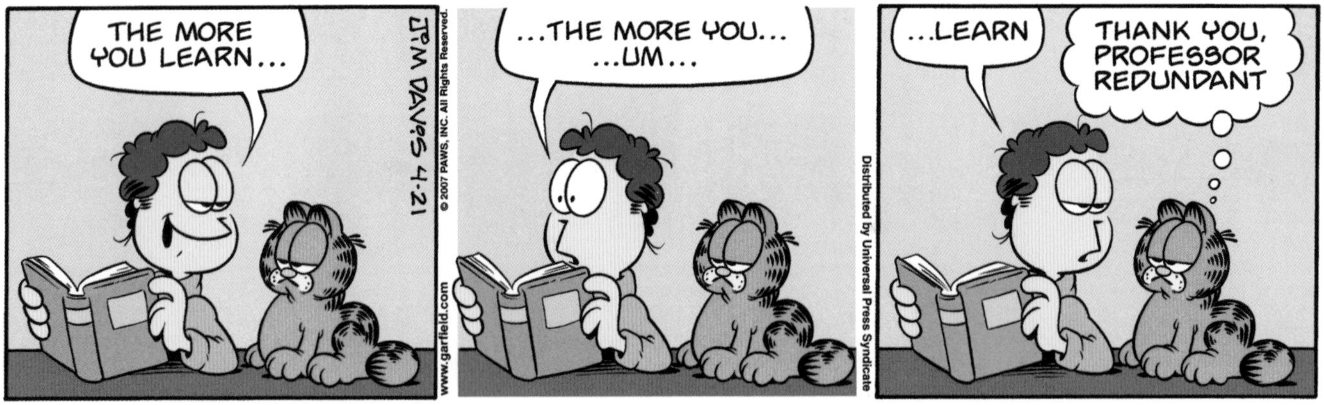
THE MORE YOU LEARN...
JIM DAVIS 4-21
© 2007 PAWS, INC. All Rights Reserved.
www.garfield.com
...THE MORE YOU...
...UM...
Distributed by Universal Press Syndicate
...LEARN
THANK YOU, PROFESSOR REDUNDANT

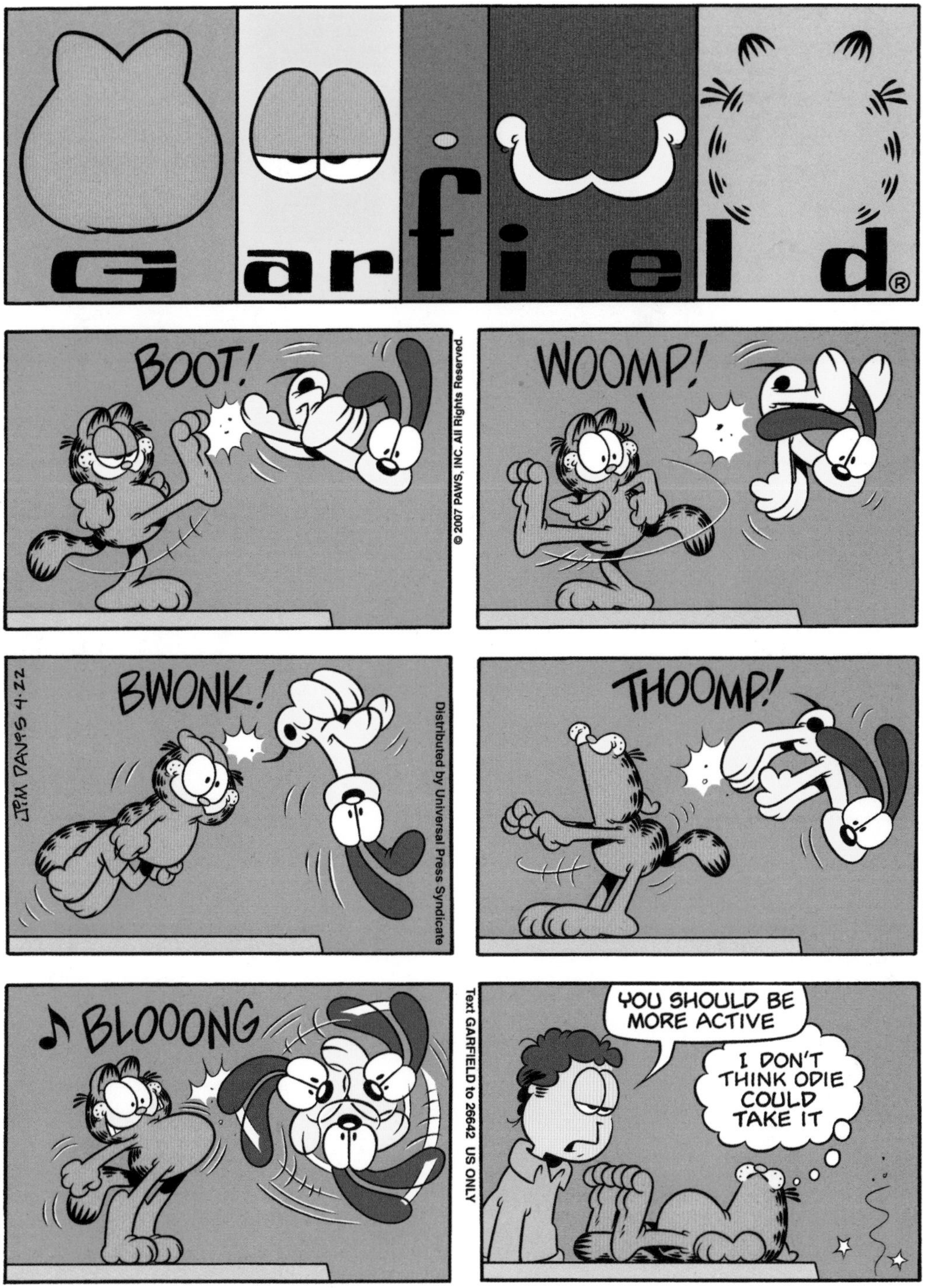
Garfield®
BOOT!
© 2007 PAWS, INC. All Rights Reserved.
WOOMP!
JIM DAVIS 4-22
BWONK!
Distributed by Universal Press Syndicate
THOOMP!
♪ BLOOONG
Text GARFIELD to 26642 US ONLY
YOU SHOULD BE MORE ACTIVE
I DON'T THINK ODIE COULD TAKE IT

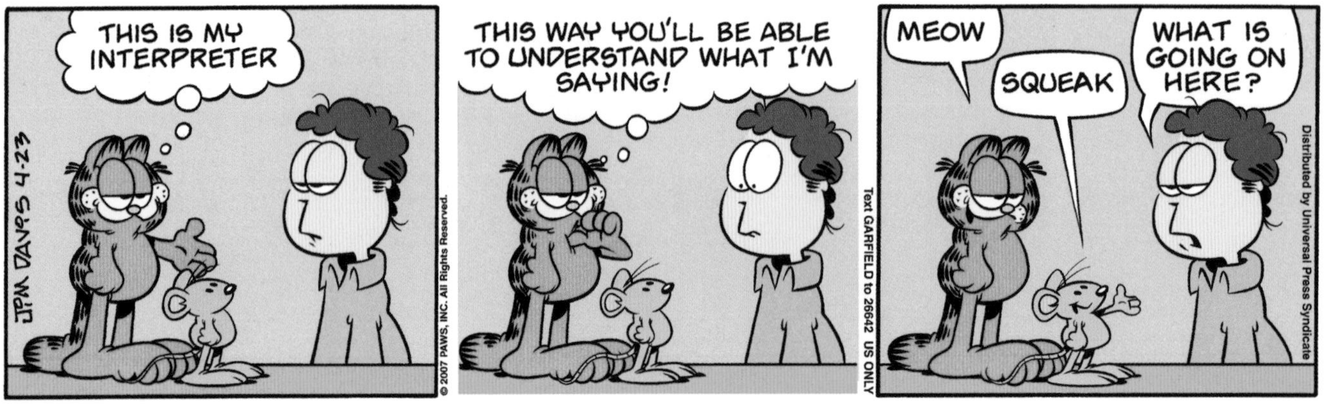
THIS IS MY INTERPRETER
JIM DAVIS 4-23
© 2007 PAWS, INC. All Rights Reserved.
THIS WAY YOU'LL BE ABLE TO UNDERSTAND WHAT I'M SAYING!
Text GARFIELD to 26642 US ONLY
MEOW
SQUEAK
WHAT IS GOING ON HERE?
Distributed by Universal Press Syndicate

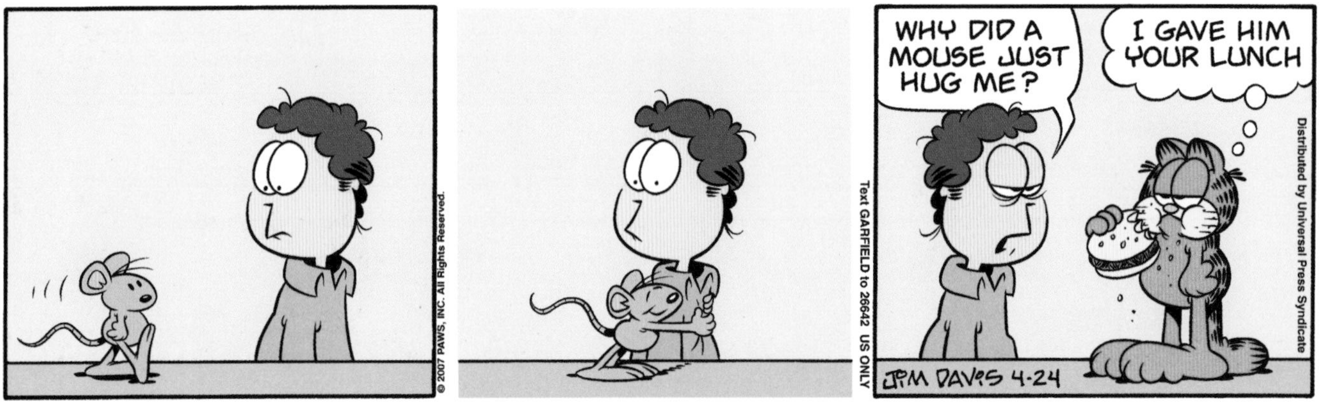
© 2007 PAWS, INC. All Rights Reserved.
Text GARFIELD to 26642 US ONLY
WHY DID A MOUSE JUST HUG ME?
I GAVE HIM YOUR LUNCH
JIM DAVIS 4-24
Distributed by Universal Press Syndicate

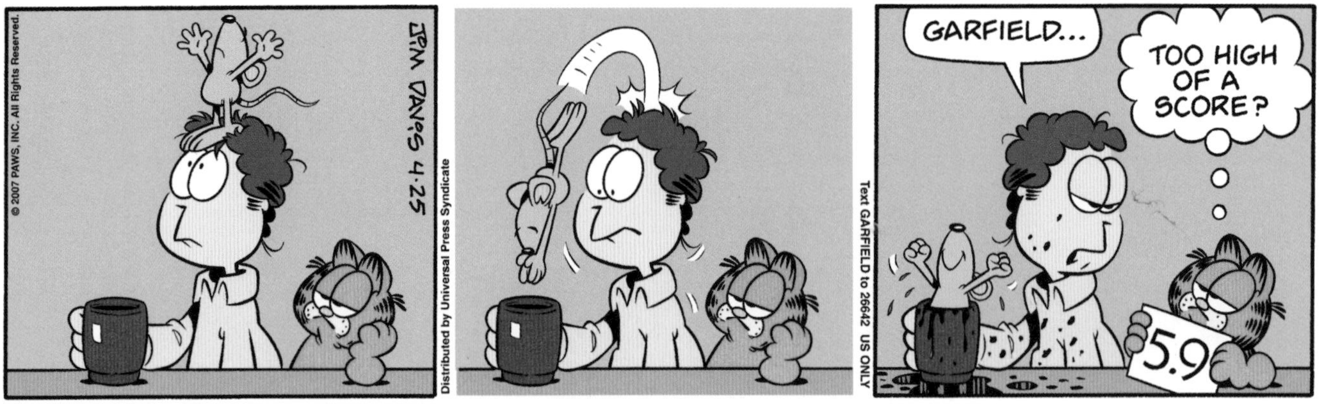
© 2007 PAWS, INC. All Rights Reserved.
JIM DAVIS 4-25
Distributed by Universal Press Syndicate
Text GARFIELD to 26642 US ONLY
GARFIELD...
TOO HIGH OF A SCORE?
5.9

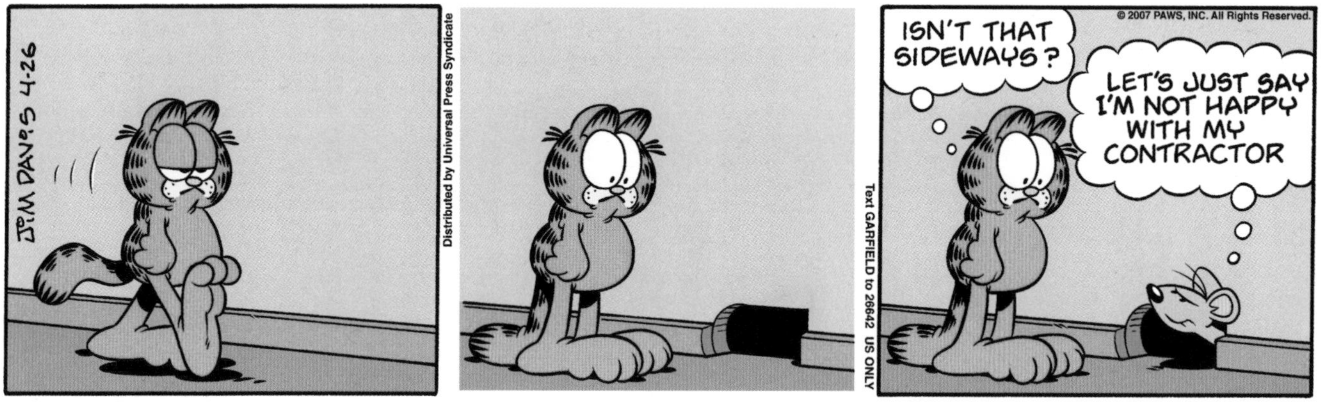
JIM DAVIS 4·26
Distributed by Universal Press Syndicate
© 2007 PAWS, INC. All Rights Reserved.
ISN'T THAT SIDEWAYS?
LET'S JUST SAY I'M NOT HAPPY WITH MY CONTRACTOR
Text GARFIELD to 26642 US ONLY

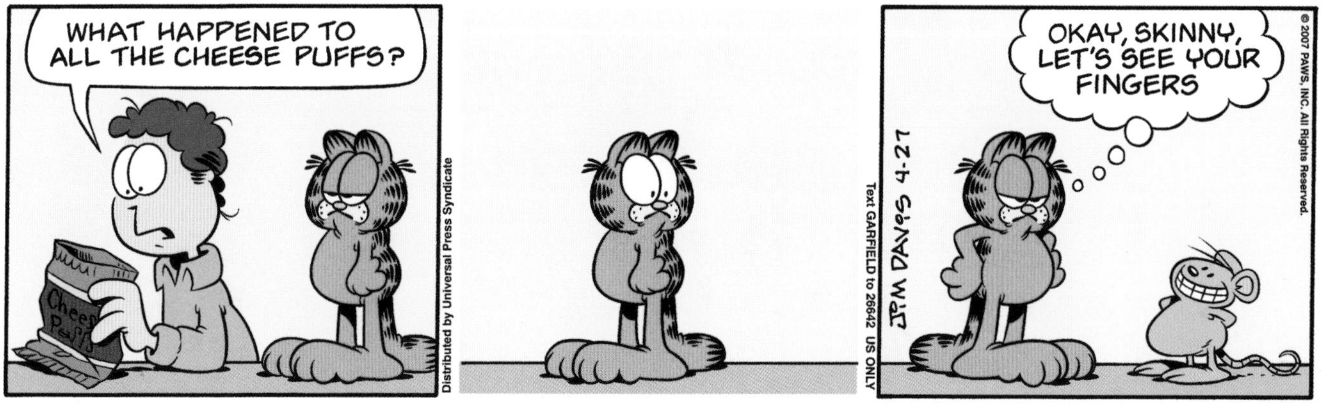
WHAT HAPPENED TO ALL THE CHEESE PUFFS?
Cheese Puffs
Distributed by Universal Press Syndicate
Text GARFIELD to 26642 US ONLY
JIM DAVIS 4·27
OKAY, SKINNY, LET'S SEE YOUR FINGERS
© 2007 PAWS, INC. All Rights Reserved.

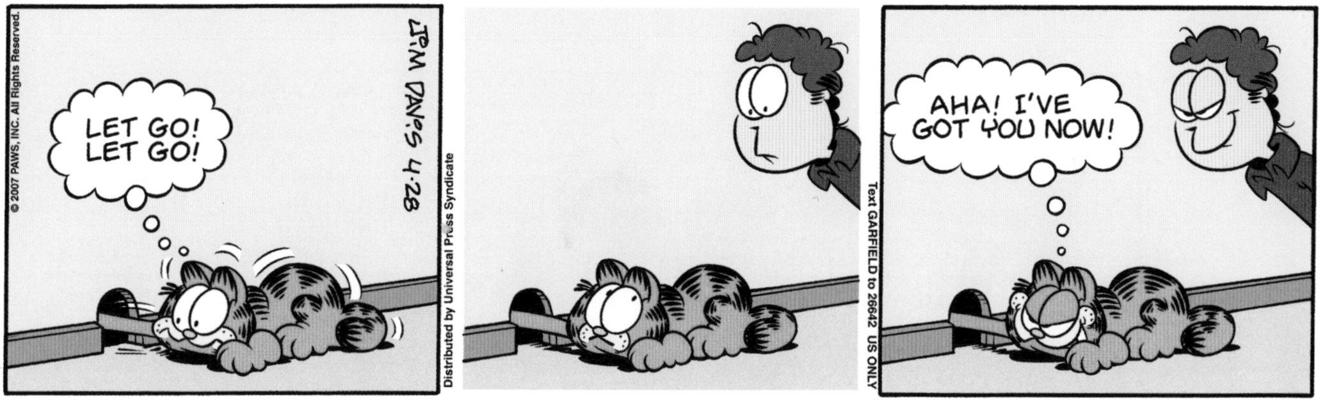
© 2007 PAWS, INC. All Rights Reserved.
LET GO! LET GO!
JIM DAVIS 4·28
Distributed by Universal Press Syndicate
Text GARFIELD to 26642 US ONLY
AHA! I'VE GOT YOU NOW!

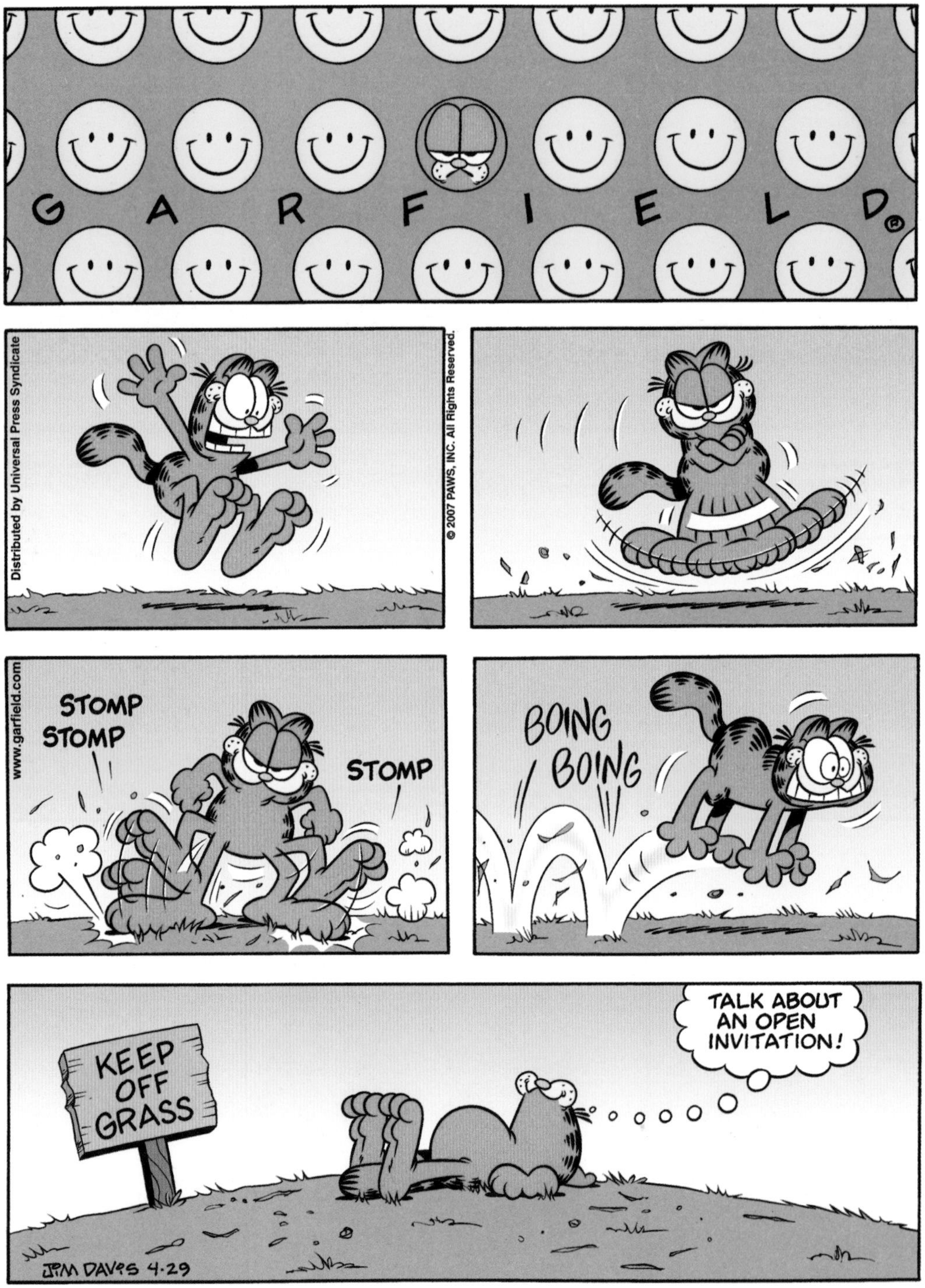
GARFIELD®
Distributed by Universal Press Syndicate
© 2007 PAWS, INC. All Rights Reserved.
www.garfield.com
STOMP
STOMP
STOMP
BOING
BOING
KEEP OFF GRASS
TALK ABOUT AN OPEN INVITATION!
JIM DAVIS 4-29

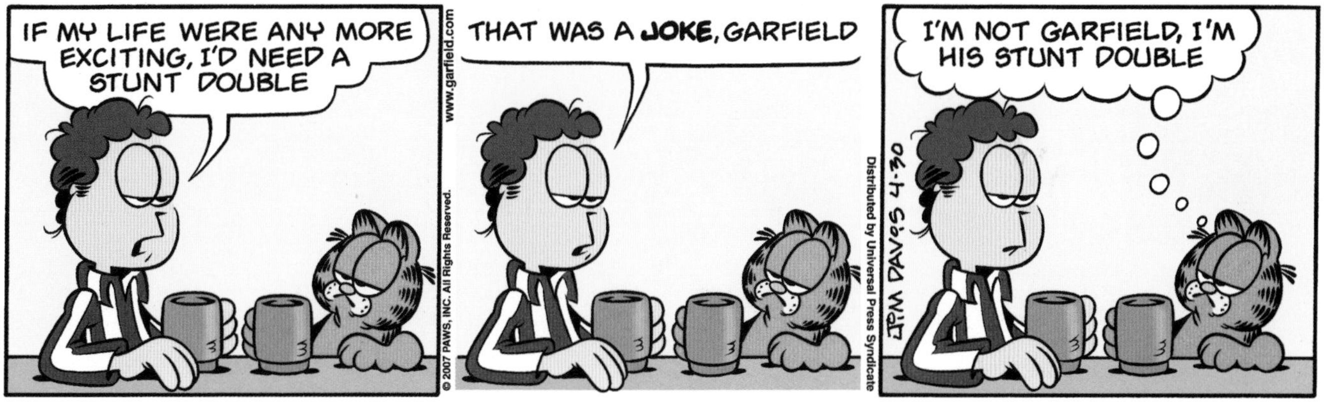
IF MY LIFE WERE ANY MORE EXCITING, I'D NEED A STUNT DOUBLE
© 2007 PAWS, INC. All Rights Reserved. www.garfield.com
THAT WAS A **JOKE**, GARFIELD
Distributed by Universal Press Syndicate
JIM DAVIS 4-30
I'M NOT GARFIELD, I'M HIS STUNT DOUBLE

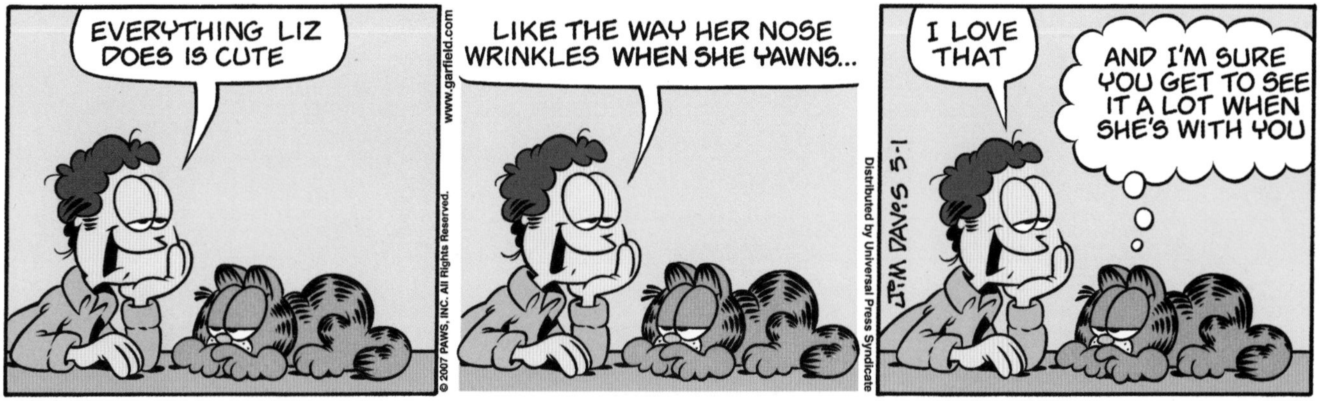
EVERYTHING LIZ DOES IS CUTE
© 2007 PAWS, INC. All Rights Reserved. www.garfield.com
LIKE THE WAY HER NOSE WRINKLES WHEN SHE YAWNS...
Distributed by Universal Press Syndicate
JIM DAVIS 5-1
I LOVE THAT
AND I'M SURE YOU GET TO SEE IT A LOT WHEN SHE'S WITH YOU

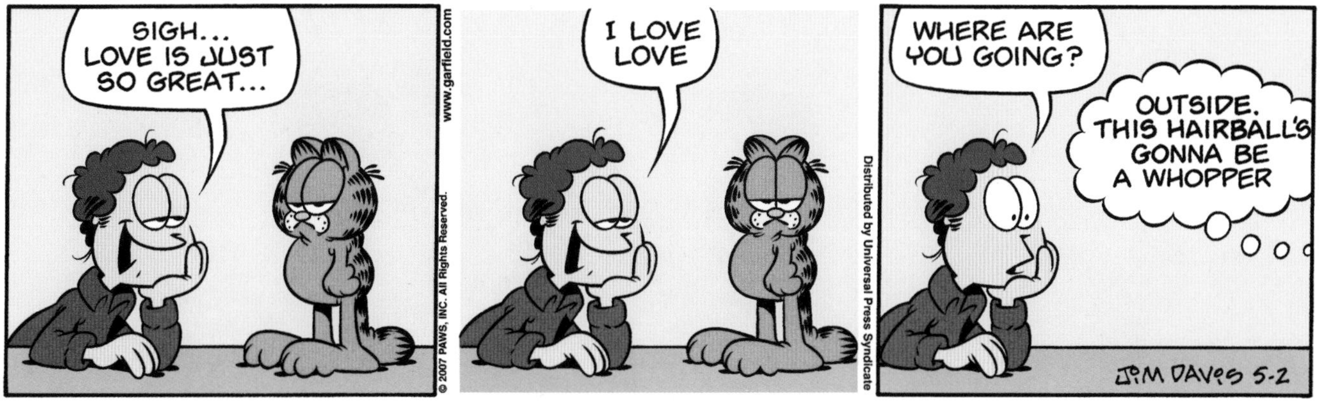
SIGH... LOVE IS JUST SO GREAT...
© 2007 PAWS, INC. All Rights Reserved. www.garfield.com
I LOVE LOVE
Distributed by Universal Press Syndicate
WHERE ARE YOU GOING?
OUTSIDE. THIS HAIRBALL'S GONNA BE A WHOPPER
JIM DAVIS 5-2

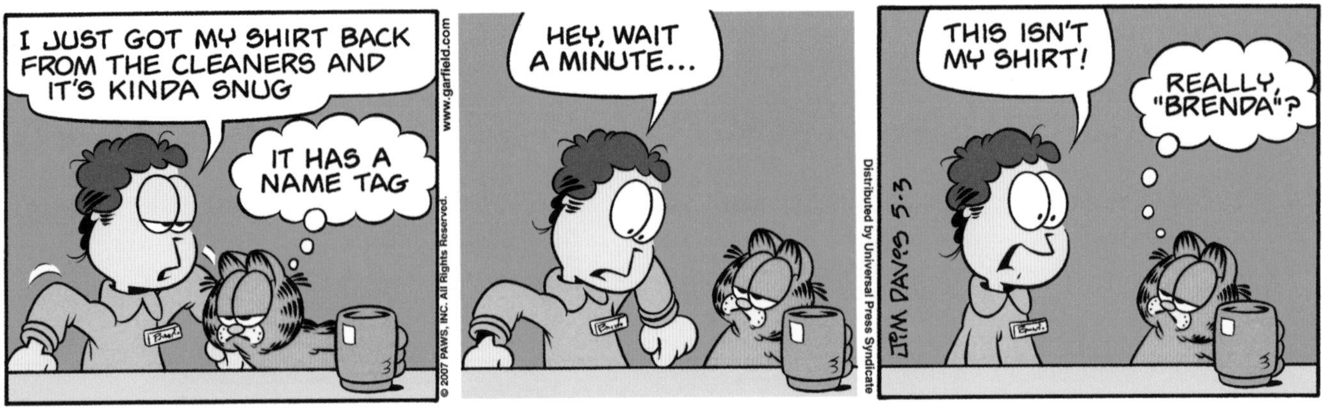
I JUST GOT MY SHIRT BACK FROM THE CLEANERS AND IT'S KINDA SNUG
IT HAS A NAME TAG
© 2007 PAWS, INC. All Rights Reserved.
www.garfield.com
HEY, WAIT A MINUTE...
Distributed by Universal Press Syndicate
JIM DAVIS 5-3
THIS ISN'T MY SHIRT!
REALLY, "BRENDA"?

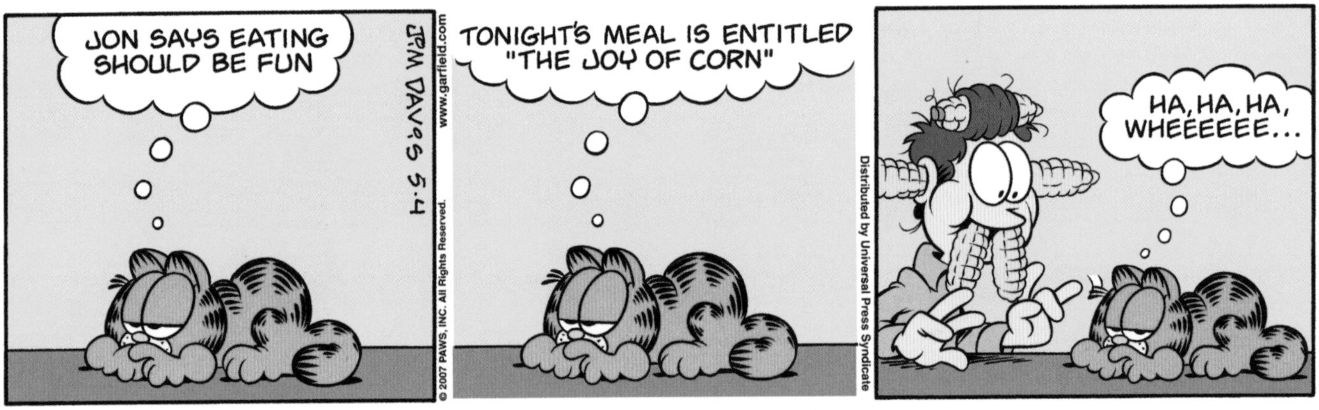
JON SAYS EATING SHOULD BE FUN
JIM DAVIS 5-4
© 2007 PAWS, INC. All Rights Reserved.
www.garfield.com
TONIGHT'S MEAL IS ENTITLED "THE JOY OF CORN"
Distributed by Universal Press Syndicate
HA, HA, HA, WHEEEEEE...

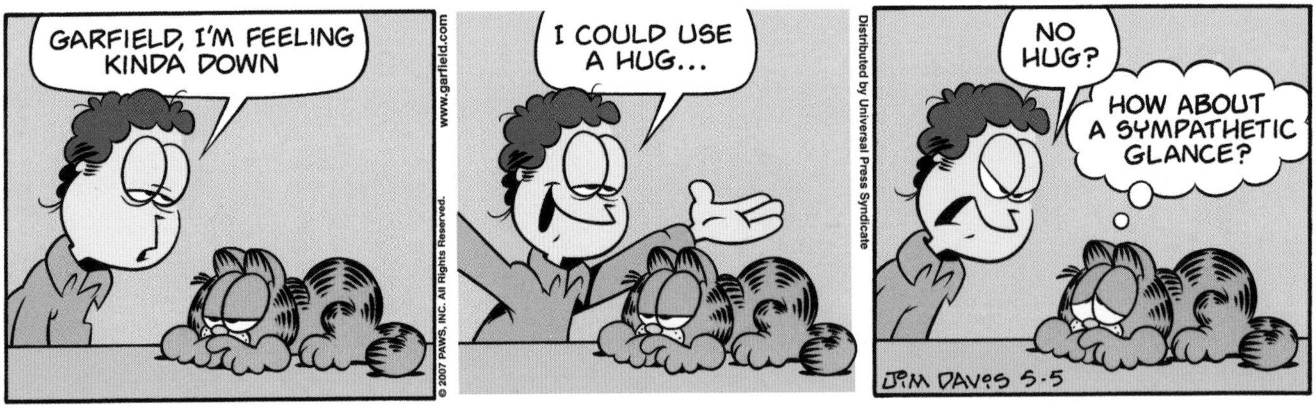
GARFIELD, I'M FEELING KINDA DOWN
© 2007 PAWS, INC. All Rights Reserved.
www.garfield.com
I COULD USE A HUG...
Distributed by Universal Press Syndicate
NO HUG?
HOW ABOUT A SYMPATHETIC GLANCE?
JIM DAVIS 5-5

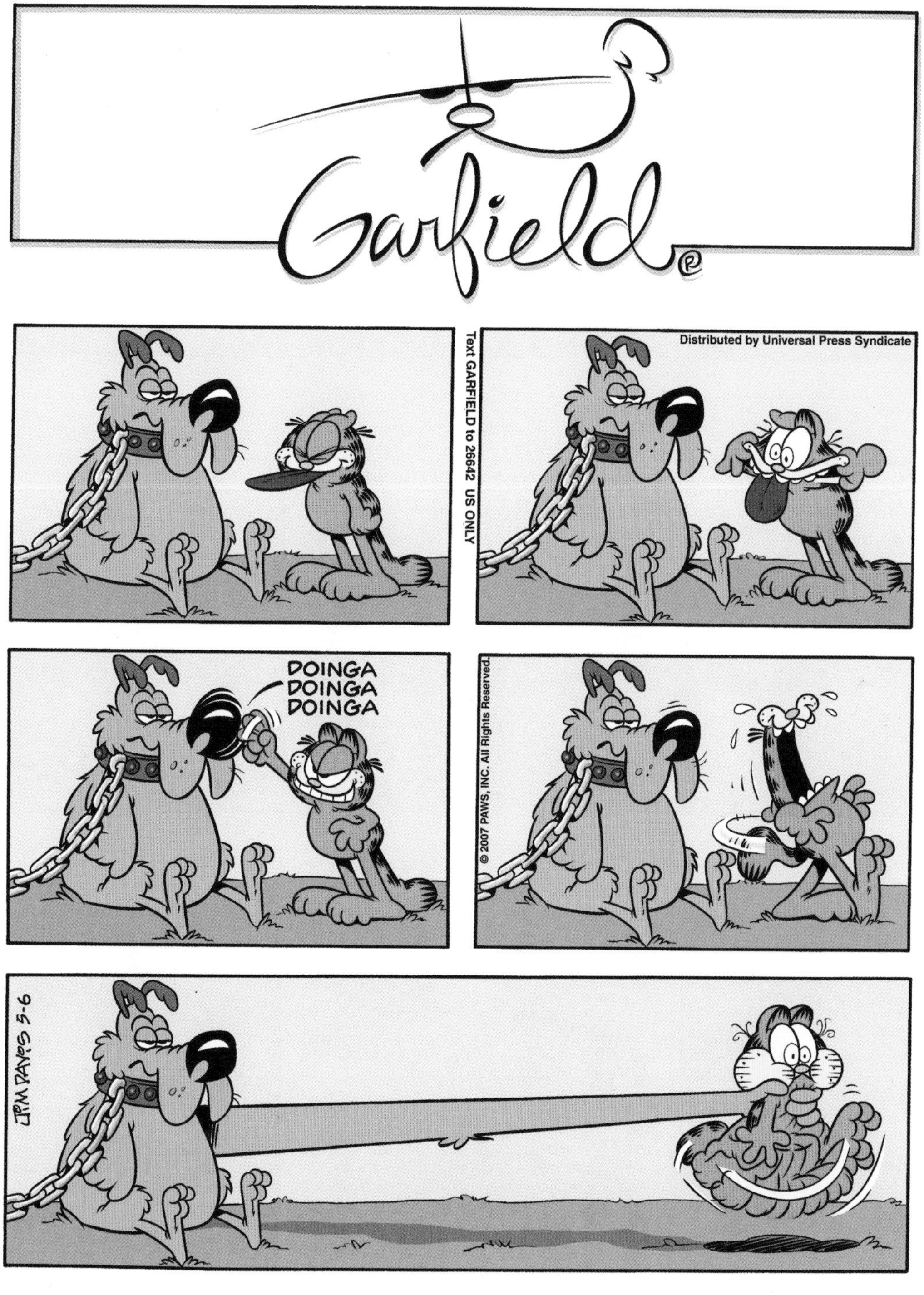
Garfield
Text GARFIELD to 26642 US ONLY
Distributed by Universal Press Syndicate
DOINGA
DOINGA
DOINGA
© 2007 PAWS, INC. All Rights Reserved.
JPM DAVIS 5-6

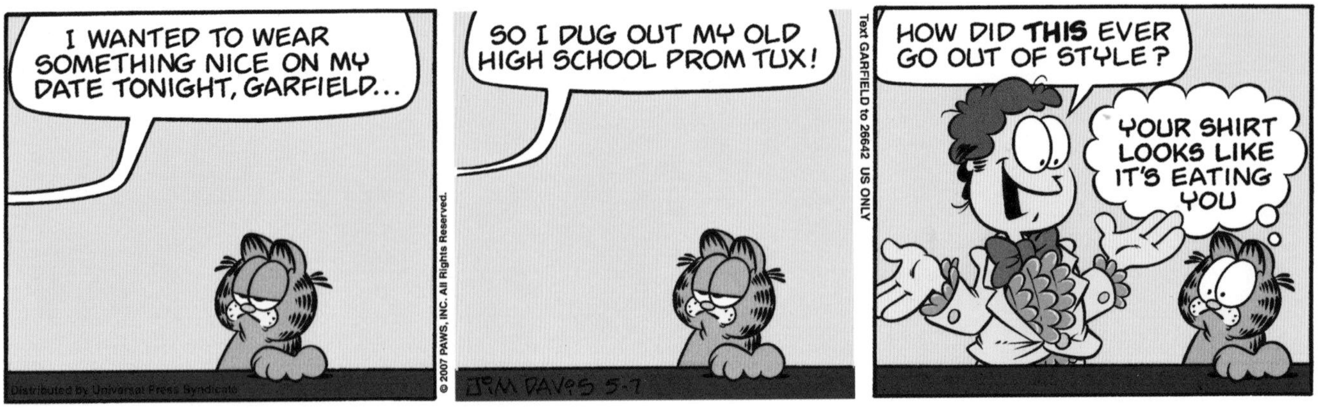
I WANTED TO WEAR SOMETHING NICE ON MY DATE TONIGHT, GARFIELD...
Distributed by Universal Press Syndicate
© 2007 PAWS, INC. All Rights Reserved.
SO I DUG OUT MY OLD HIGH SCHOOL PROM TUX!
JIM DAVIS 5-7
Text GARFIELD to 26642 US ONLY
HOW DID **THIS** EVER GO OUT OF STYLE?
YOUR SHIRT LOOKS LIKE IT'S EATING YOU

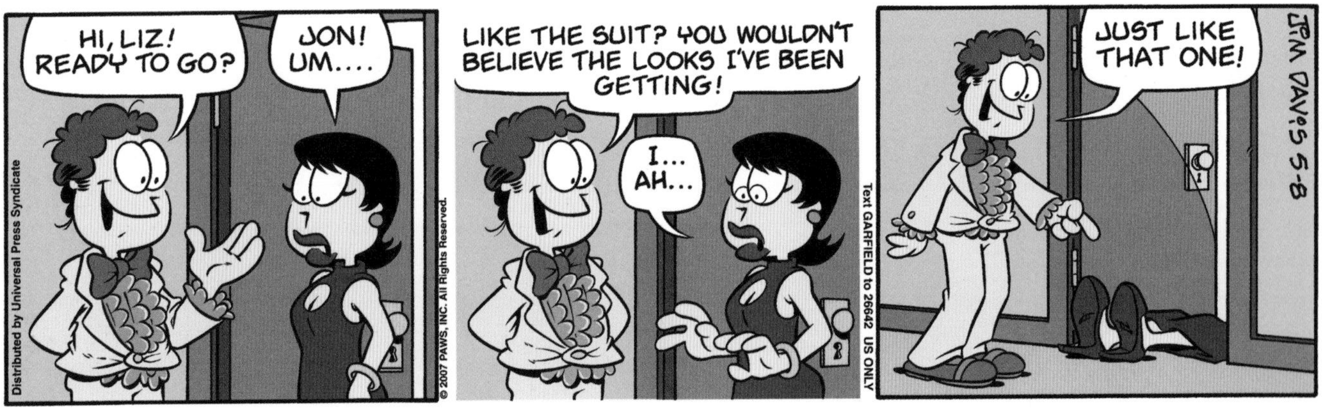
HI, LIZ! READY TO GO?
JON! UM....
Distributed by Universal Press Syndicate
© 2007 PAWS, INC. All Rights Reserved.
LIKE THE SUIT? YOU WOULDN'T BELIEVE THE LOOKS I'VE BEEN GETTING!
I... AH...
Text GARFIELD to 26642 US ONLY
JUST LIKE THAT ONE!
JIM DAVIS 5-8

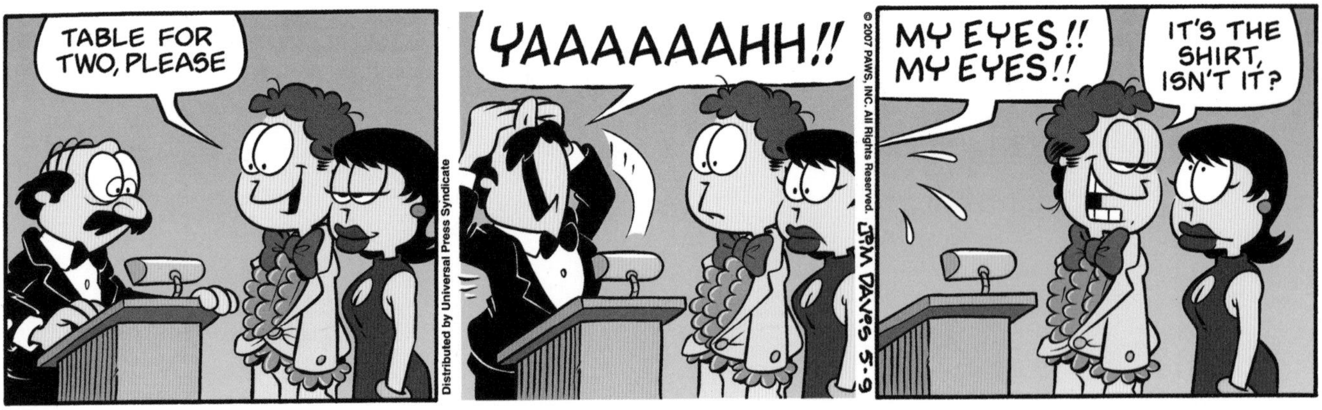
TABLE FOR TWO, PLEASE
Distributed by Universal Press Syndicate
YAAAAAAHH!!
© 2007 PAWS, INC. All Rights Reserved.
JIM DAVIS 5-9
MY EYES!! MY EYES!!
IT'S THE SHIRT, ISN'T IT?

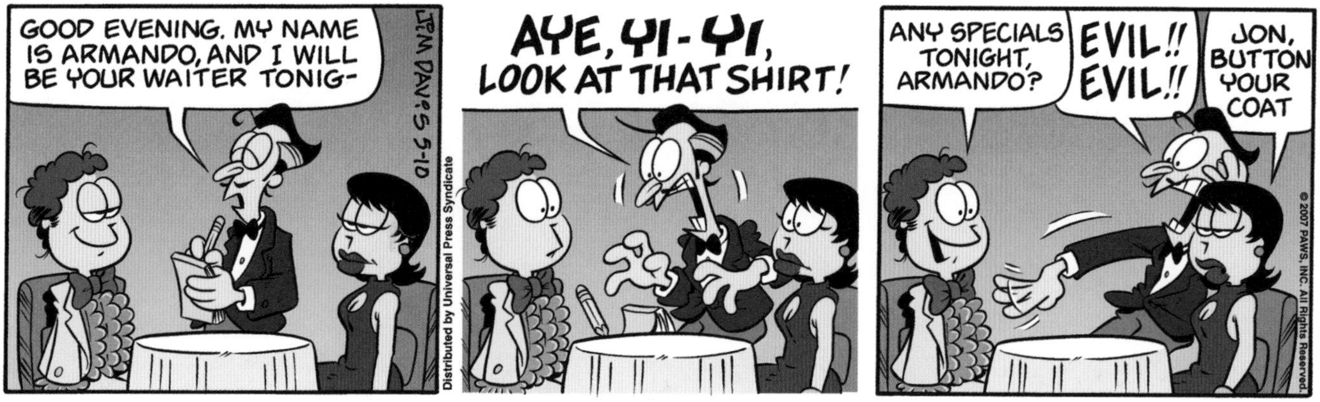
GOOD EVENING. MY NAME IS ARMANDO, AND I WILL BE YOUR WAITER TONIG-
JIM DAVIS 5-10
Distributed by Universal Press Syndicate
AYE, YI-YI, LOOK AT THAT SHIRT!
ANY SPECIALS TONIGHT, ARMANDO?
EVIL!! EVIL!!
JON, BUTTON YOUR COAT
© 2007 PAWS, INC. All Rights Reserved.

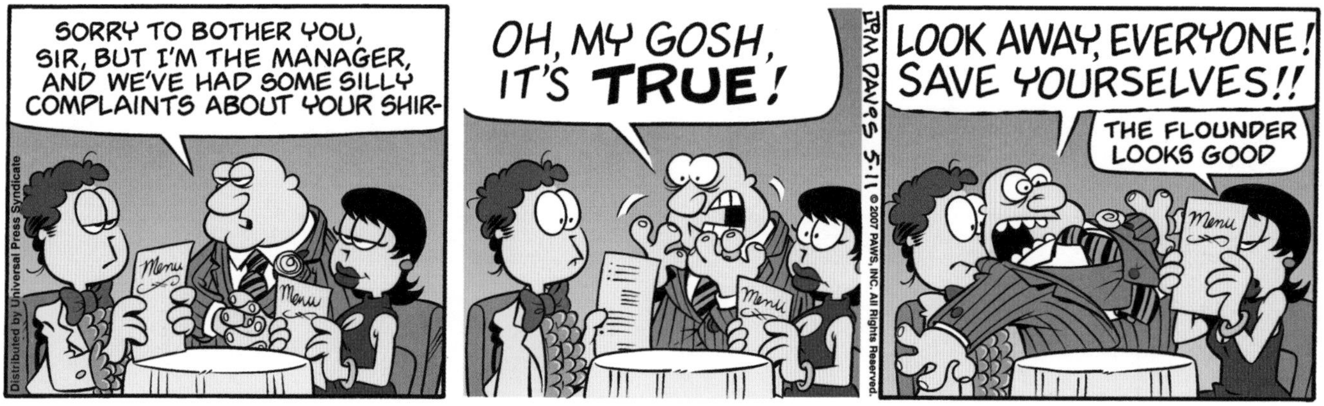
SORRY TO BOTHER YOU, SIR, BUT I'M THE MANAGER, AND WE'VE HAD SOME SILLY COMPLAINTS ABOUT YOUR SHIR-
Distributed by Universal Press Syndicate
Menu
Menu
OH, MY GOSH, IT'S **TRUE**!
JIM DAVIS 5-11
© 2007 PAWS, INC. All Rights Reserved.
Menu
LOOK AWAY, EVERYONE! SAVE YOURSELVES!!
THE FLOUNDER LOOKS GOOD
Menu

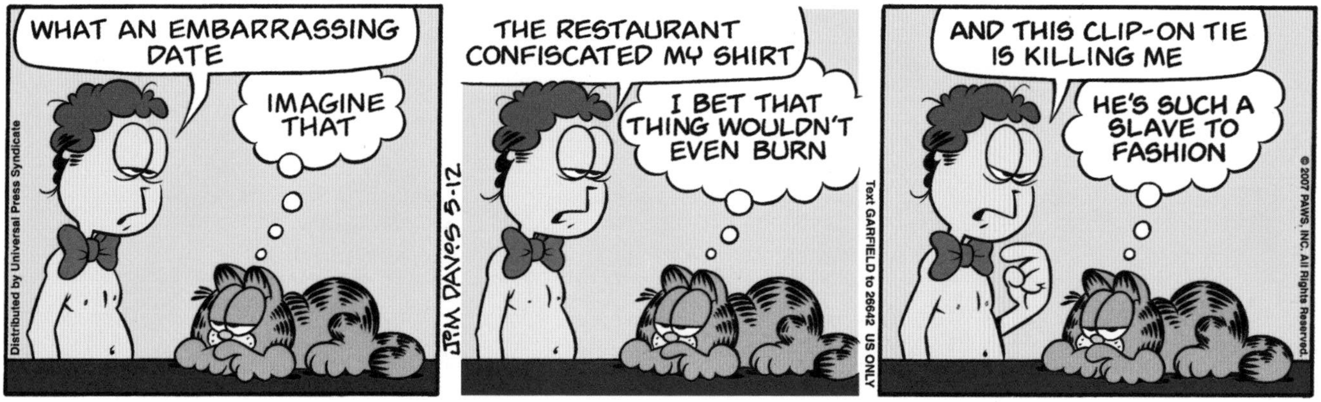
WHAT AN EMBARRASSING DATE
IMAGINE THAT
Distributed by Universal Press Syndicate
JIM DAVIS 5-12
THE RESTAURANT CONFISCATED MY SHIRT
I BET THAT THING WOULDN'T EVEN BURN
Text GARFIELD to 26642 US ONLY
AND THIS CLIP-ON TIE IS KILLING ME
HE'S SUCH A SLAVE TO FASHION
© 2007 PAWS, INC. All Rights Reserved.

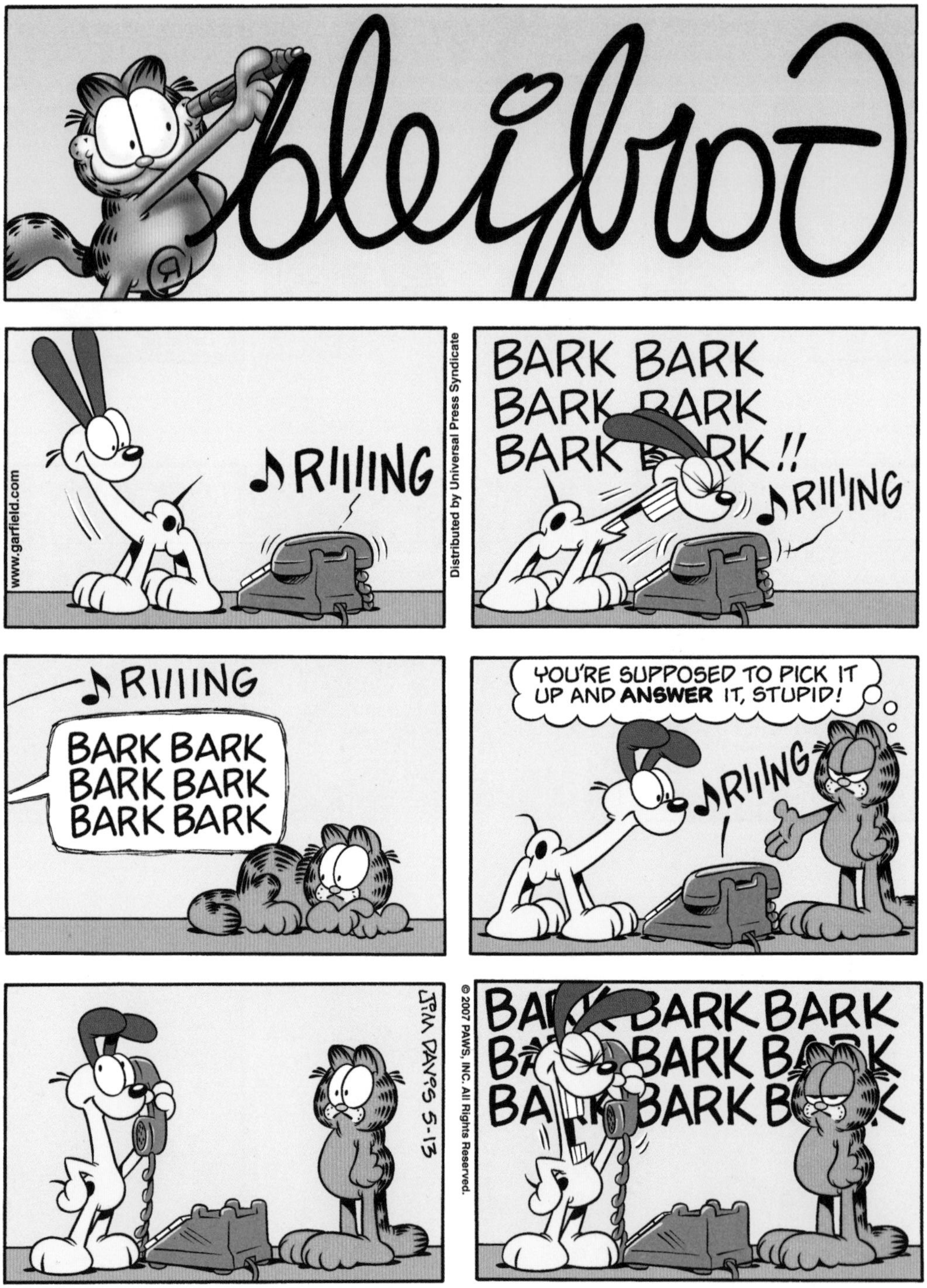
www.garfield.com
♪RIIIING
Distributed by Universal Press Syndicate
BARK BARK BARK BARK BARK BARK!!
♪RIIIING
♪RIIIING
BARK BARK BARK BARK BARK BARK
YOU'RE SUPPOSED TO PICK IT UP AND **ANSWER** IT, STUPID!
♪RIIING
JPM DAVIS 5-13
© 2007 PAWS, INC. All Rights Reserved.
BARK BARK BARK
BARK BARK BARK
BARK BARK BARK

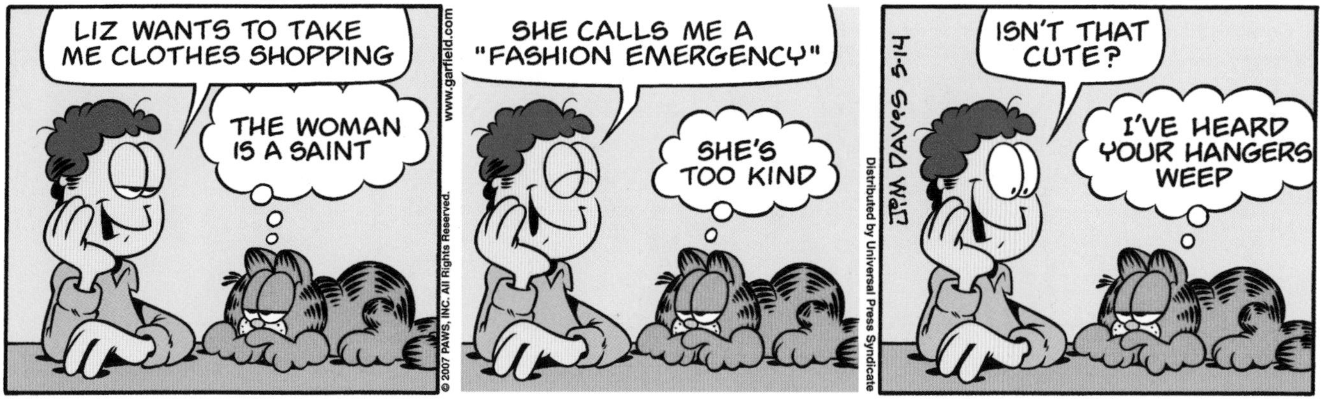
LIZ WANTS TO TAKE ME CLOTHES SHOPPING
THE WOMAN IS A SAINT
SHE CALLS ME A "FASHION EMERGENCY"
SHE'S TOO KIND
ISN'T THAT CUTE?
I'VE HEARD YOUR HANGERS WEEP
JIM DAVIS 5-14
© 2007 PAWS, INC. All Rights Reserved. www.garfield.com
Distributed by Universal Press Syndicate

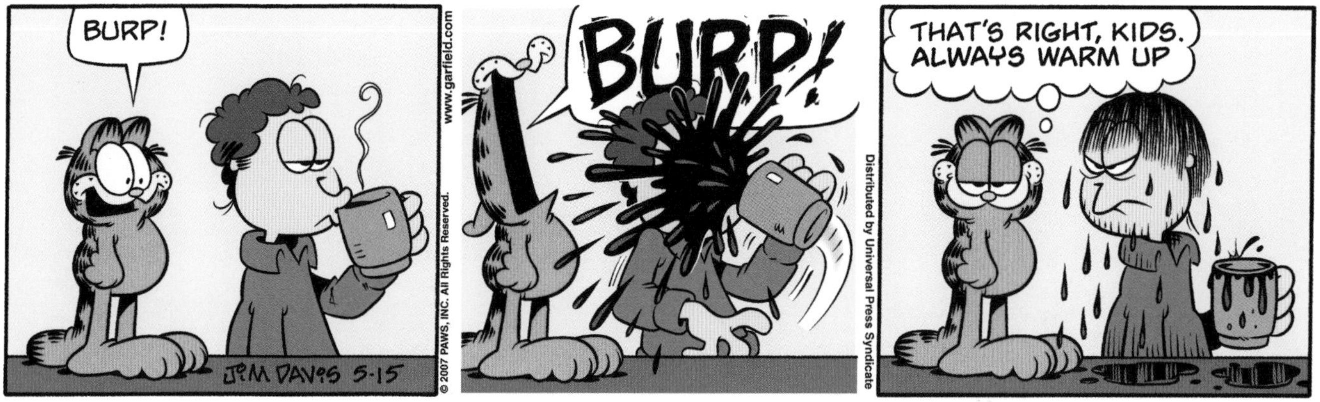
BURP!
JIM DAVIS 5-15
BURP!
THAT'S RIGHT, KIDS. ALWAYS WARM UP
© 2007 PAWS, INC. All Rights Reserved. www.garfield.com
Distributed by Universal Press Syndicate

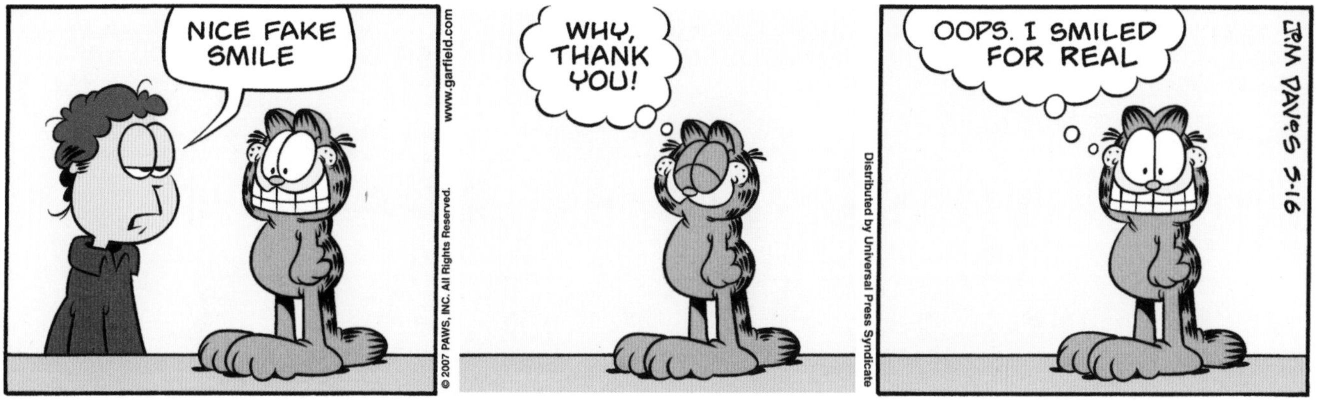
NICE FAKE SMILE
WHY, THANK YOU!
OOPS. I SMILED FOR REAL
JIM DAVIS 5-16
© 2007 PAWS, INC. All Rights Reserved. www.garfield.com
Distributed by Universal Press Syndicate

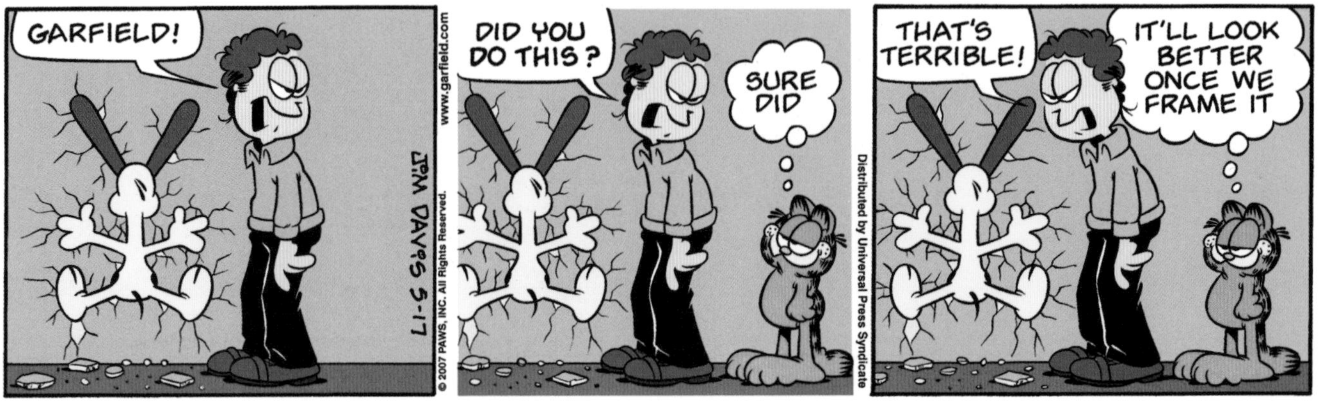
GARFIELD!
© 2007 PAWS, INC. All Rights Reserved. www.garfield.com
DID YOU DO THIS?
SURE DID
Distributed by Universal Press Syndicate
THAT'S TERRIBLE!
IT'LL LOOK BETTER ONCE WE FRAME IT

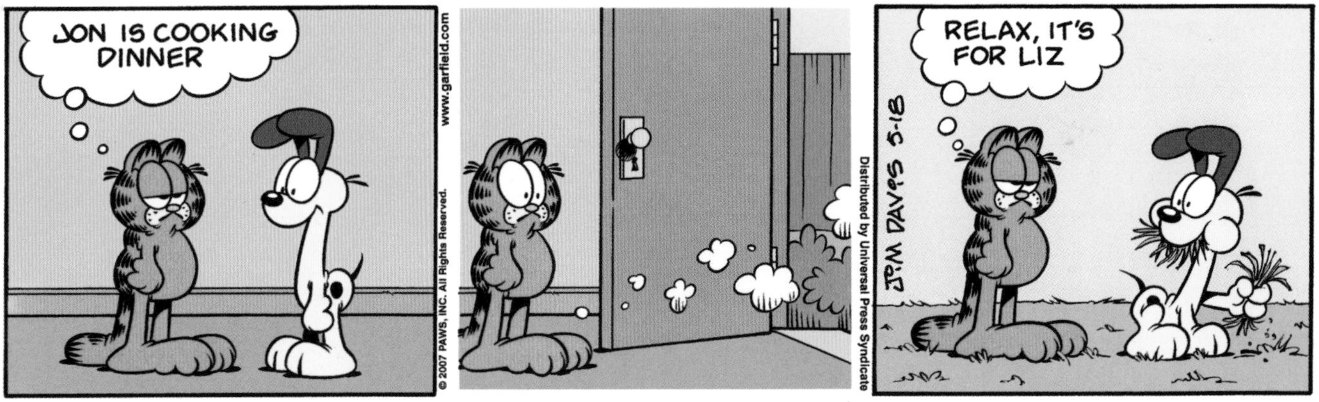
JON IS COOKING DINNER
© 2007 PAWS, INC. All Rights Reserved. www.garfield.com
Distributed by Universal Press Syndicate
RELAX, IT'S FOR LIZ

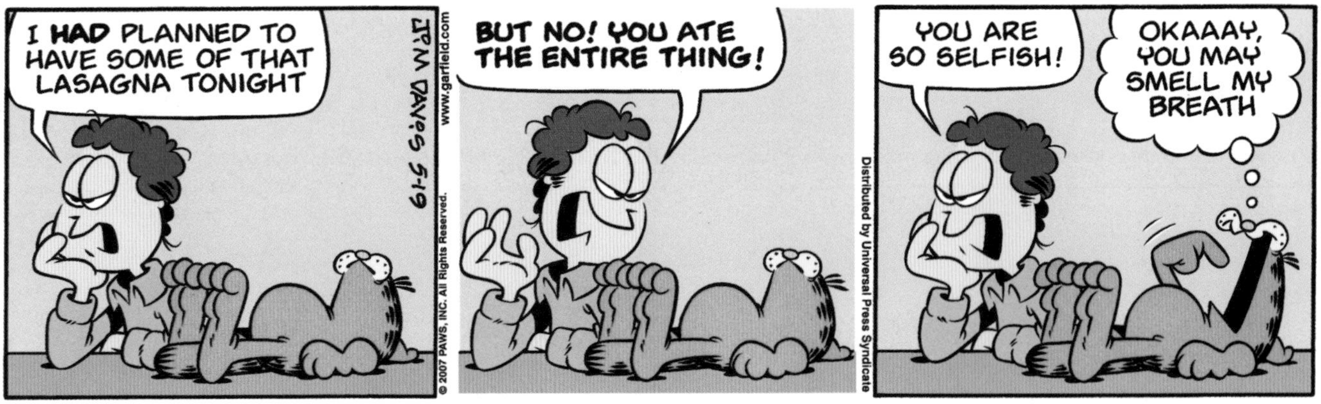
I HAD PLANNED TO HAVE SOME OF THAT LASAGNA TONIGHT
© 2007 PAWS, INC. All Rights Reserved. www.garfield.com
BUT NO! YOU ATE THE ENTIRE THING!
Distributed by Universal Press Syndicate
YOU ARE SO SELFISH!
OKAAAY, YOU MAY SMELL MY BREATH

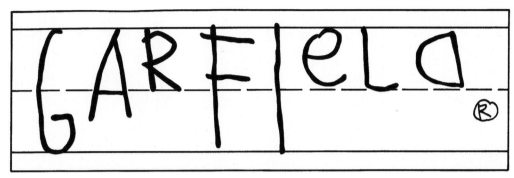

© 2007 PAWS, INC. All Rights Reserved.

Text GARFIELD to 26642 US ONLY

HEY, YOU BREWED A NEW POT!

SIP

JIM DAVIS 5-20

WANT SOME?

NAH

Distributed by Universal Press Syndicate

TOO WEAK FOR ME

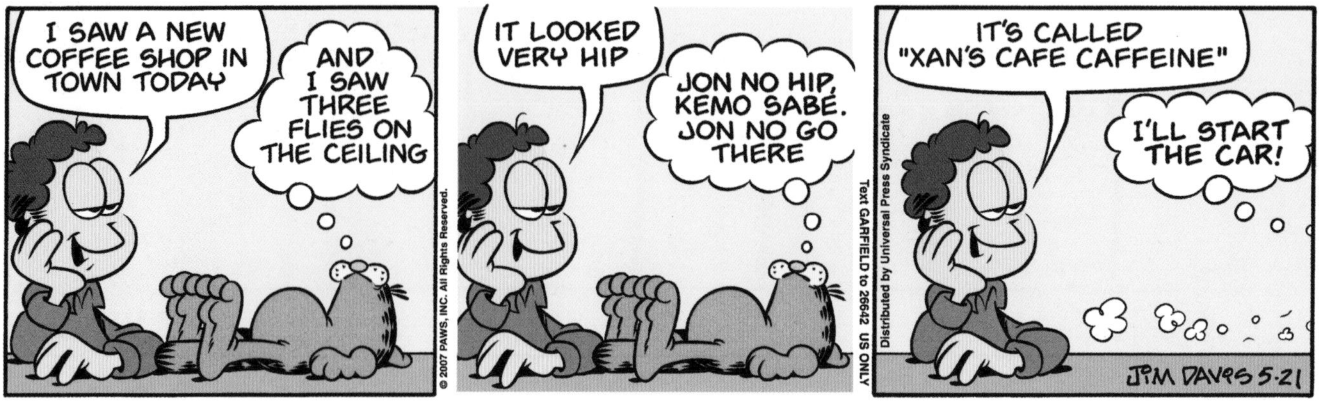
I SAW A NEW COFFEE SHOP IN TOWN TODAY
AND I SAW THREE FLIES ON THE CEILING
© 2007 PAWS, INC. All Rights Reserved.
IT LOOKED VERY HIP
JON NO HIP, KEMO SABÉ. JON NO GO THERE
Text GARFIELD to 26642 US ONLY
Distributed by Universal Press Syndicate
IT'S CALLED "XAN'S CAFE CAFFEINE"
I'LL START THE CAR!
JIM DAVIS 5-21

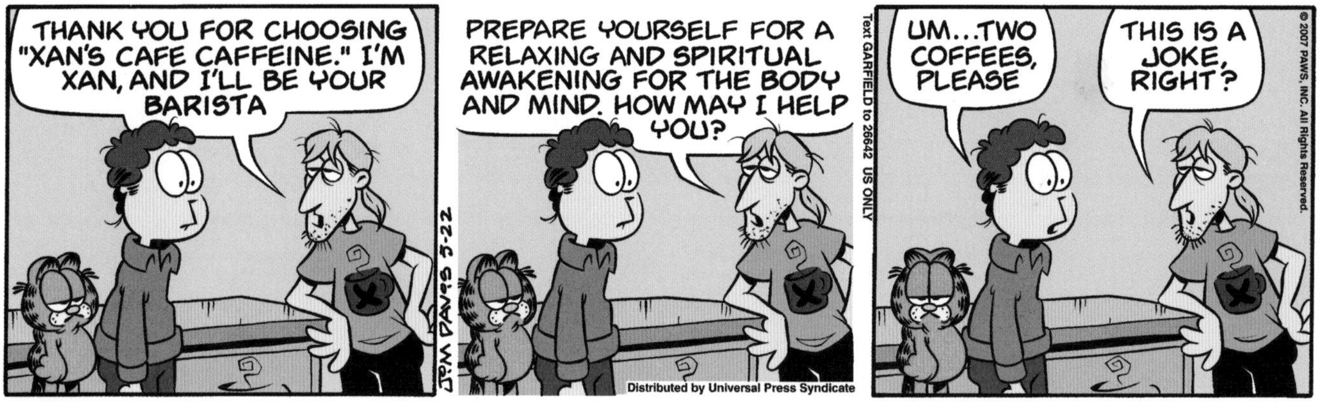
THANK YOU FOR CHOOSING "XAN'S CAFE CAFFEINE." I'M XAN, AND I'LL BE YOUR BARISTA
JIM DAVIS 5-22
PREPARE YOURSELF FOR A RELAXING AND SPIRITUAL AWAKENING FOR THE BODY AND MIND. HOW MAY I HELP YOU?
Distributed by Universal Press Syndicate
Text GARFIELD to 26642 US ONLY
UM...TWO COFFEES, PLEASE
THIS IS A JOKE, RIGHT?
© 2007 PAWS, INC. All Rights Reserved.

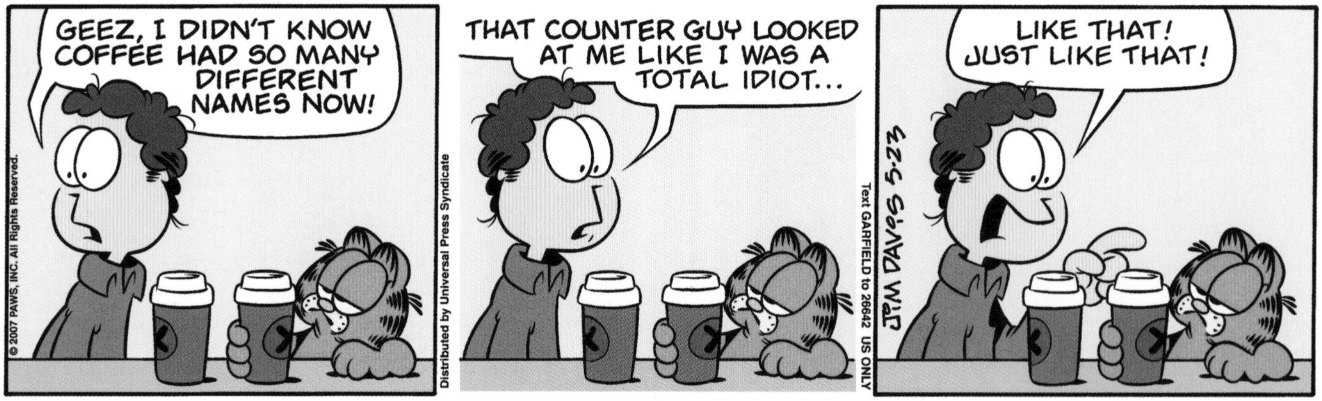
GEEZ, I DIDN'T KNOW COFFEE HAD SO MANY DIFFERENT NAMES NOW!
© 2007 PAWS, INC. All Rights Reserved.
Distributed by Universal Press Syndicate
THAT COUNTER GUY LOOKED AT ME LIKE I WAS A TOTAL IDIOT...
Text GARFIELD to 26642 US ONLY
JIM DAVIS 5-23
LIKE THAT! JUST LIKE THAT!

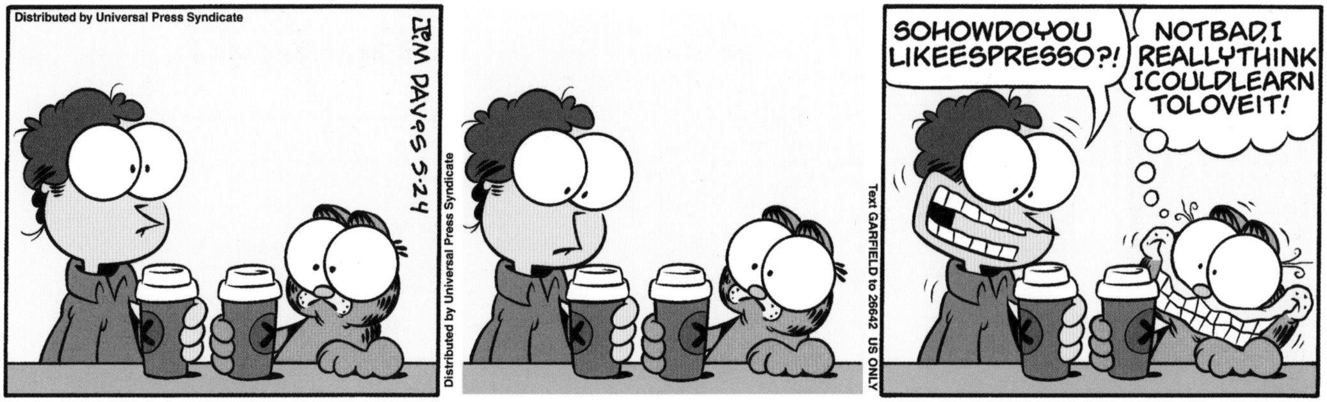
Distributed by Universal Press Syndicate
JIM DAVIS 5·24
Distributed by Universal Press Syndicate
Text GARFIELD to 26642 US ONLY
SOHOWDOYOU LIKEESPRESSO?!
NOTBAD,I REALLYTHINK ICOULDLEARN TOLOVEIT!

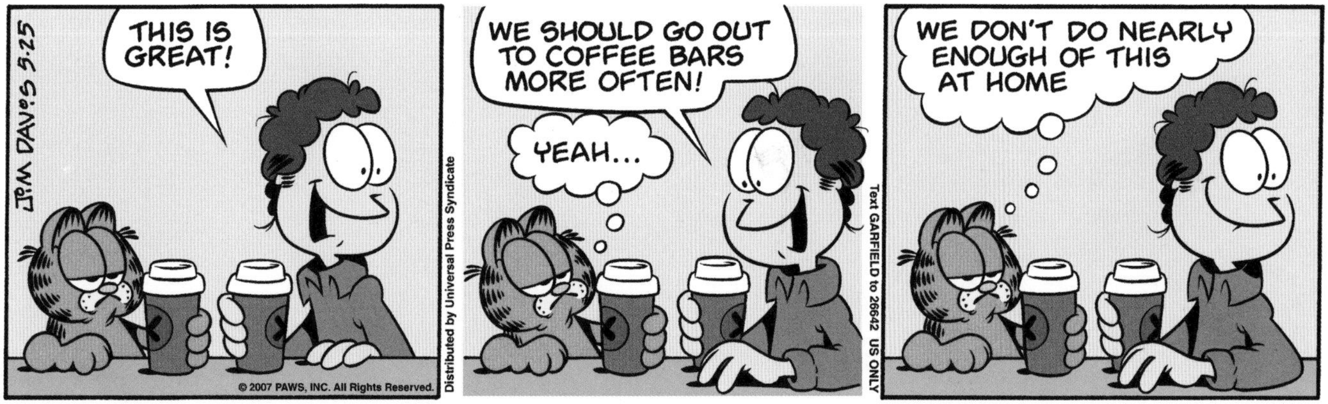
JIM DAVIS 5·25
THIS IS GREAT!
© 2007 PAWS, INC. All Rights Reserved.
Distributed by Universal Press Syndicate
WE SHOULD GO OUT TO COFFEE BARS MORE OFTEN!
YEAH...
Text GARFIELD to 26642 US ONLY
WE DON'T DO NEARLY ENOUGH OF THIS AT HOME

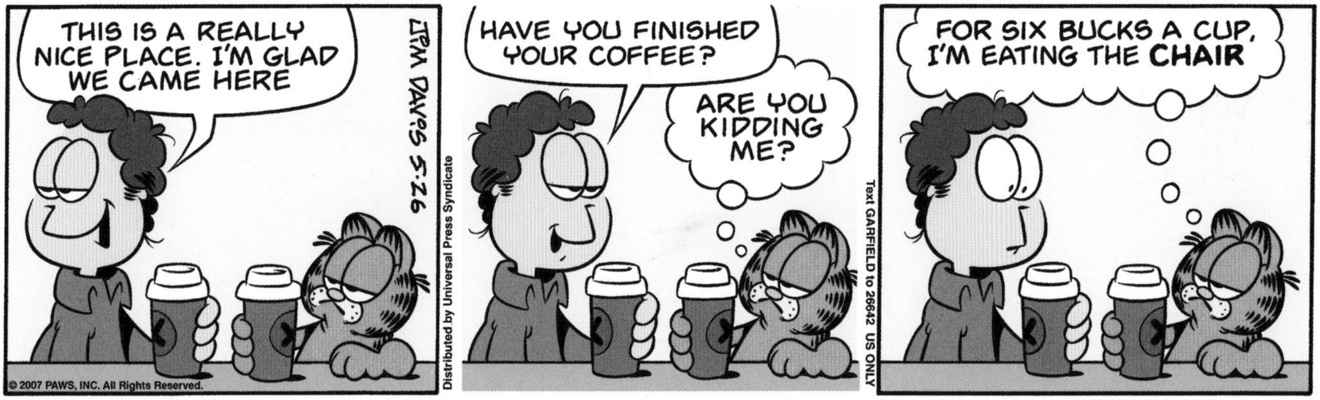
THIS IS A REALLY NICE PLACE. I'M GLAD WE CAME HERE
JIM DAVIS 5·26
© 2007 PAWS, INC. All Rights Reserved.
Distributed by Universal Press Syndicate
HAVE YOU FINISHED YOUR COFFEE?
ARE YOU KIDDING ME?
Text GARFIELD to 26642 US ONLY
FOR SIX BUCKS A CUP, I'M EATING THE **CHAIR**

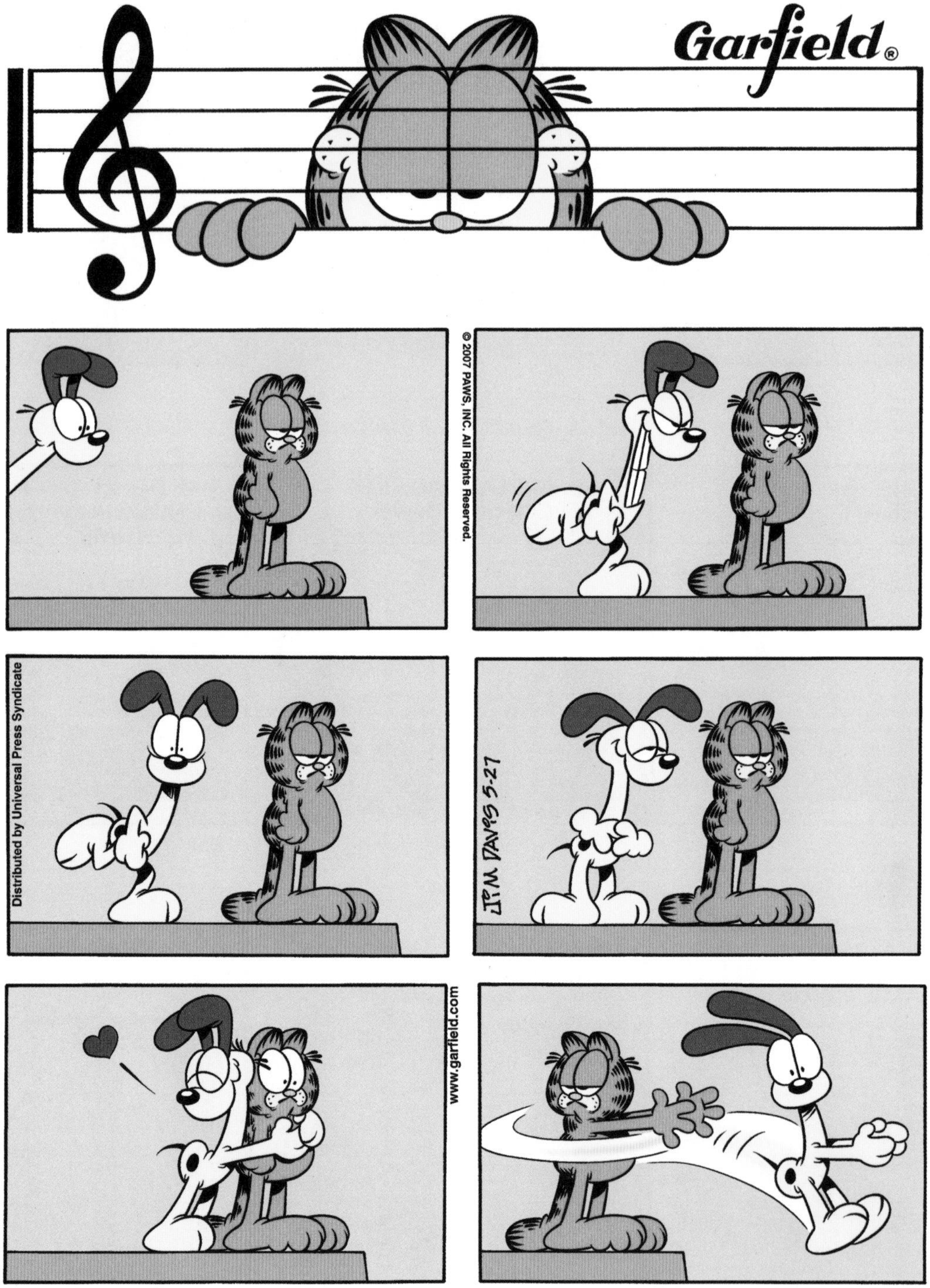
Garfield®
© 2007 PAWS, INC. All Rights Reserved.
Distributed by Universal Press Syndicate
JIM DAVIS 5-27
www.garfield.com

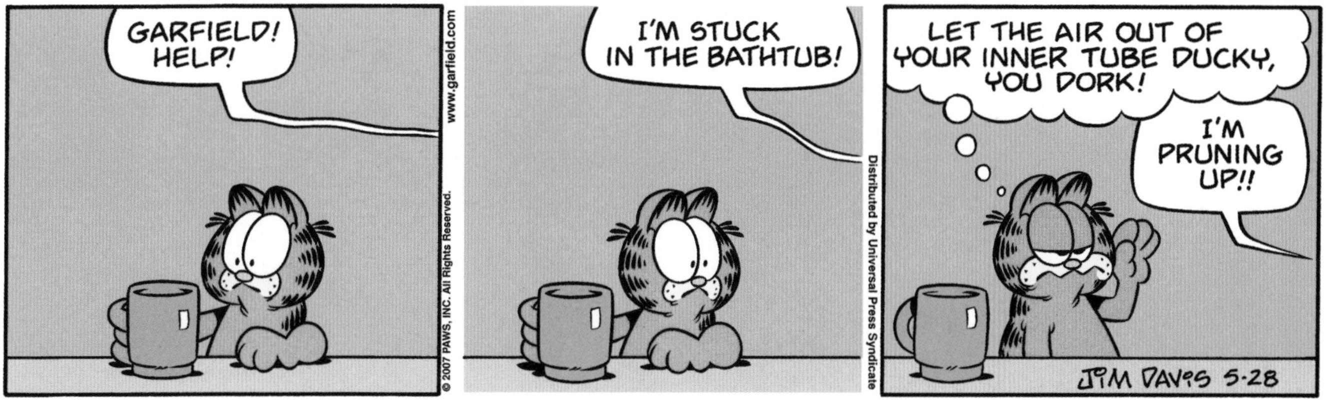
GARFIELD! HELP!
I'M STUCK IN THE BATHTUB!
LET THE AIR OUT OF YOUR INNER TUBE DUCKY, YOU DORK!
I'M PRUNING UP!!
JIM DAVIS 5-28
© 2007 PAWS, INC. All Rights Reserved. www.garfield.com
Distributed by Universal Press Syndicate

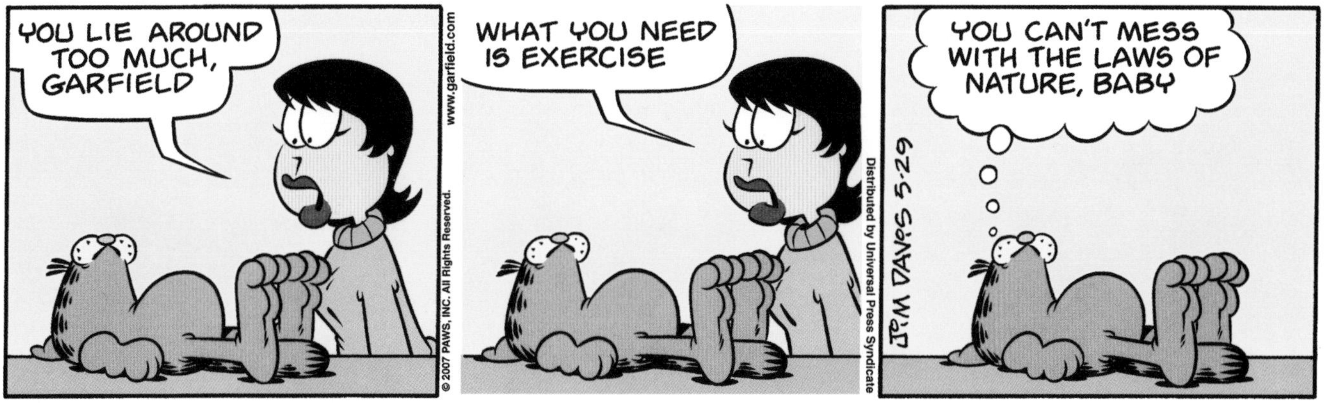
YOU LIE AROUND TOO MUCH, GARFIELD
WHAT YOU NEED IS EXERCISE
YOU CAN'T MESS WITH THE LAWS OF NATURE, BABY
JIM DAVIS 5-29
© 2007 PAWS, INC. All Rights Reserved. www.garfield.com
Distributed by Universal Press Syndicate

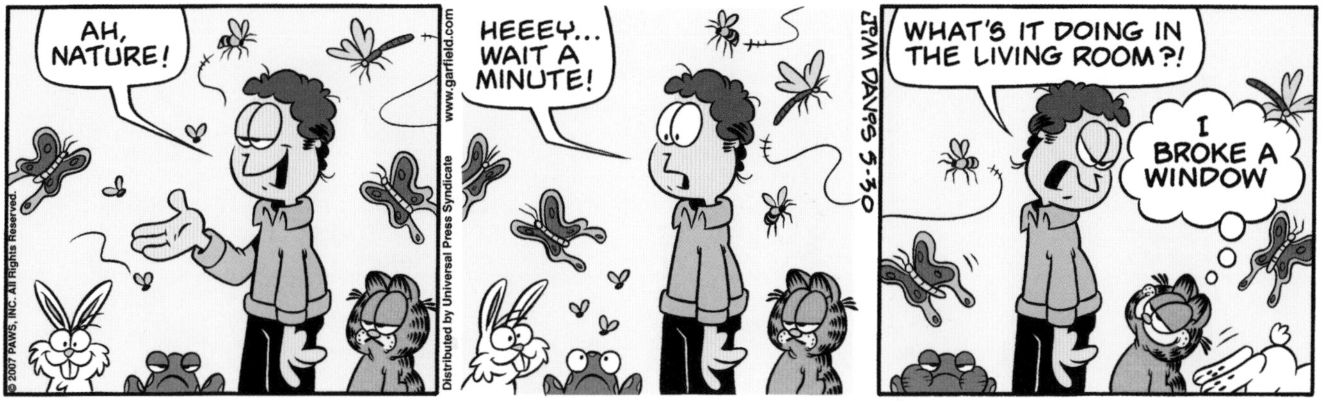
AH, NATURE!
HEEEY... WAIT A MINUTE!
WHAT'S IT DOING IN THE LIVING ROOM?!
I BROKE A WINDOW
JIM DAVIS 5-30
© 2007 PAWS, INC. All Rights Reserved. www.garfield.com
Distributed by Universal Press Syndicate

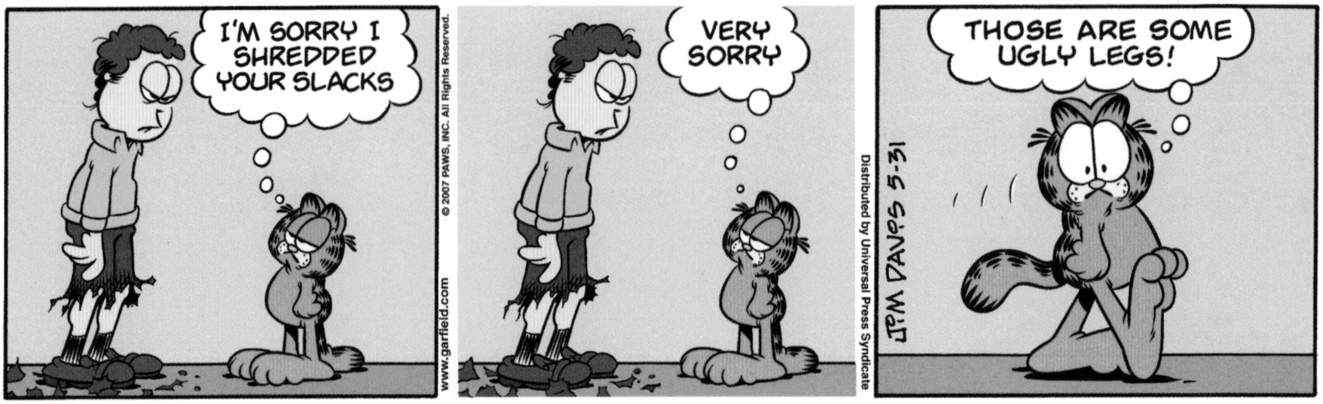
I'M SORRY I SHREDDED YOUR SLACKS
© 2007 PAWS, INC. All Rights Reserved.
www.garfield.com
VERY SORRY
Distributed by Universal Press Syndicate
JIM DAVIS 5-31
THOSE ARE SOME UGLY LEGS!

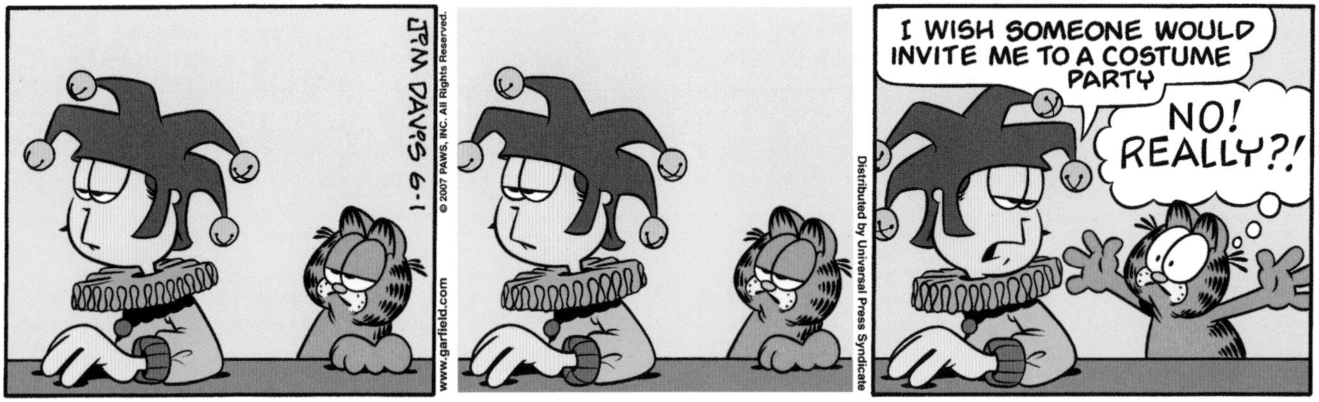
JIM DAVIS 6-1
© 2007 PAWS, INC. All Rights Reserved.
www.garfield.com
Distributed by Universal Press Syndicate
I WISH SOMEONE WOULD INVITE ME TO A COSTUME PARTY
NO! REALLY?!

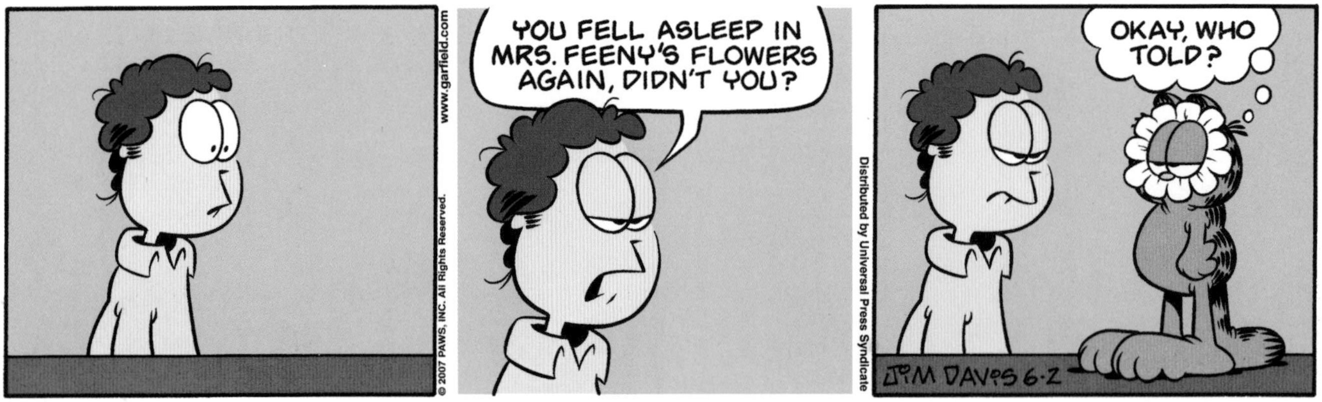
© 2007 PAWS, INC. All Rights Reserved.
www.garfield.com
YOU FELL ASLEEP IN MRS. FEENY'S FLOWERS AGAIN, DIDN'T YOU?
Distributed by Universal Press Syndicate
OKAY, WHO TOLD?
JIM DAVIS 6-2

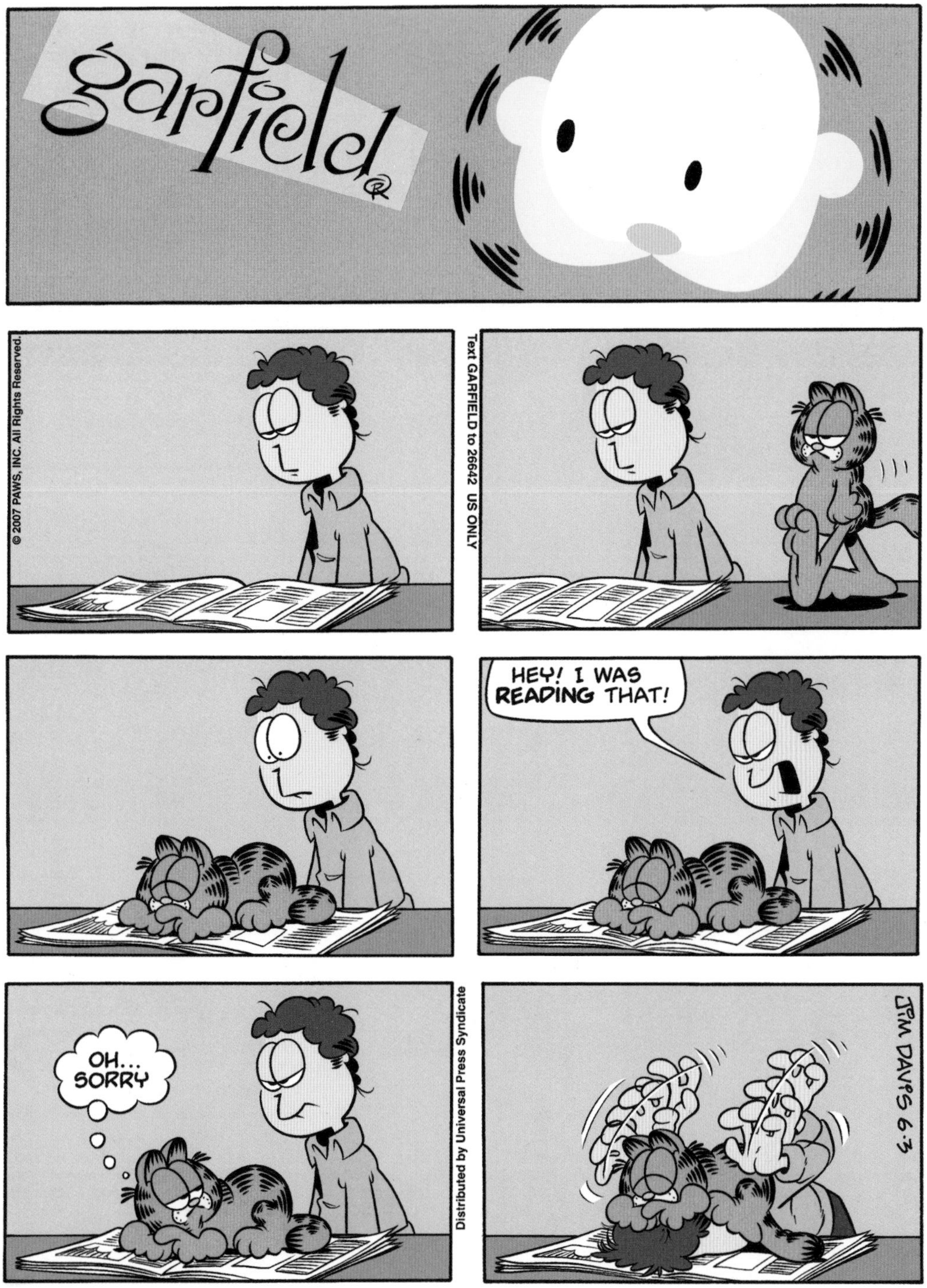
garfield
© 2007 PAWS, INC. All Rights Reserved.
Text GARFIELD to 26642 US ONLY
HEY! I WAS READING THAT!
OH... SORRY
Distributed by Universal Press Syndicate
JIM DAVIS 6-3

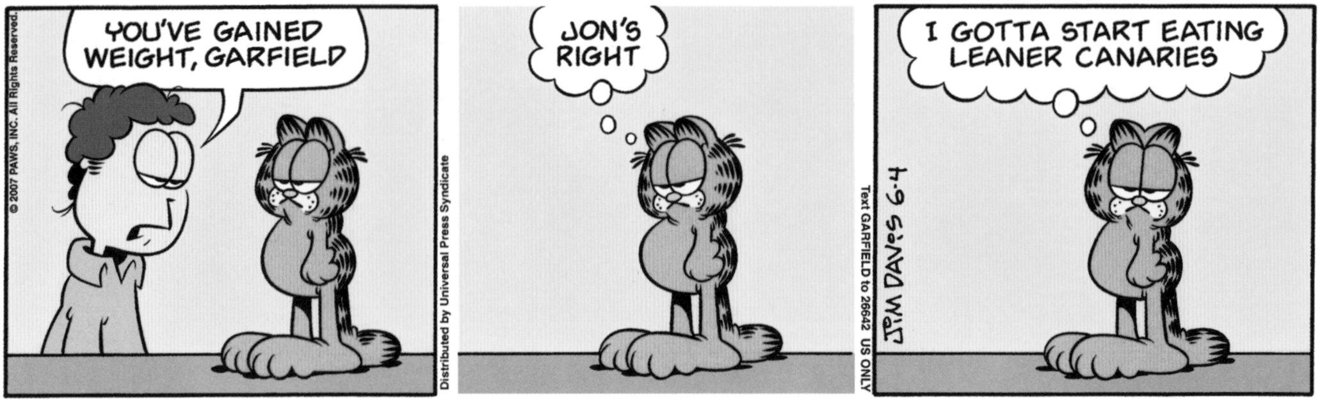
YOU'VE GAINED WEIGHT, GARFIELD
JON'S RIGHT
I GOTTA START EATING LEANER CANARIES

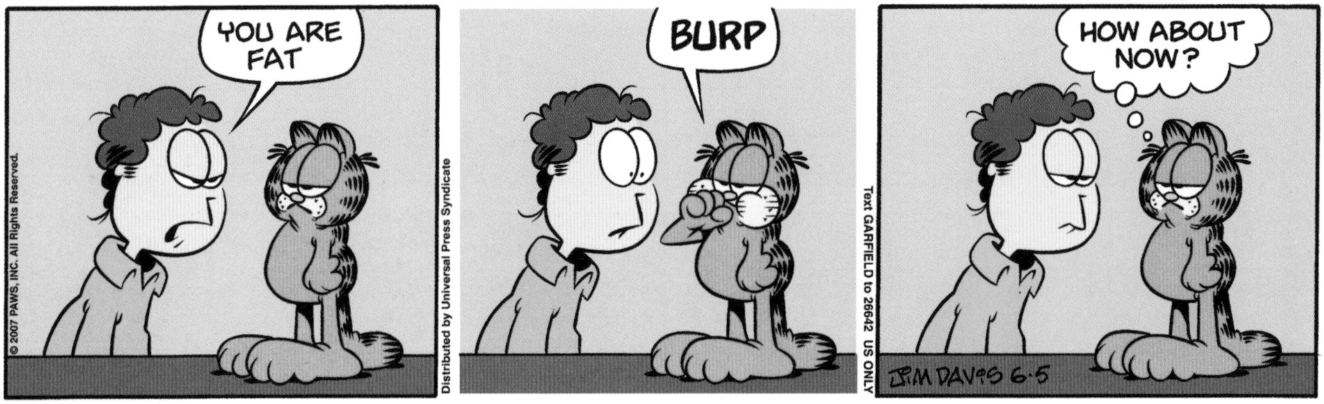
YOU ARE FAT
BURP
HOW ABOUT NOW?

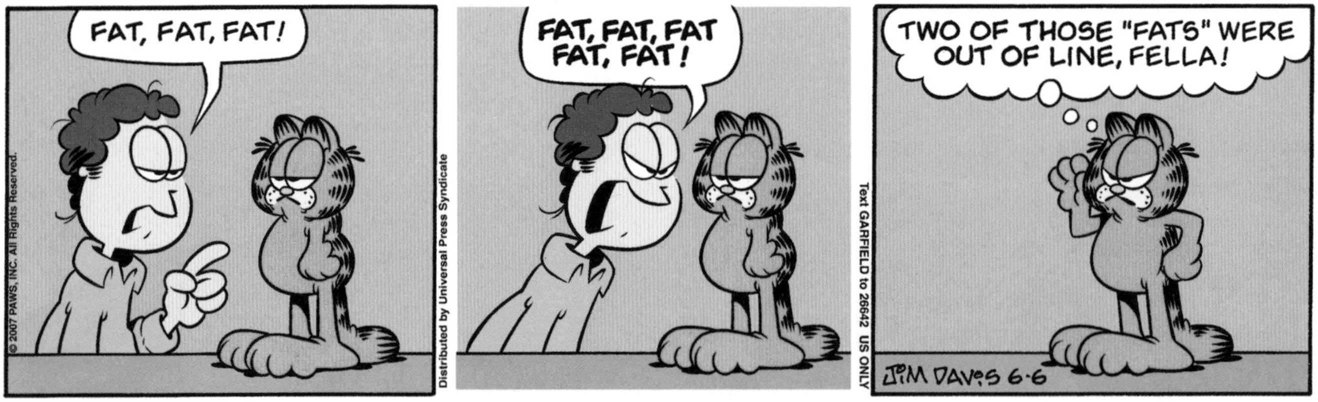
FAT, FAT, FAT!
FAT, FAT, FAT FAT, FAT!
TWO OF THOSE "FATS" WERE OUT OF LINE, FELLA!

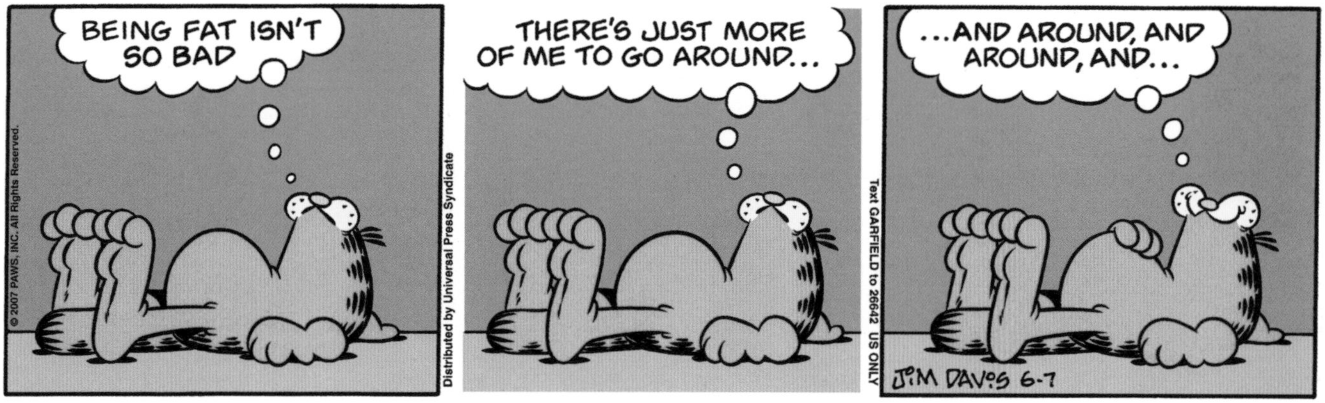
BEING FAT ISN'T SO BAD
© 2007 PAWS, INC. All Rights Reserved.
Distributed by Universal Press Syndicate
THERE'S JUST MORE OF ME TO GO AROUND...
Text GARFIELD to 26642 US ONLY
...AND AROUND, AND AROUND, AND...
JIM DAVIS 6-7

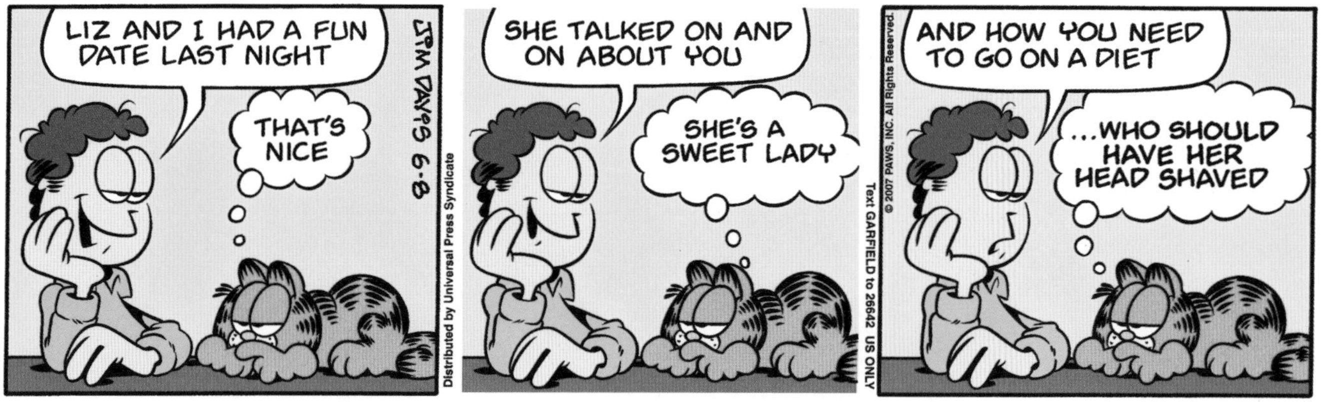
LIZ AND I HAD A FUN DATE LAST NIGHT
THAT'S NICE
JIM DAVIS 6-8
Distributed by Universal Press Syndicate
SHE TALKED ON AND ON ABOUT YOU
SHE'S A SWEET LADY
Text GARFIELD to 26642 US ONLY
© 2007 PAWS, INC. All Rights Reserved.
AND HOW YOU NEED TO GO ON A DIET
...WHO SHOULD HAVE HER HEAD SHAVED

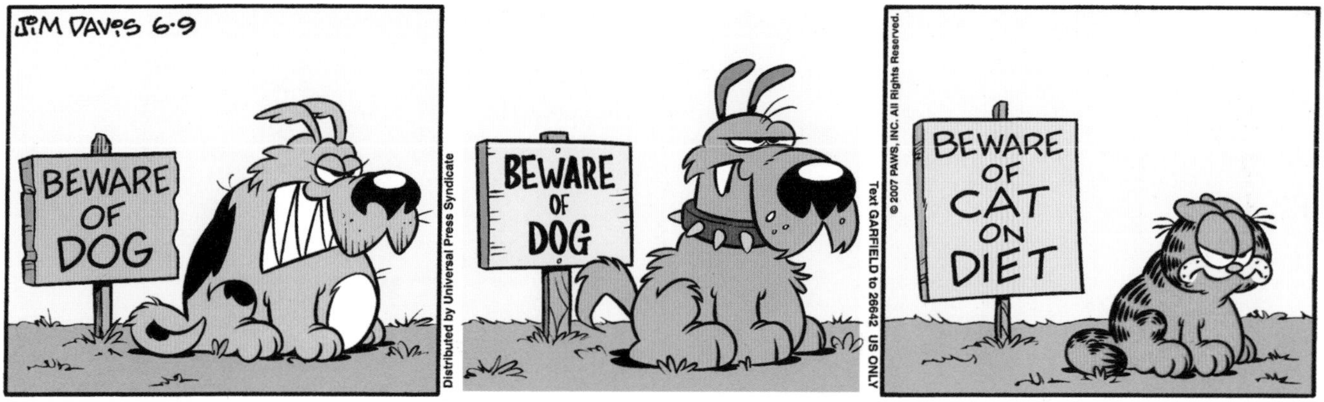
JIM DAVIS 6-9
BEWARE OF DOG
Distributed by Universal Press Syndicate
BEWARE OF DOG
Text GARFIELD to 26642 US ONLY
© 2007 PAWS, INC. All Rights Reserved.
BEWARE OF CAT ON DIET

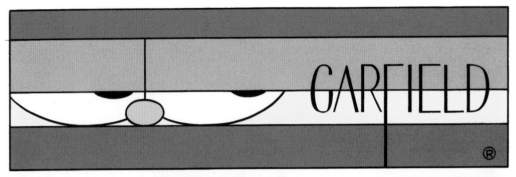

www.garfield.com

BYE, LIZ...YEAH... ME, TOO...

Distributed by Universal Press Syndicate

YOU WANT ME TO WHAT?!

LIZ, I CAN'T KISS THE PHONE...MY CAT IS WATCHING

JIM DAVIS 6-10

© 2007 PAWS, INC. All Rights Reserved.

YEAH, I KNOW THAT SOUNDS WEIRD

JUST TRUST ME ON THIS

ONE TIME FOR THE CAMERA PHONE, COME ON!

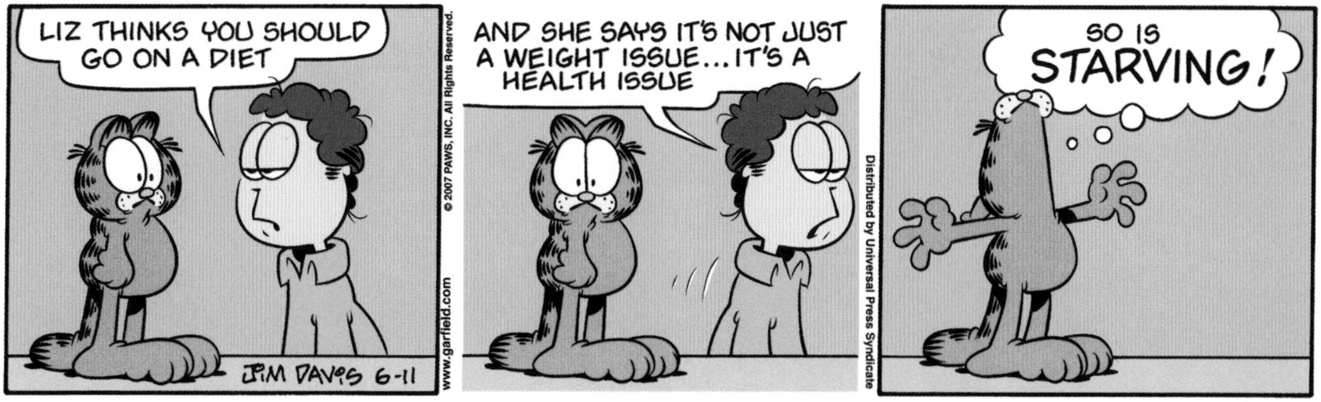
LIZ THINKS YOU SHOULD GO ON A DIET
JIM DAVIS 6-11
© 2007 PAWS, INC. All Rights Reserved.
www.garfield.com
AND SHE SAYS IT'S NOT JUST A WEIGHT ISSUE... IT'S A HEALTH ISSUE
Distributed by Universal Press Syndicate
SO IS STARVING!

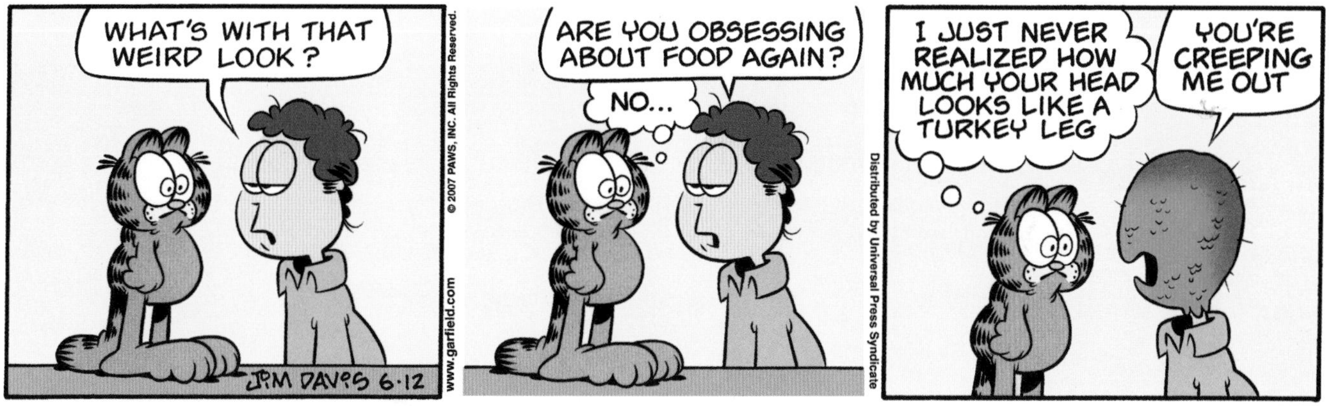
WHAT'S WITH THAT WEIRD LOOK?
JIM DAVIS 6-12
© 2007 PAWS, INC. All Rights Reserved.
www.garfield.com
ARE YOU OBSESSING ABOUT FOOD AGAIN?
NO...
Distributed by Universal Press Syndicate
I JUST NEVER REALIZED HOW MUCH YOUR HEAD LOOKS LIKE A TURKEY LEG
YOU'RE CREEPING ME OUT

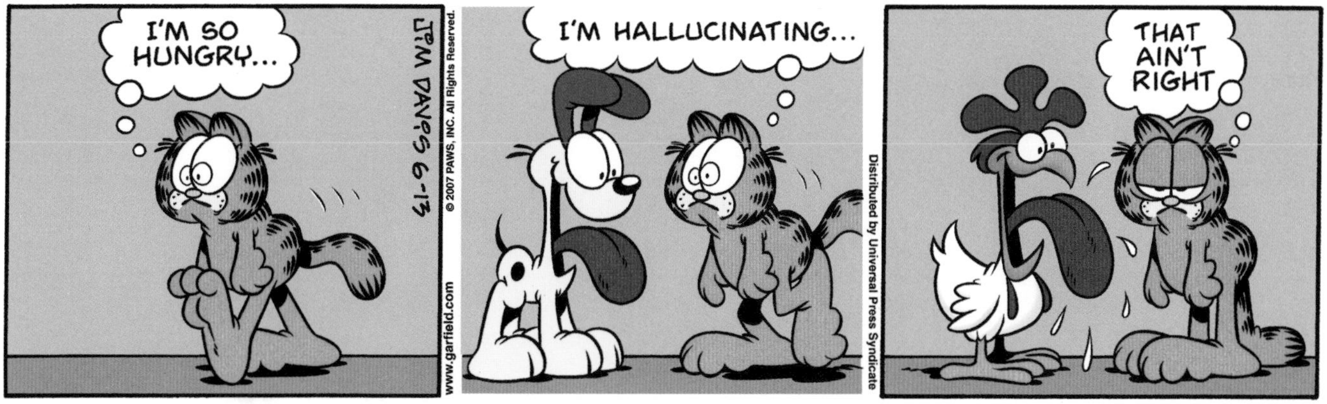
I'M SO HUNGRY...
JIM DAVIS 6-13
© 2007 PAWS, INC. All Rights Reserved.
www.garfield.com
I'M HALLUCINATING...
Distributed by Universal Press Syndicate
THAT AIN'T RIGHT

TOP 50 REASONS TO PARTY!

Somewhere in the world it's Happy Hour

You finally got your sock drawer organized

Nostradamus prophesied it

You want to listen to all 10,000 songs on your MP3 player

You can't think of anything boring to do

You've invested heavily in piñatas

They just passed a law abolishing Mondays

It's a good way to meet your local law enforcement officials

You don't want to offend the Party Gods

Elvis told you to in a dream

You're tired of playing charades by yourself

You look great in a toga

It's the only exercise you get

You're considering it as a career

You're carrying a party gene

The moon is in a party phase

Because it's daytime

Because it's nighttime

Maturity is overrated

You're dying to wear your new lampshade

You finally potty trained your virtual pet

Your yo-yo stock went up a point

Your place could use a good trashing

The fun content of your blood is too low

You have a bad reputation to uphold

It's exactly one week later than this time last week

Fun is a terrible thing to waste

You're not getting any younger

You're having a good hair day

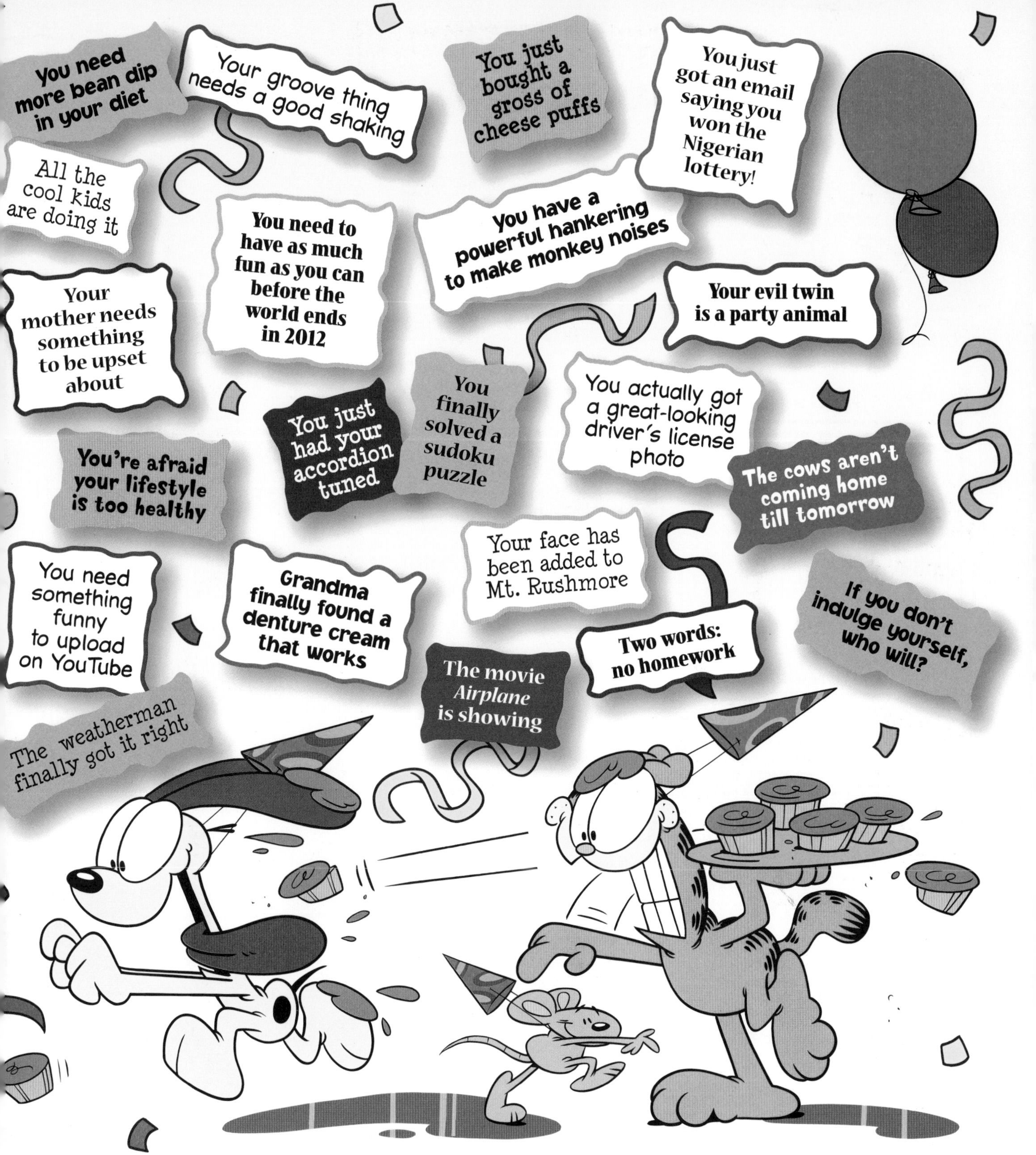
You need more bean dip in your diet
Your groove thing needs a good shaking
You just bought a gross of cheese puffs
You just got an email saying you won the Nigerian lottery!
All the cool kids are doing it
You need to have as much fun as you can before the world ends in 2012
You have a powerful hankering to make monkey noises
Your mother needs something to be upset about
Your evil twin is a party animal
You just had your accordion tuned
You finally solved a sudoku puzzle
You actually got a great-looking driver's license photo
You're afraid your lifestyle is too healthy
The cows aren't coming home till tomorrow
Your face has been added to Mt. Rushmore
You need something funny to upload on YouTube
Grandma finally found a denture cream that works
If you don't indulge yourself, who will?
Two words: no homework
The movie Airplane is showing
The weatherman finally got it right

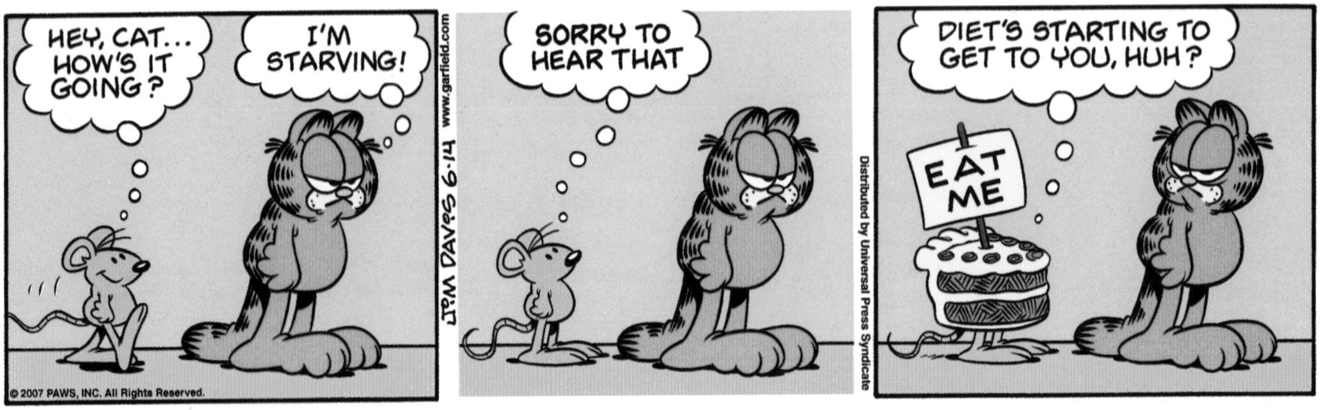
HEY, CAT... HOW'S IT GOING?
I'M STARVING!
SORRY TO HEAR THAT
DIET'S STARTING TO GET TO YOU, HUH?
EAT ME
JIM DAVIS 6-14
www.garfield.com
© 2007 PAWS, INC. All Rights Reserved.
Distributed by Universal Press Syndicate

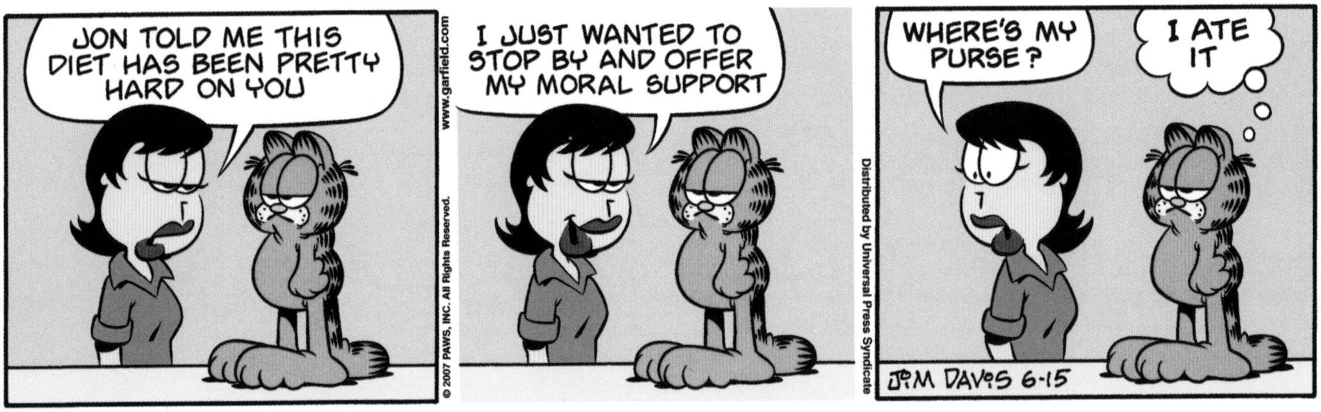
JON TOLD ME THIS DIET HAS BEEN PRETTY HARD ON YOU
I JUST WANTED TO STOP BY AND OFFER MY MORAL SUPPORT
WHERE'S MY PURSE?
I ATE IT
JIM DAVIS 6-15
www.garfield.com
© 2007 PAWS, INC. All Rights Reserved.
Distributed by Universal Press Syndicate

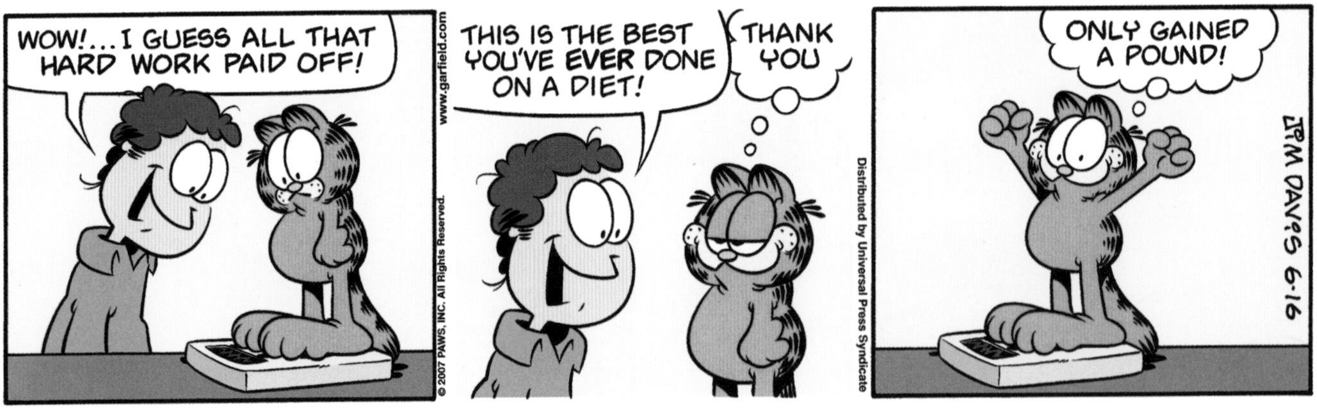
WOW!... I GUESS ALL THAT HARD WORK PAID OFF!
THIS IS THE BEST YOU'VE EVER DONE ON A DIET!
THANK YOU
ONLY GAINED A POUND!
JIM DAVIS 6-16
www.garfield.com
© 2007 PAWS, INC. All Rights Reserved.
Distributed by Universal Press Syndicate

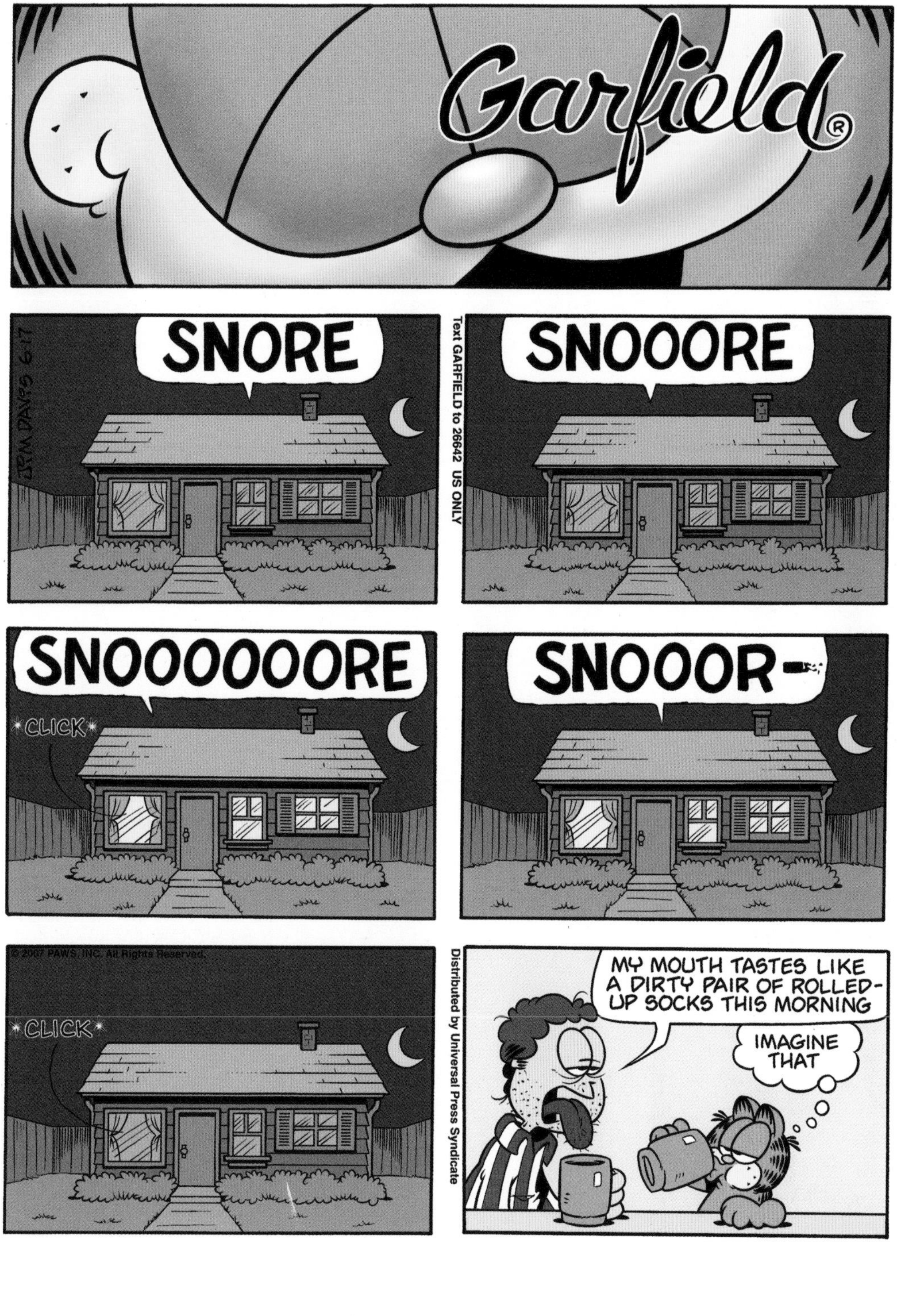
Garfield®
JIM DAVIS 6-17
SNORE
Text GARFIELD to 26642 US ONLY
SNOOORE
SNOOOOOORE
CLICK
SNOOOR-
© 2007 PAWS, INC. All Rights Reserved.
CLICK
Distributed by Universal Press Syndicate
MY MOUTH TASTES LIKE A DIRTY PAIR OF ROLLED-UP SOCKS THIS MORNING
IMAGINE THAT

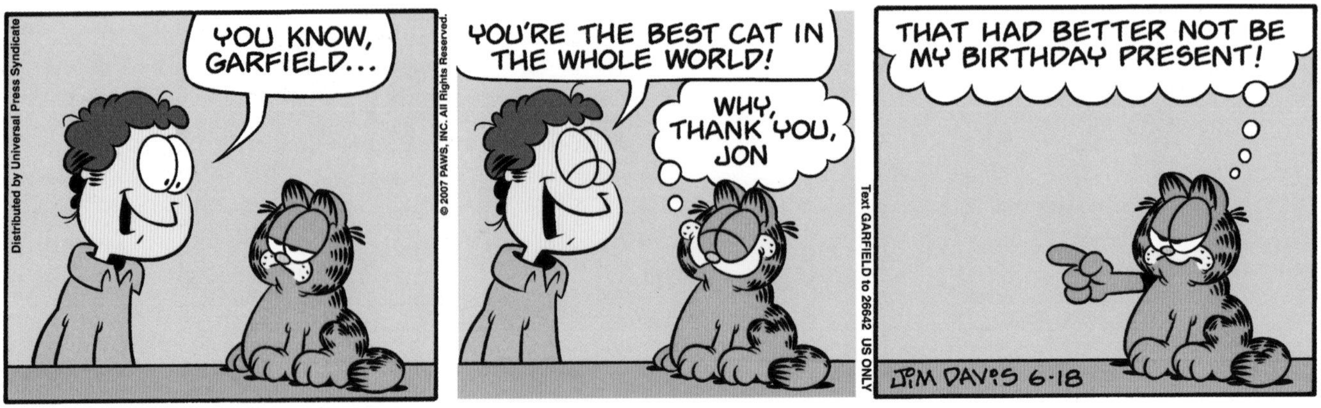
Distributed by Universal Press Syndicate
YOU KNOW, GARFIELD...
© 2007 PAWS, INC. All Rights Reserved.
YOU'RE THE BEST CAT IN THE WHOLE WORLD!
WHY, THANK YOU, JON
Text GARFIELD to 26642 US ONLY
THAT HAD BETTER NOT BE MY BIRTHDAY PRESENT!
JIM DAVIS 6-18

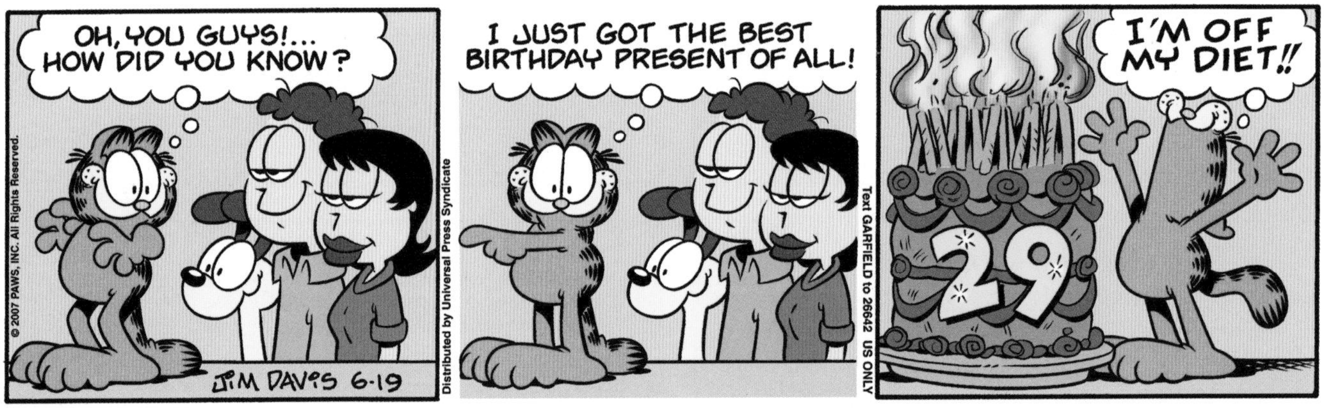
© 2007 PAWS, INC. All Rights Reserved.
OH, YOU GUYS!... HOW DID YOU KNOW?
JIM DAVIS 6-19
Distributed by Universal Press Syndicate
I JUST GOT THE BEST BIRTHDAY PRESENT OF ALL!
Text GARFIELD to 26642 US ONLY
I'M OFF MY DIET!!
29

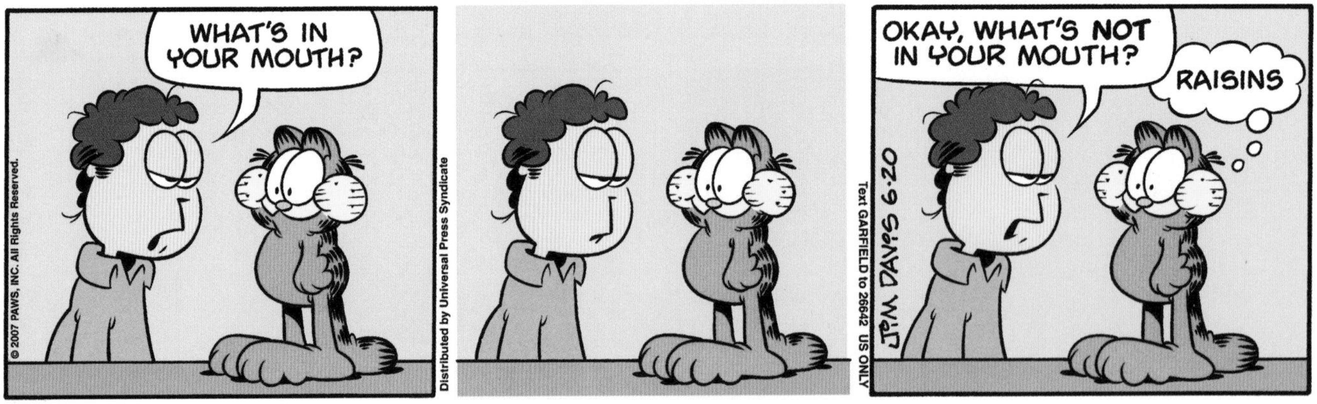
© 2007 PAWS, INC. All Rights Reserved.
WHAT'S IN YOUR MOUTH?
Distributed by Universal Press Syndicate
Text GARFIELD to 26642 US ONLY
JIM DAVIS 6-20
OKAY, WHAT'S NOT IN YOUR MOUTH?
RAISINS

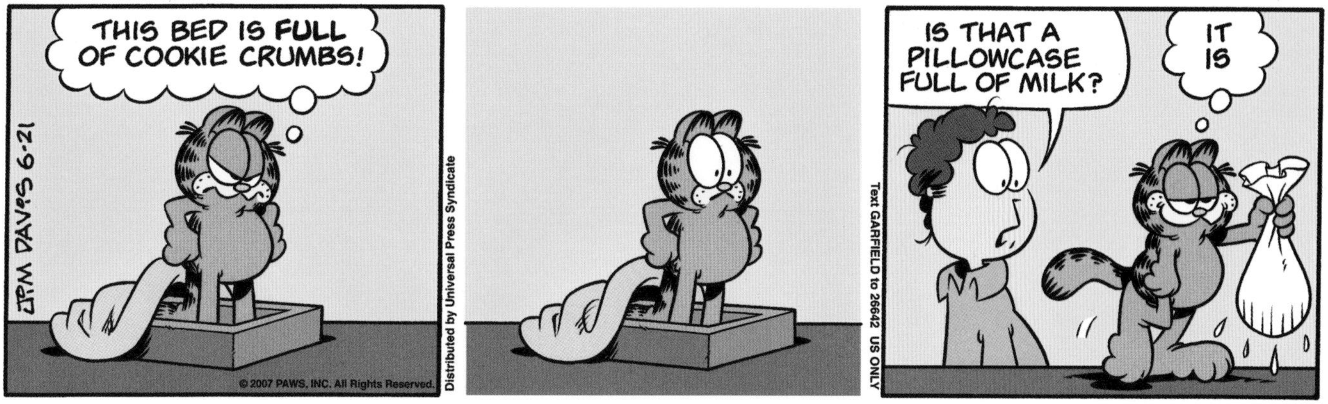
THIS BED IS FULL OF COOKIE CRUMBS!
JIM DAVIS 6-21
© 2007 PAWS, INC. All Rights Reserved.
Distributed by Universal Press Syndicate
Text GARFIELD to 26642 US ONLY
IS THAT A PILLOWCASE FULL OF MILK?
IT IS

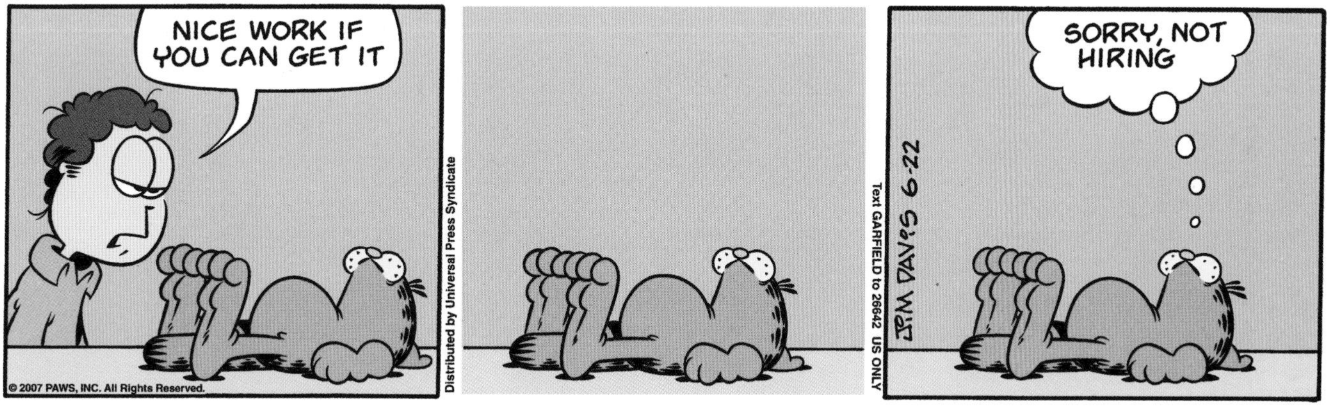
NICE WORK IF YOU CAN GET IT
© 2007 PAWS, INC. All Rights Reserved.
Distributed by Universal Press Syndicate
Text GARFIELD to 26642 US ONLY
JIM DAVIS 6-22
SORRY, NOT HIRING

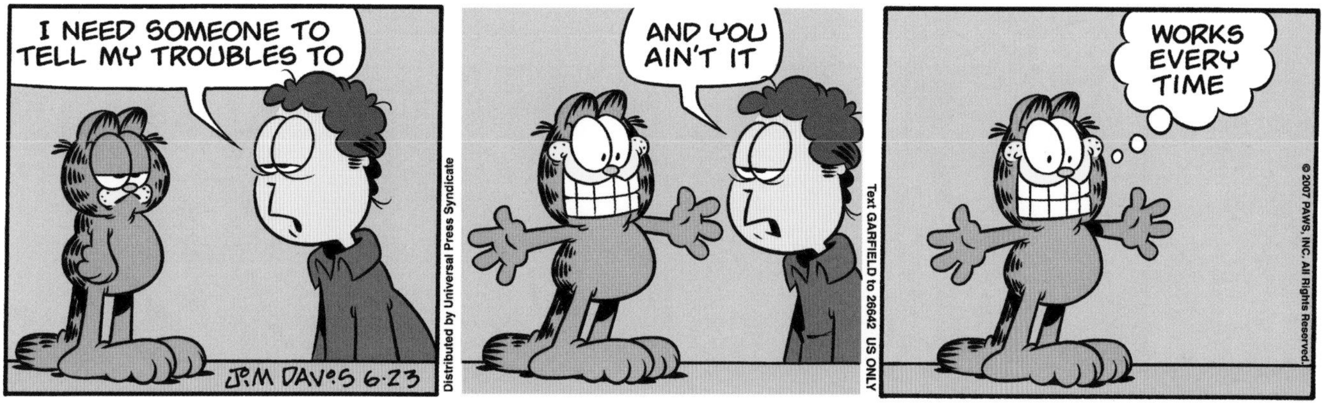
I NEED SOMEONE TO TELL MY TROUBLES TO
JIM DAVIS 6-23
Distributed by Universal Press Syndicate
AND YOU AIN'T IT
Text GARFIELD to 26642 US ONLY
WORKS EVERY TIME
© 2007 PAWS, INC. All Rights Reserved.

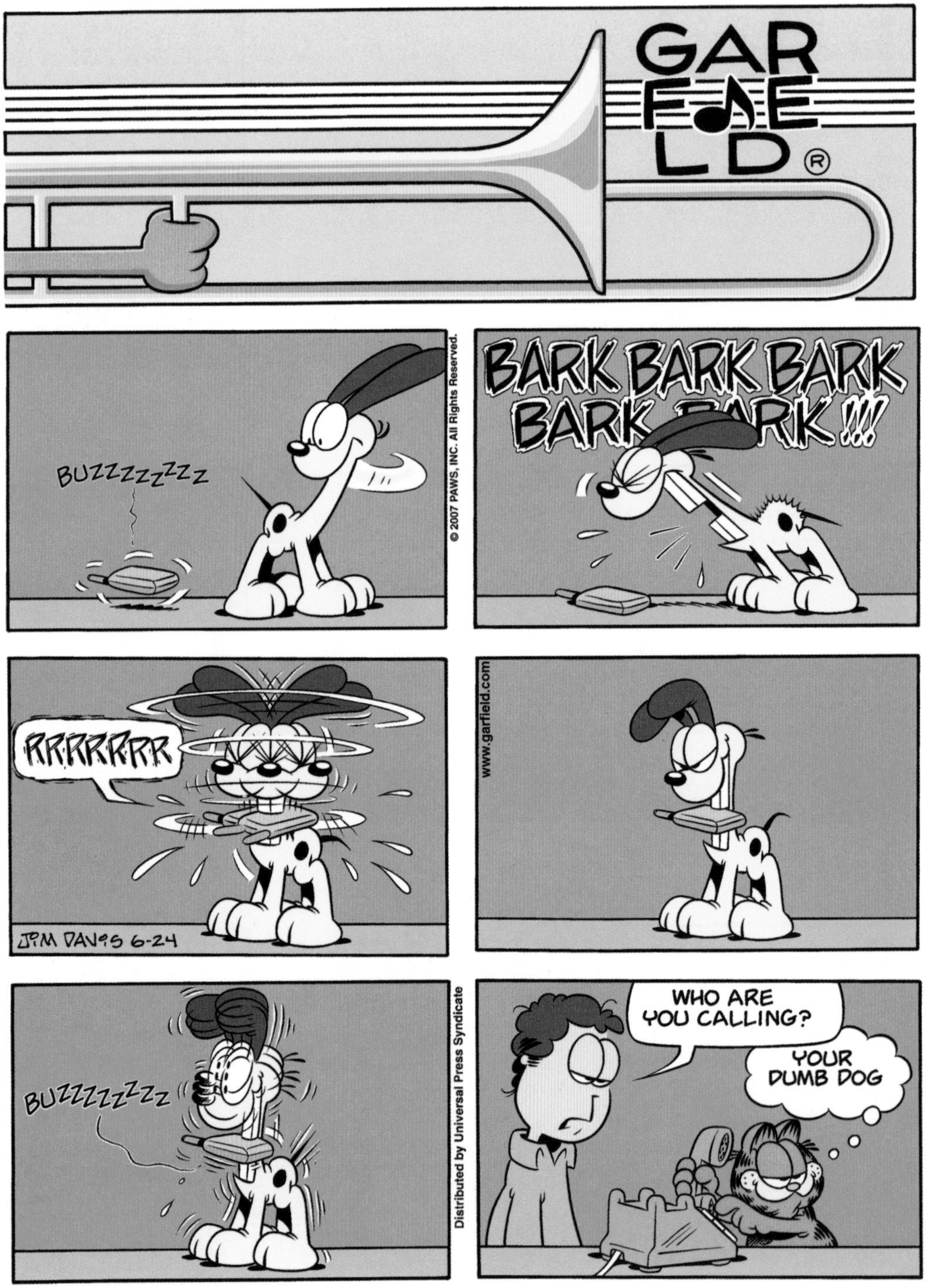
GARFIELD ®
BUZZZZZZZZZ
© 2007 PAWS, INC. All Rights Reserved.
BARK BARK BARK
BARK ARK!!!
RRRRRRRR
www.garfield.com
JIM DAVIS 6-24
BUZZZZZZZZZ
Distributed by Universal Press Syndicate
WHO ARE YOU CALLING?
YOUR DUMB DOG

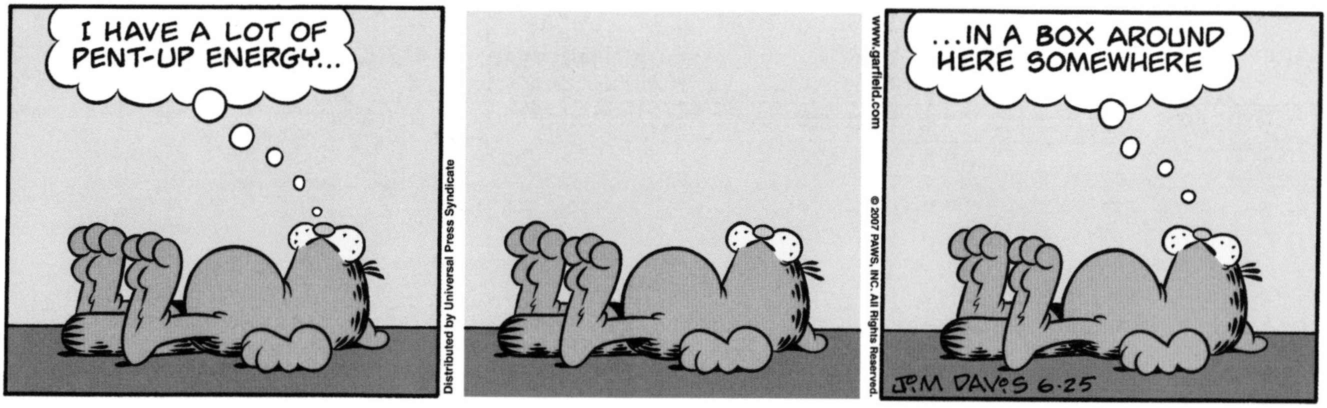
I HAVE A LOT OF PENT-UP ENERGY...
...IN A BOX AROUND HERE SOMEWHERE
JIM DAVIS 6-25
Distributed by Universal Press Syndicate
www.garfield.com
© 2007 PAWS, INC. All Rights Reserved.

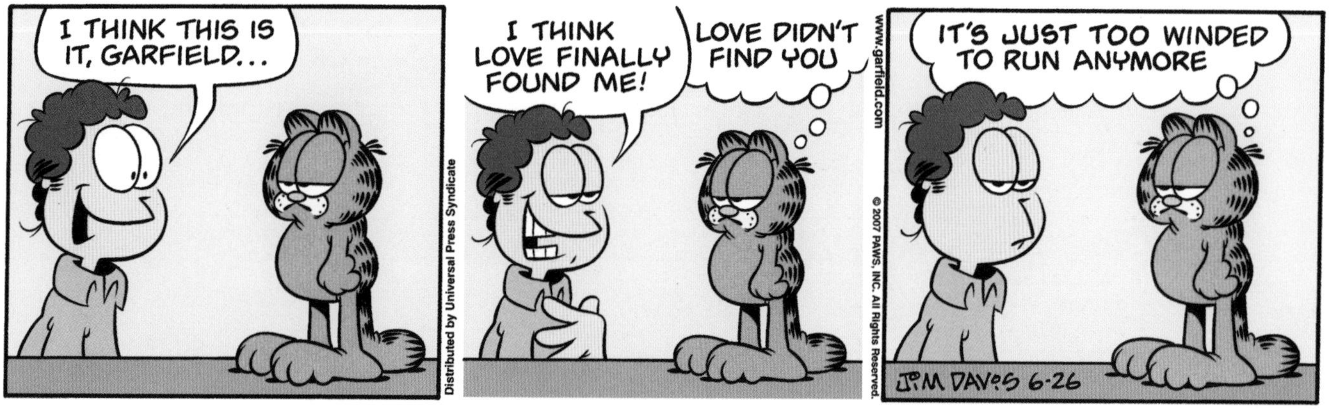
I THINK THIS IS IT, GARFIELD...
I THINK LOVE FINALLY FOUND ME!
LOVE DIDN'T FIND YOU
IT'S JUST TOO WINDED TO RUN ANYMORE
JIM DAVIS 6-26
Distributed by Universal Press Syndicate
www.garfield.com
© 2007 PAWS, INC. All Rights Reserved.

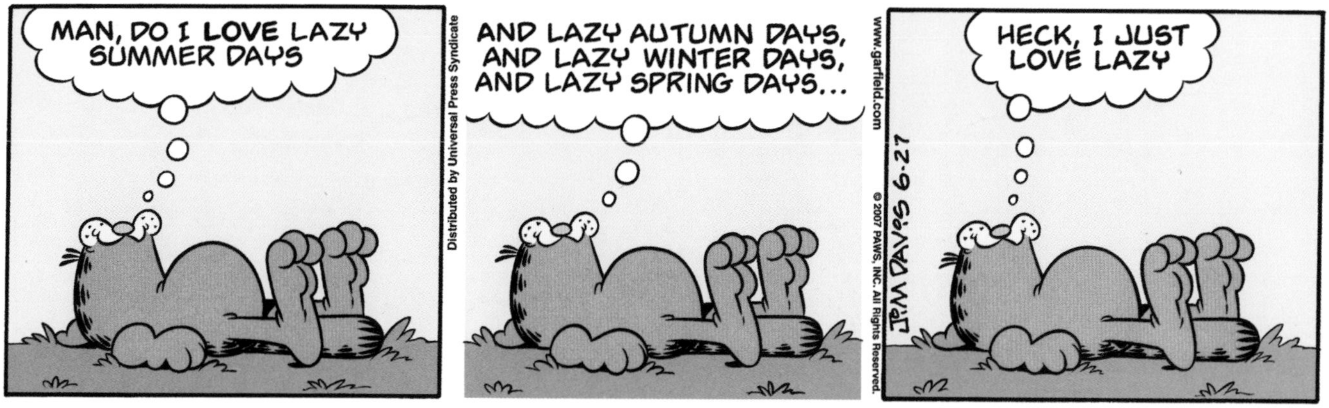
MAN, DO I LOVE LAZY SUMMER DAYS
AND LAZY AUTUMN DAYS, AND LAZY WINTER DAYS, AND LAZY SPRING DAYS...
HECK, I JUST LOVE LAZY
JIM DAVIS 6-27
Distributed by Universal Press Syndicate
www.garfield.com
© 2007 PAWS, INC. All Rights Reserved.

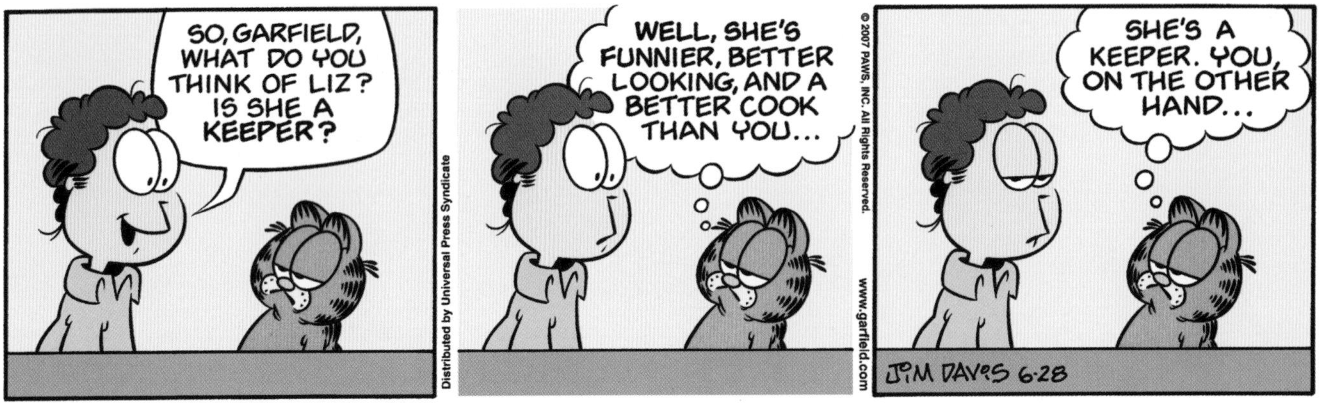
SO, GARFIELD, WHAT DO YOU THINK OF LIZ? IS SHE A KEEPER?
Distributed by Universal Press Syndicate
WELL, SHE'S FUNNIER, BETTER LOOKING, AND A BETTER COOK THAN YOU...
© 2007 PAWS, INC. All Rights Reserved.
www.garfield.com
SHE'S A KEEPER. YOU, ON THE OTHER HAND...
JIM DAVIS 6-28

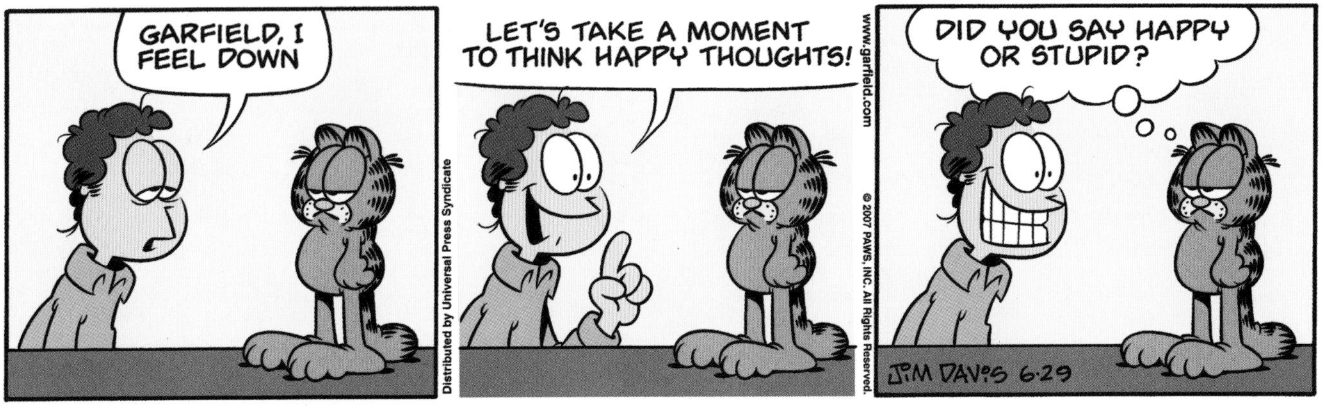
GARFIELD, I FEEL DOWN
Distributed by Universal Press Syndicate
LET'S TAKE A MOMENT TO THINK HAPPY THOUGHTS!
www.garfield.com
© 2007 PAWS, INC. All Rights Reserved.
DID YOU SAY HAPPY OR STUPID?
JIM DAVIS 6-29

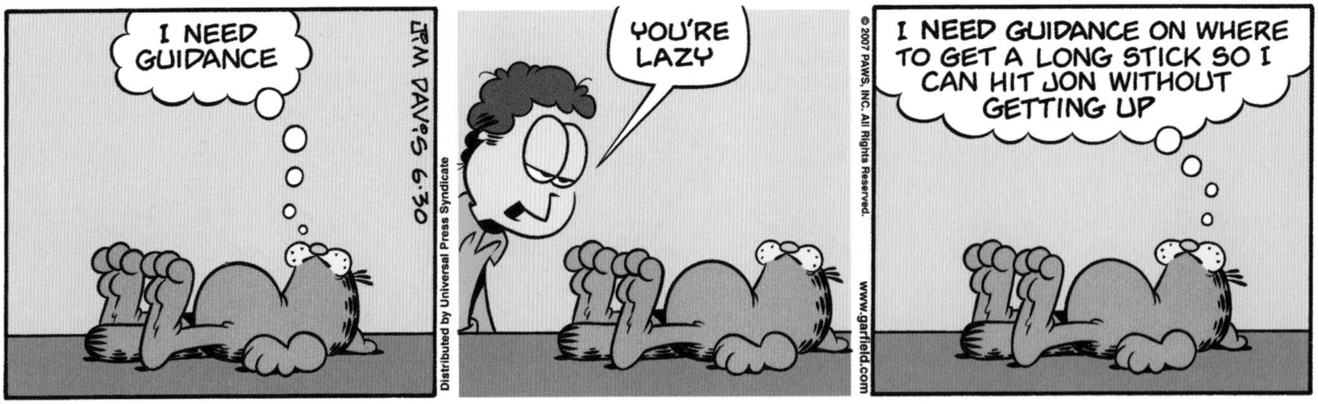
I NEED GUIDANCE
JIM DAVIS 6-30
Distributed by Universal Press Syndicate
YOU'RE LAZY
© 2007 PAWS, INC. All Rights Reserved.
www.garfield.com
I NEED GUIDANCE ON WHERE TO GET A LONG STICK SO I CAN HIT JON WITHOUT GETTING UP

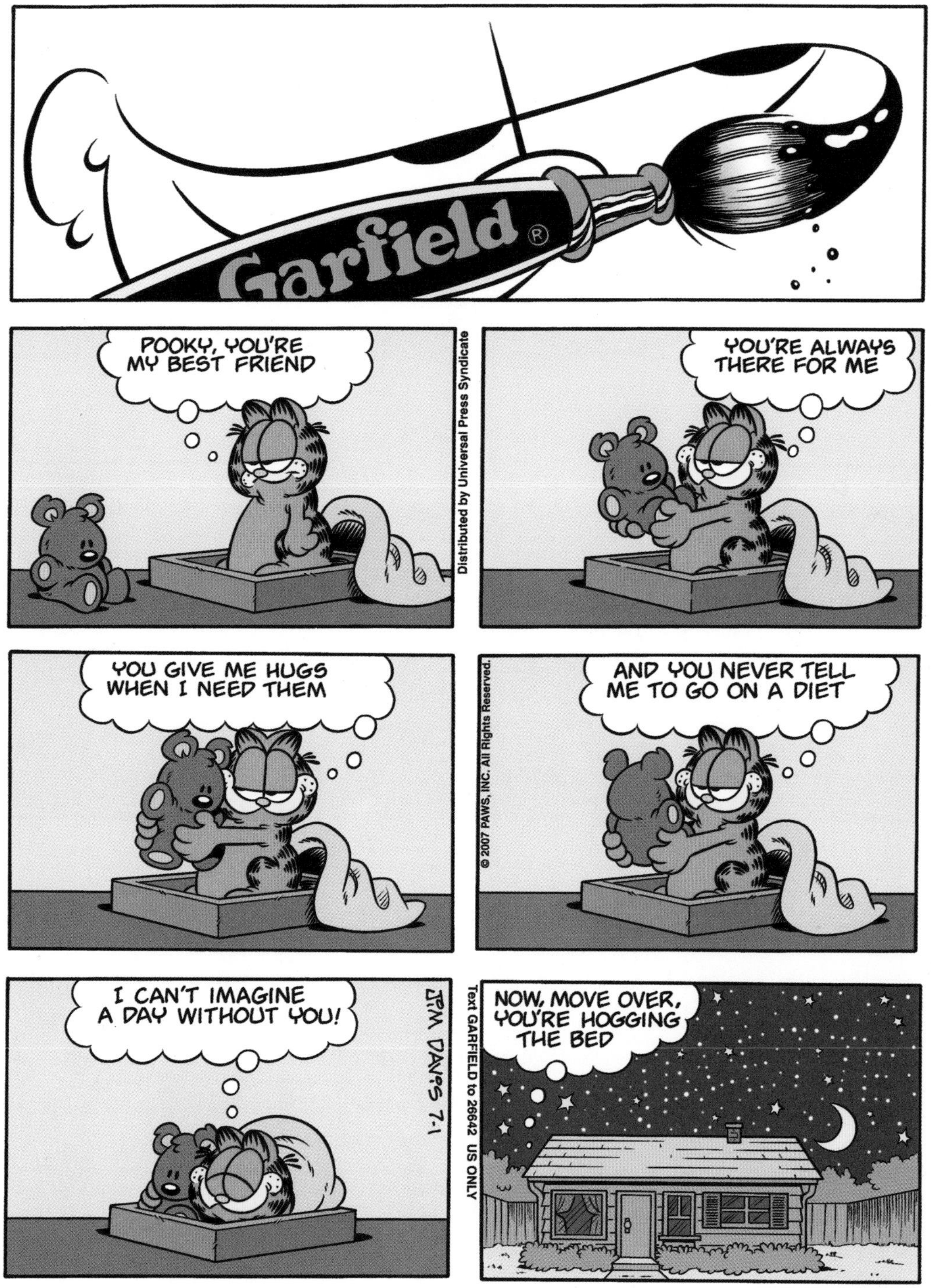
Garfield®
POOKY, YOU'RE MY BEST FRIEND
Distributed by Universal Press Syndicate
YOU'RE ALWAYS THERE FOR ME
YOU GIVE ME HUGS WHEN I NEED THEM
© 2007 PAWS, INC. All Rights Reserved.
AND YOU NEVER TELL ME TO GO ON A DIET
I CAN'T IMAGINE A DAY WITHOUT YOU!
JIM DAVIS 7-1
Text GARFIELD to 26642 US ONLY
NOW, MOVE OVER, YOU'RE HOGGING THE BED

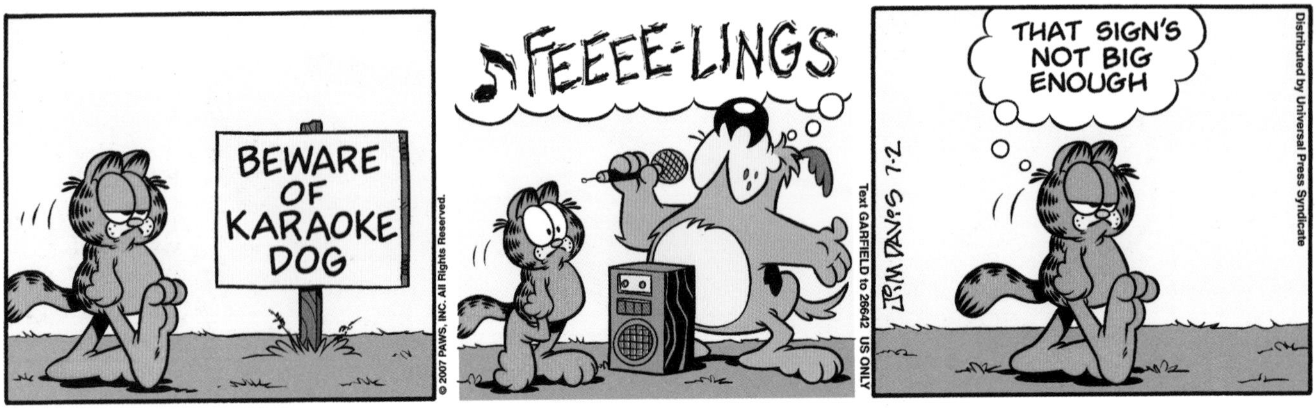
BEWARE OF KARAOKE DOG
FEEEE-LINGS
THAT SIGN'S NOT BIG ENOUGH
JPM DAVPS 7-2
© 2007 PAWS, INC. All Rights Reserved.
Text GARFIELD to 26642 US ONLY
Distributed by Universal Press Syndicate

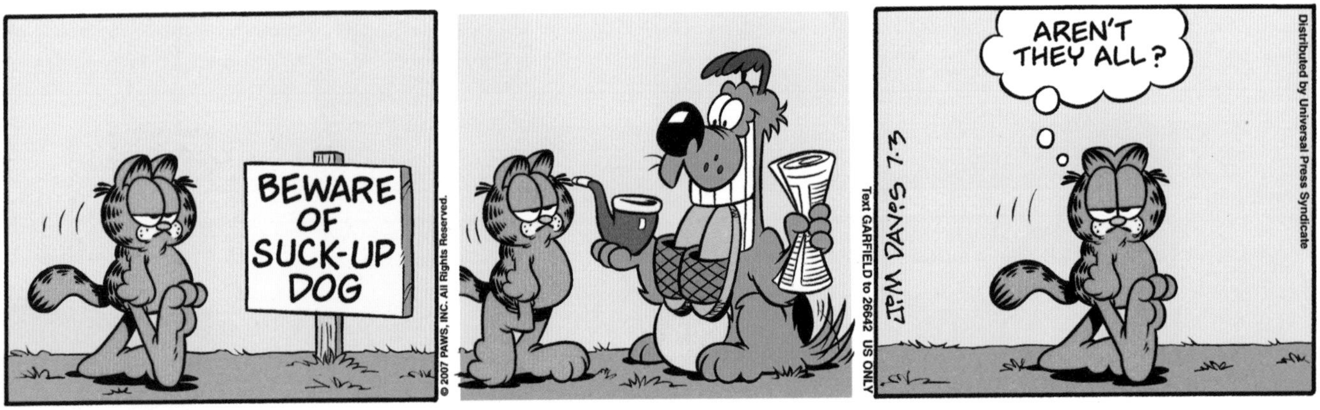
BEWARE OF SUCK-UP DOG
AREN'T THEY ALL?
JPM DAVPS 7-3
© 2007 PAWS, INC. All Rights Reserved.
Text GARFIELD to 26642 US ONLY
Distributed by Universal Press Syndicate

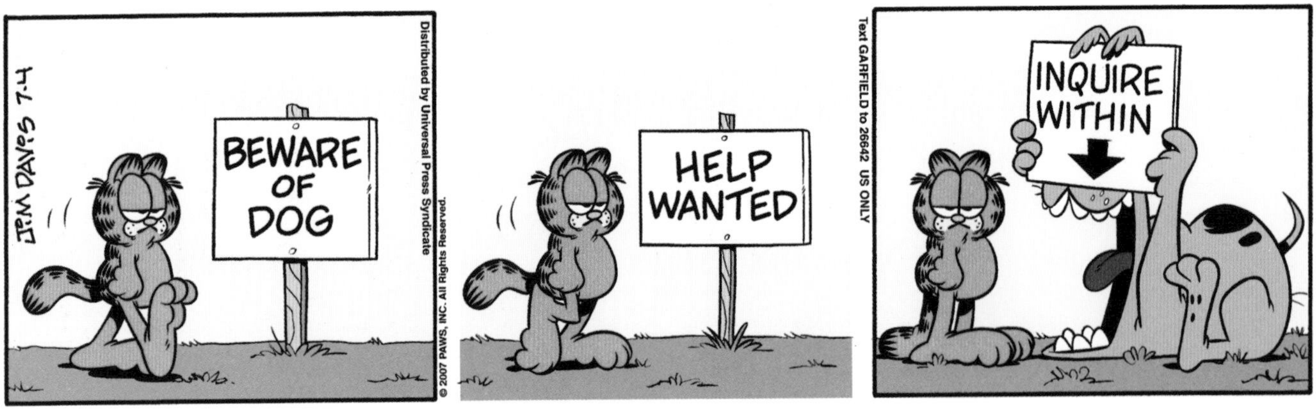
BEWARE OF DOG
HELP WANTED
INQUIRE WITHIN
JPM DAVPS 7-4
© 2007 PAWS, INC. All Rights Reserved.
Text GARFIELD to 26642 US ONLY
Distributed by Universal Press Syndicate

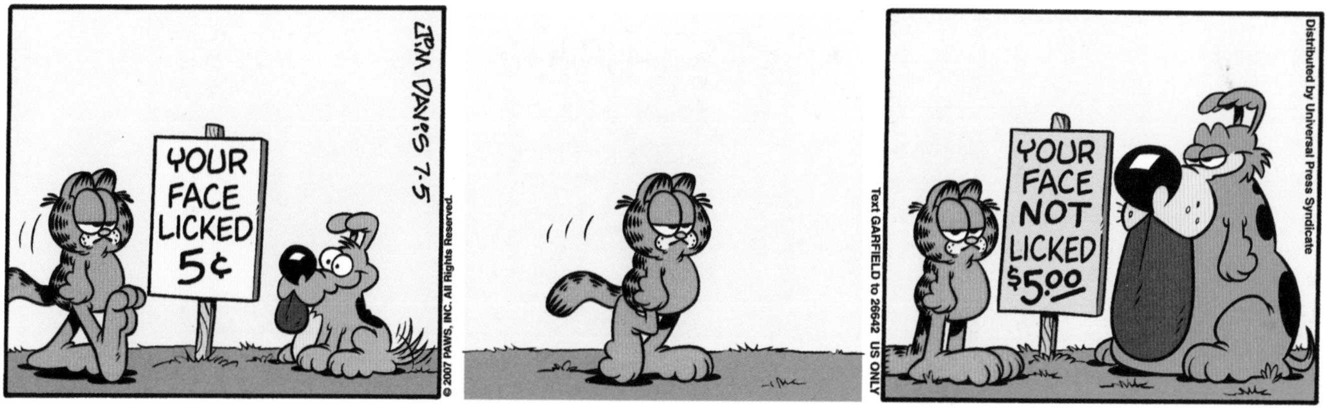
JIM DAVIS 7-5
YOUR FACE LICKED 5¢
© 2007 PAWS, INC. All Rights Reserved.
Text GARFIELD to 26642 US ONLY
YOUR FACE NOT LICKED $5.00
Distributed by Universal Press Syndicate

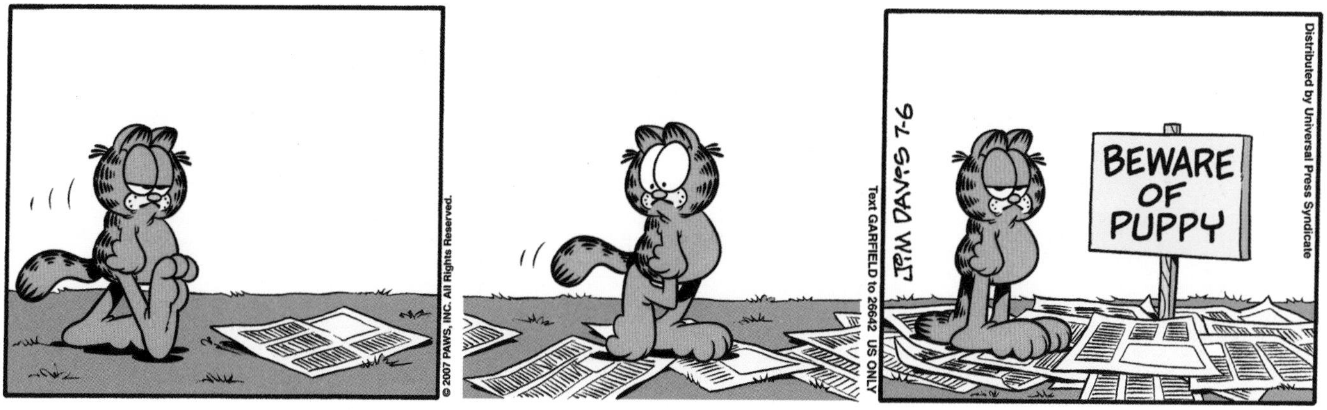
© 2007 PAWS, INC. All Rights Reserved.
Text GARFIELD to 26642 US ONLY
JIM DAVIS 7-6
BEWARE OF PUPPY
Distributed by Universal Press Syndicate

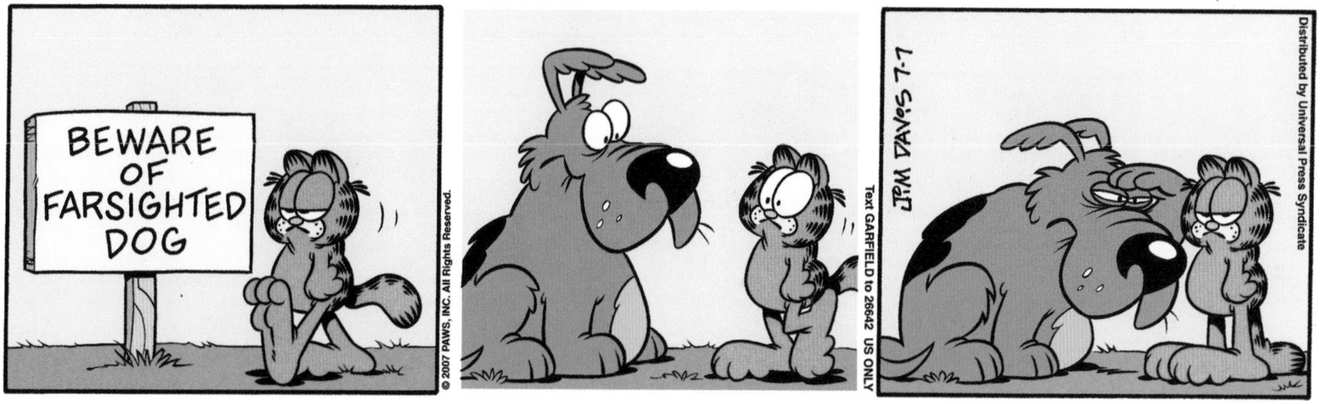
BEWARE OF FARSIGHTED DOG
© 2007 PAWS, INC. All Rights Reserved.
Text GARFIELD to 26642 US ONLY
JIM DAVIS 7-7
Distributed by Universal Press Syndicate

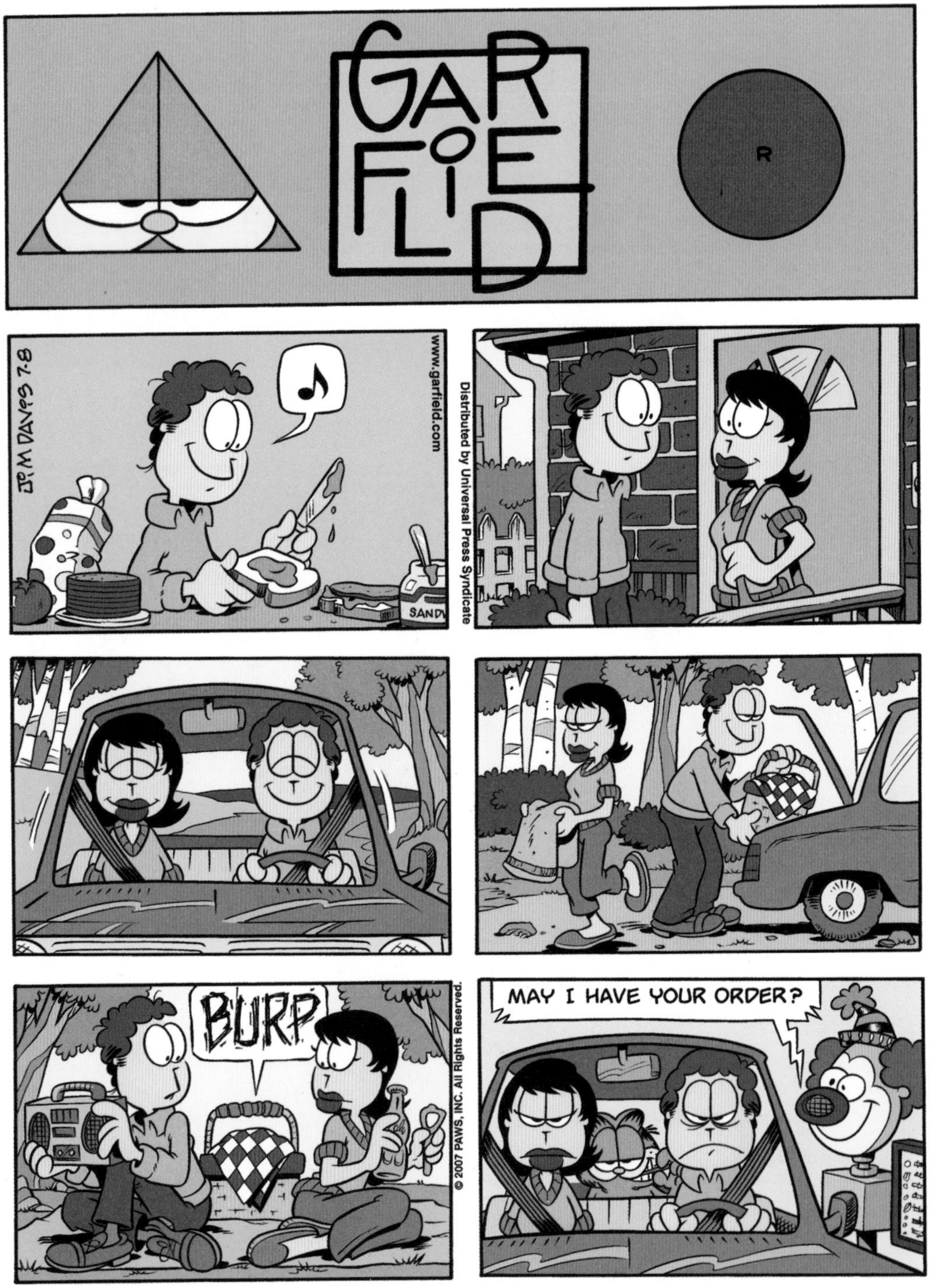
GARFIELD
R
JPM DAVPS 7-8
www.garfield.com
Distributed by Universal Press Syndicate
SANDW
BURP
© 2007 PAWS, INC. All Rights Reserved.
MAY I HAVE YOUR ORDER?

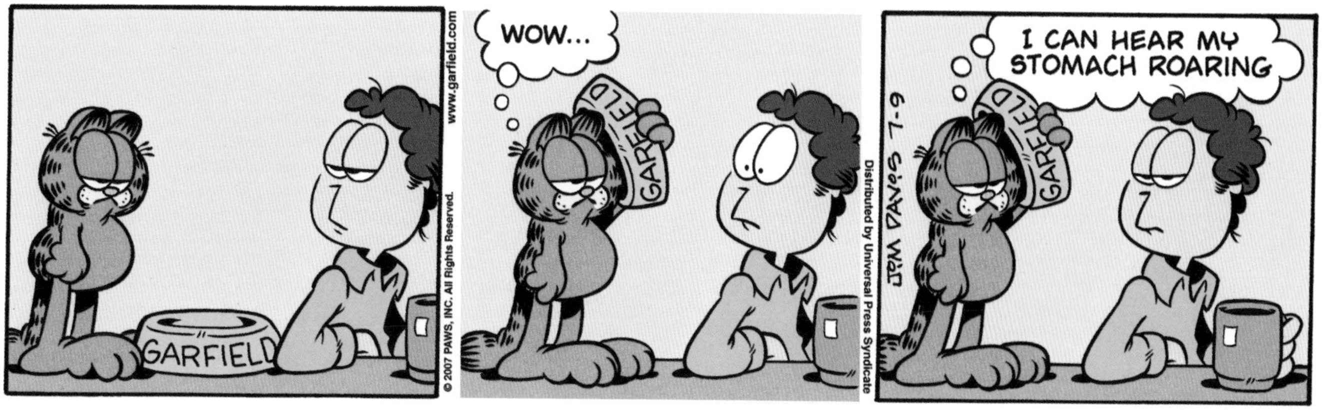
© 2007 PAWS, INC. All Rights Reserved. www.garfield.com
GARFIELD
WOW...
GARFIELD
Distributed by Universal Press Syndicate
JIM DAVIS 7-9
I CAN HEAR MY STOMACH ROARING
GARFIELD

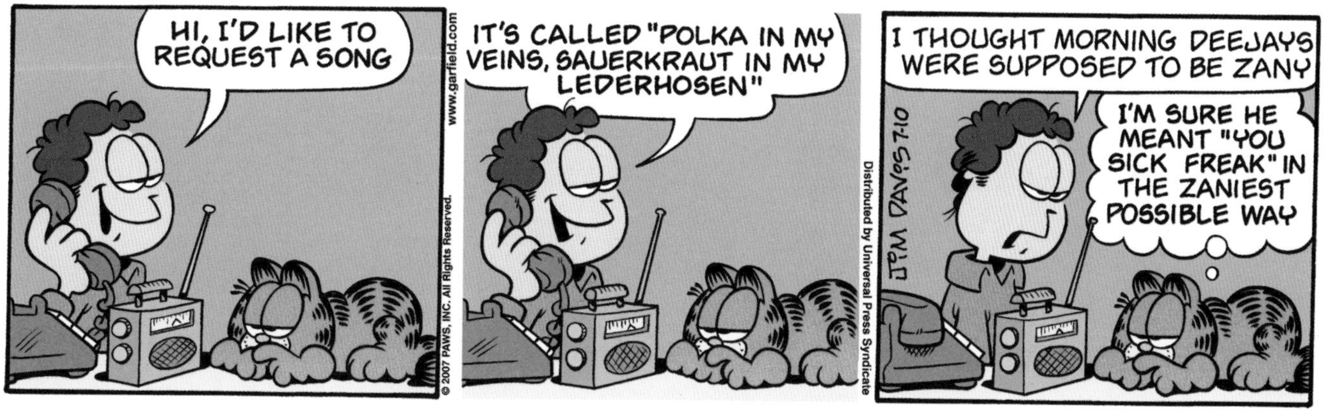
HI, I'D LIKE TO REQUEST A SONG
© 2007 PAWS, INC. All Rights Reserved. www.garfield.com
IT'S CALLED "POLKA IN MY VEINS, SAUERKRAUT IN MY LEDERHOSEN"
Distributed by Universal Press Syndicate
JIM DAVIS 7-10
I THOUGHT MORNING DEEJAYS WERE SUPPOSED TO BE ZANY
I'M SURE HE MEANT "YOU SICK FREAK" IN THE ZANIEST POSSIBLE WAY

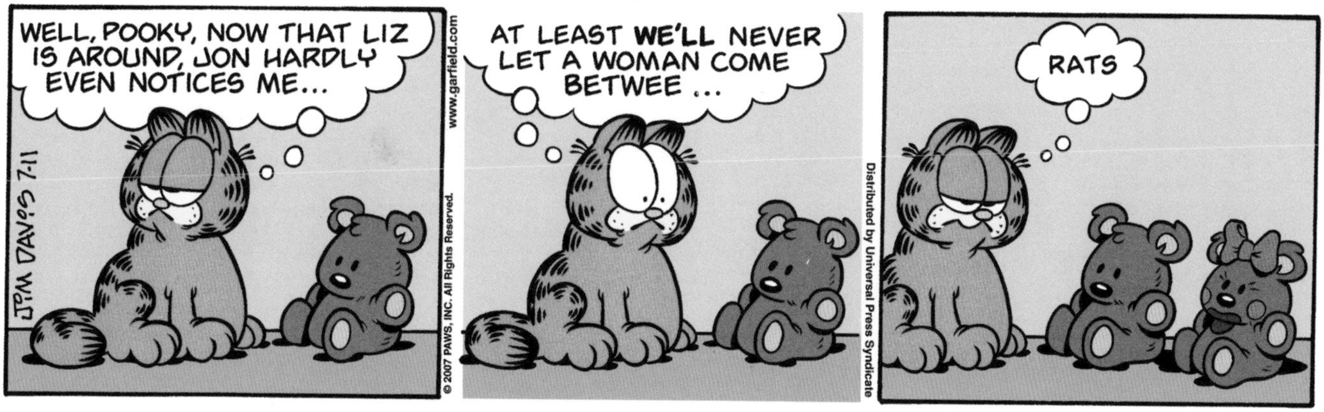
WELL, POOKY, NOW THAT LIZ IS AROUND, JON HARDLY EVEN NOTICES ME...
JIM DAVIS 7-11
© 2007 PAWS, INC. All Rights Reserved. www.garfield.com
AT LEAST **WE'LL** NEVER LET A WOMAN COME BETWEE ...
Distributed by Universal Press Syndicate
RATS

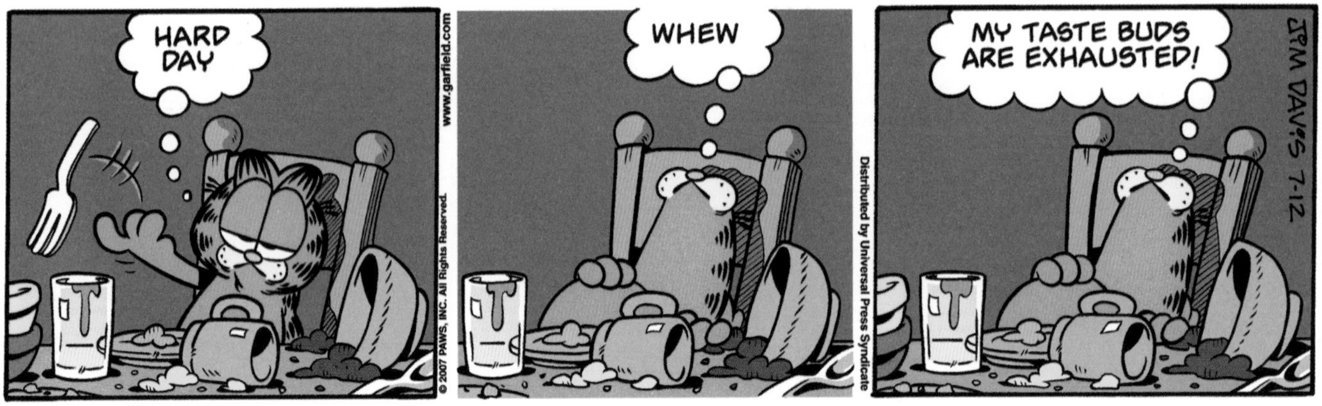
HARD DAY
WHEW
MY TASTE BUDS ARE EXHAUSTED!
JIM DAVIS 7-12
www.garfield.com
© 2007 PAWS, INC. All Rights Reserved.
Distributed by Universal Press Syndicate

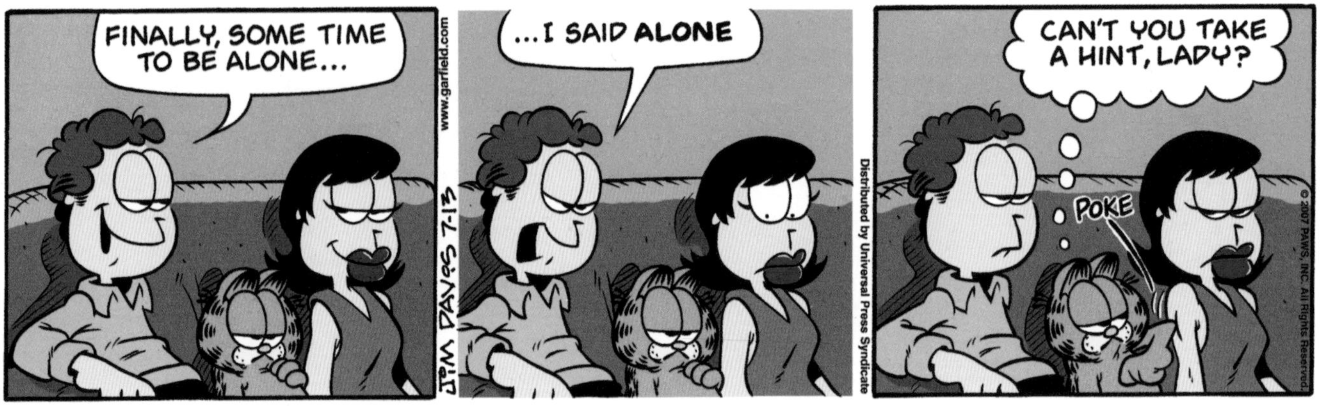
FINALLY, SOME TIME TO BE ALONE...
...I SAID ALONE
CAN'T YOU TAKE A HINT, LADY?
POKE
JIM DAVIS 7-13
www.garfield.com
Distributed by Universal Press Syndicate
© 2007 PAWS, INC. All Rights Reserved.

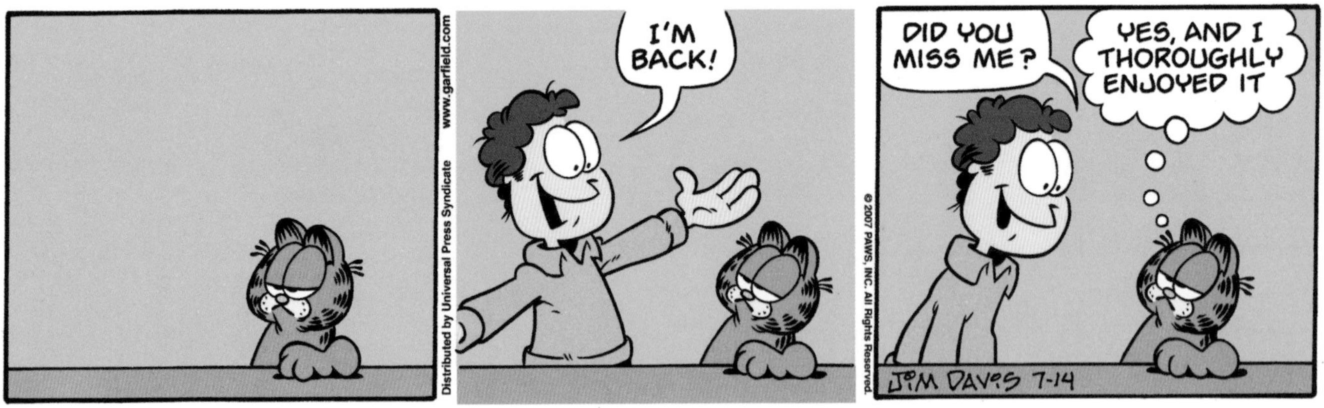
I'M BACK!
DID YOU MISS ME?
YES, AND I THOROUGHLY ENJOYED IT
JIM DAVIS 7-14
www.garfield.com
Distributed by Universal Press Syndicate
© 2007 PAWS, INC. All Rights Reserved.

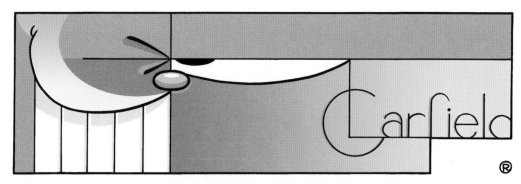

Text GARFIELD to 26642 US ONLY

© 2007 PAWS, INC. All Rights Reserved.

Distributed by Universal Press Syndicate

GET OFF OF MY NEWSPAPER!!

YOU KNOW, ALL YOU HAD TO DO WAS ASK

THERE'S NO NEED TO LOSE YOUR TEMPER

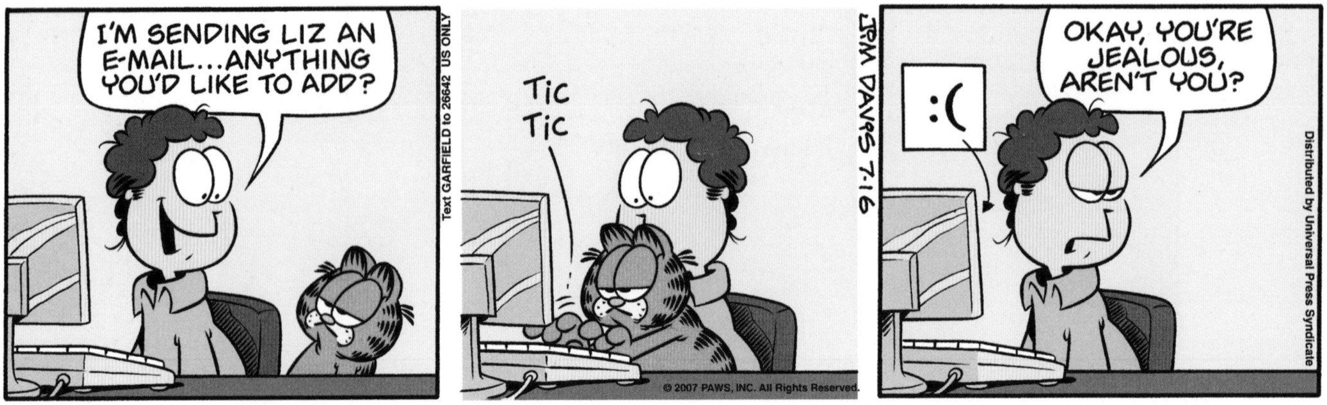
I'M SENDING LIZ AN E-MAIL...ANYTHING YOU'D LIKE TO ADD?
Text GARFIELD to 26642 US ONLY
Tic
Tic
© 2007 PAWS, INC. All Rights Reserved.
JPM DAVIS 7-16
:(
OKAY, YOU'RE JEALOUS, AREN'T YOU?
Distributed by Universal Press Syndicate

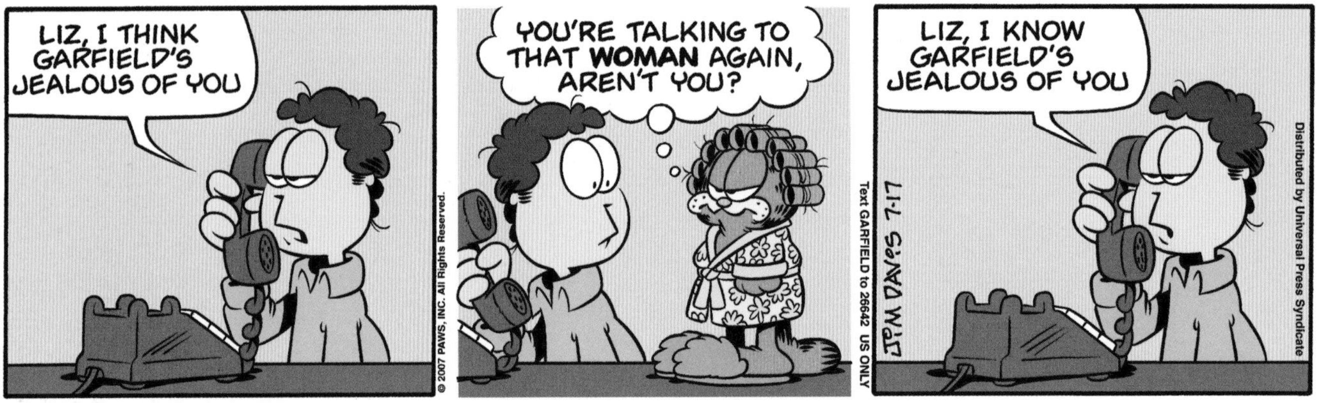
LIZ, I THINK GARFIELD'S JEALOUS OF YOU
© 2007 PAWS, INC. All Rights Reserved.
YOU'RE TALKING TO THAT **WOMAN** AGAIN, AREN'T YOU?
Text GARFIELD to 26642 US ONLY
JPM DAVIS 7-17
LIZ, I KNOW GARFIELD'S JEALOUS OF YOU
Distributed by Universal Press Syndicate

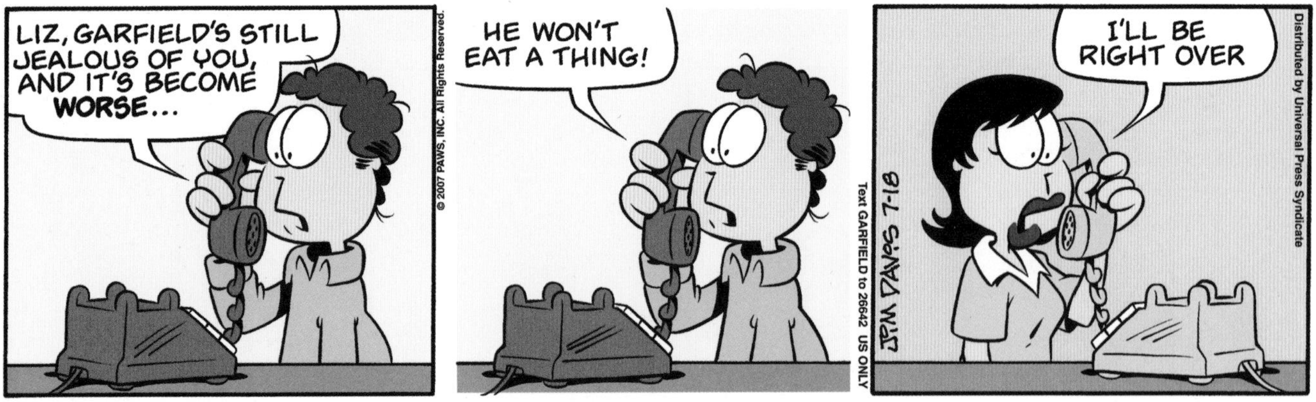
LIZ, GARFIELD'S STILL JEALOUS OF YOU, AND IT'S BECOME **WORSE**...
© 2007 PAWS, INC. All Rights Reserved.
HE WON'T EAT A THING!
Text GARFIELD to 26642 US ONLY
JPM DAVIS 7-18
I'LL BE RIGHT OVER
Distributed by Universal Press Syndicate

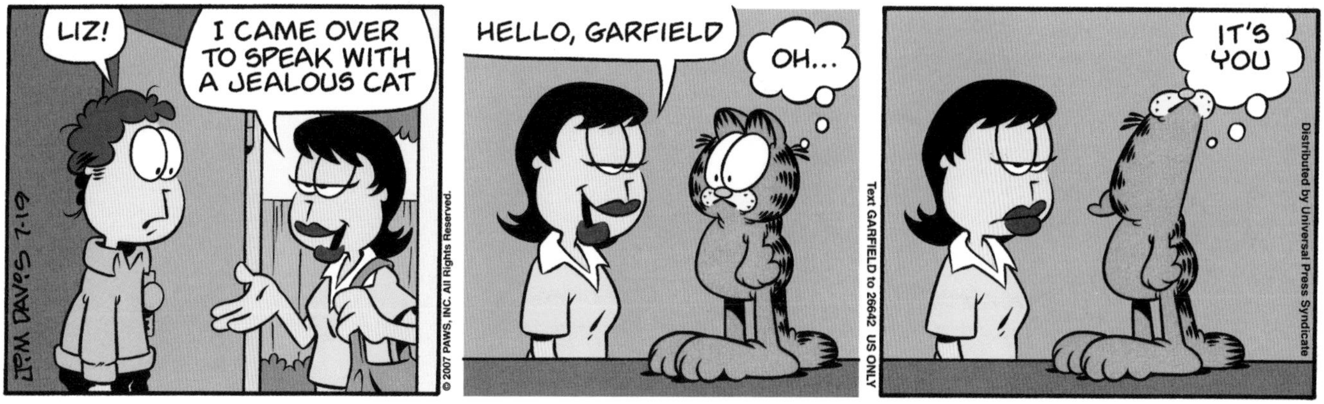
LIZ!
I CAME OVER TO SPEAK WITH A JEALOUS CAT
HELLO, GARFIELD
OH...
IT'S YOU
JIM DAVIS 7-19
© 2007 PAWS, INC. All Rights Reserved.
Text GARFIELD to 26642 US ONLY
Distributed by Universal Press Syndicate

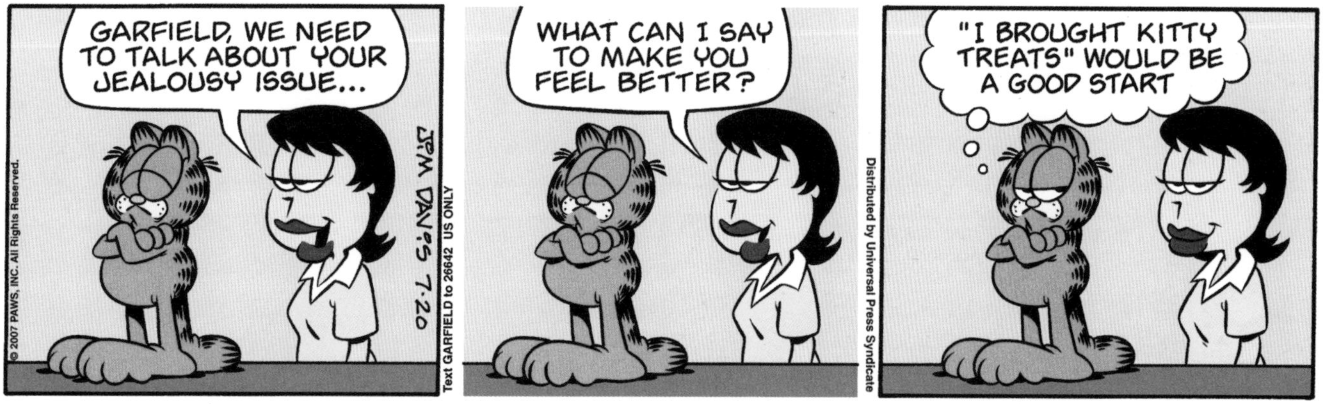
GARFIELD, WE NEED TO TALK ABOUT YOUR JEALOUSY ISSUE...
JIM DAVIS 7-20
WHAT CAN I SAY TO MAKE YOU FEEL BETTER?
"I BROUGHT KITTY TREATS" WOULD BE A GOOD START
© 2007 PAWS, INC. All Rights Reserved.
Text GARFIELD to 26642 US ONLY
Distributed by Universal Press Syndicate

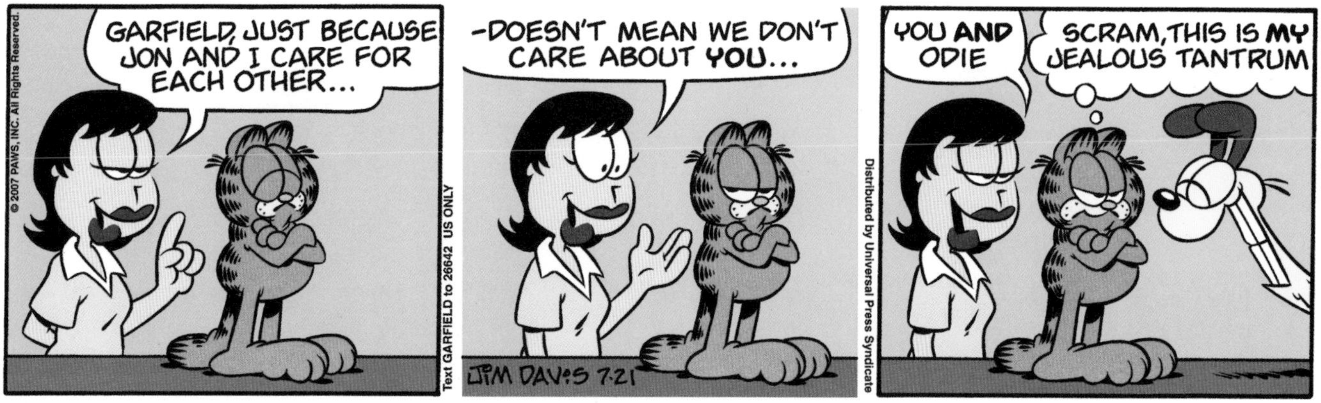
GARFIELD, JUST BECAUSE JON AND I CARE FOR EACH OTHER...
-DOESN'T MEAN WE DON'T CARE ABOUT **YOU**...
YOU **AND** ODIE
SCRAM, THIS IS **MY** JEALOUS TANTRUM
JIM DAVIS 7-21
© 2007 PAWS, INC. All Rights Reserved.
Text GARFIELD to 26642 US ONLY
Distributed by Universal Press Syndicate

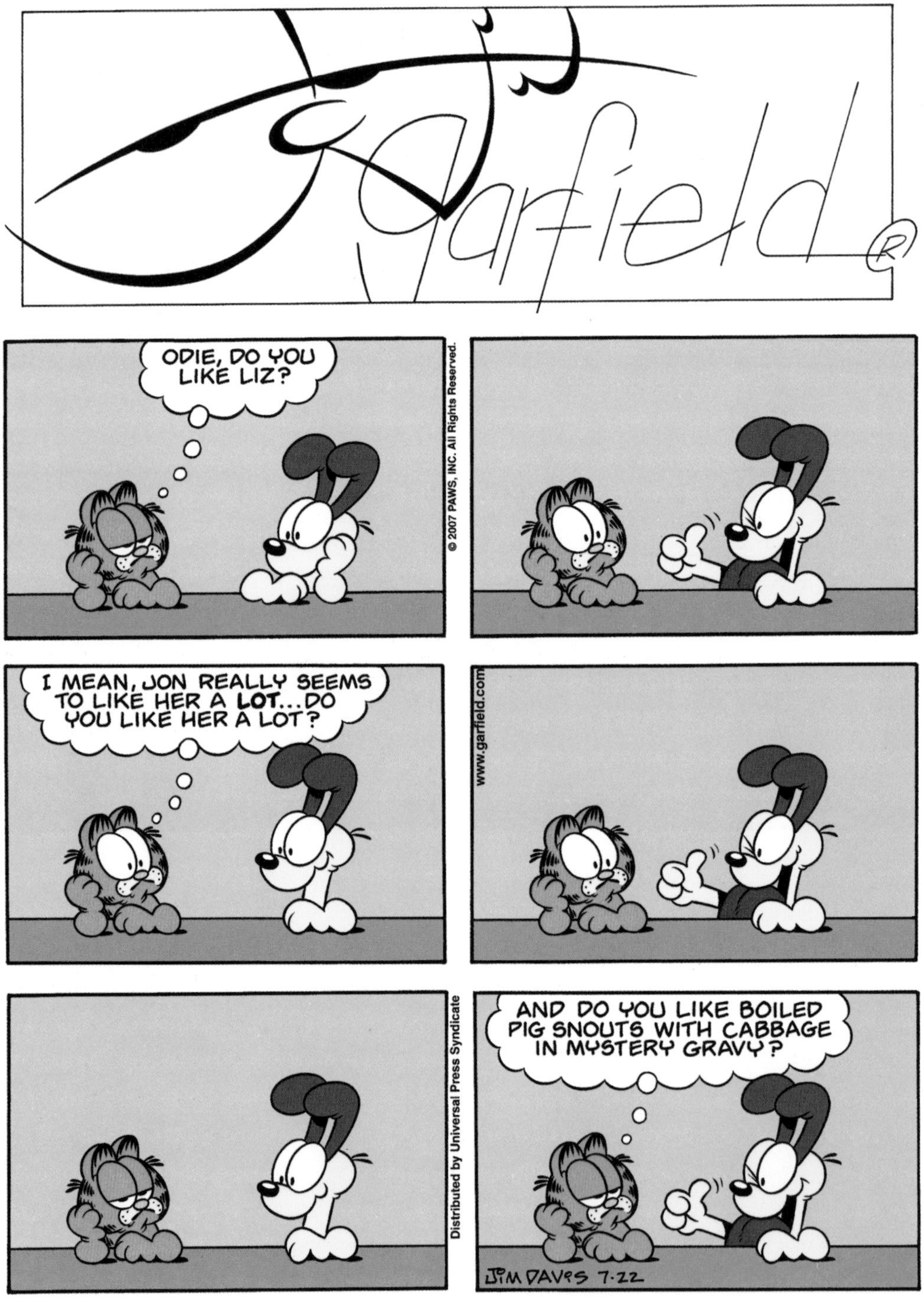
Garfield®
ODIE, DO YOU LIKE LIZ?
© 2007 PAWS, INC. All Rights Reserved.
I MEAN, JON REALLY SEEMS TO LIKE HER A **LOT**... DO YOU LIKE HER A LOT?
www.garfield.com
Distributed by Universal Press Syndicate
AND DO YOU LIKE BOILED PIG SNOUTS WITH CABBAGE IN MYSTERY GRAVY?
JIM DAVIS 7-22

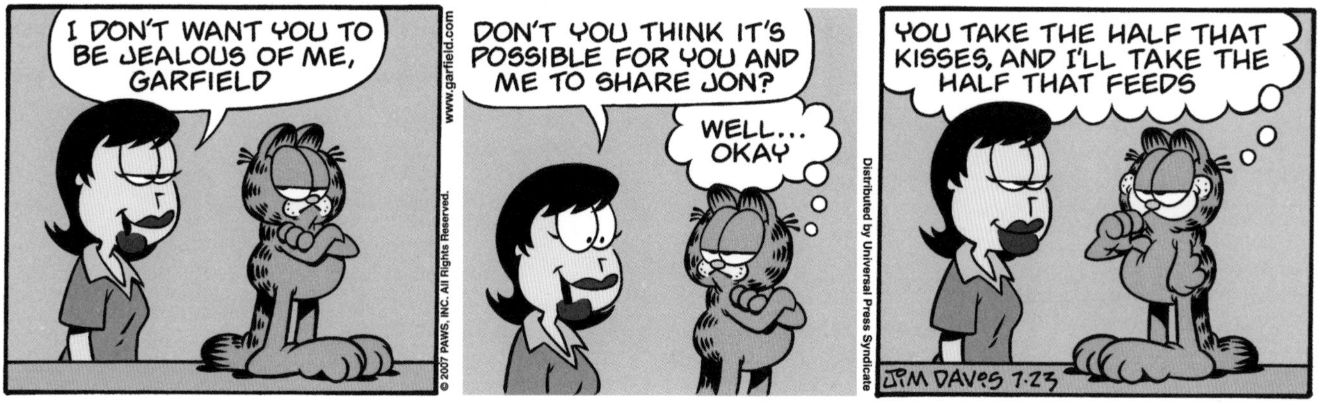
I DON'T WANT YOU TO BE JEALOUS OF ME, GARFIELD
© 2007 PAWS, INC. All Rights Reserved. www.garfield.com
DON'T YOU THINK IT'S POSSIBLE FOR YOU AND ME TO SHARE JON?
WELL... OKAY
Distributed by Universal Press Syndicate
YOU TAKE THE HALF THAT KISSES, AND I'LL TAKE THE HALF THAT FEEDS
7-23

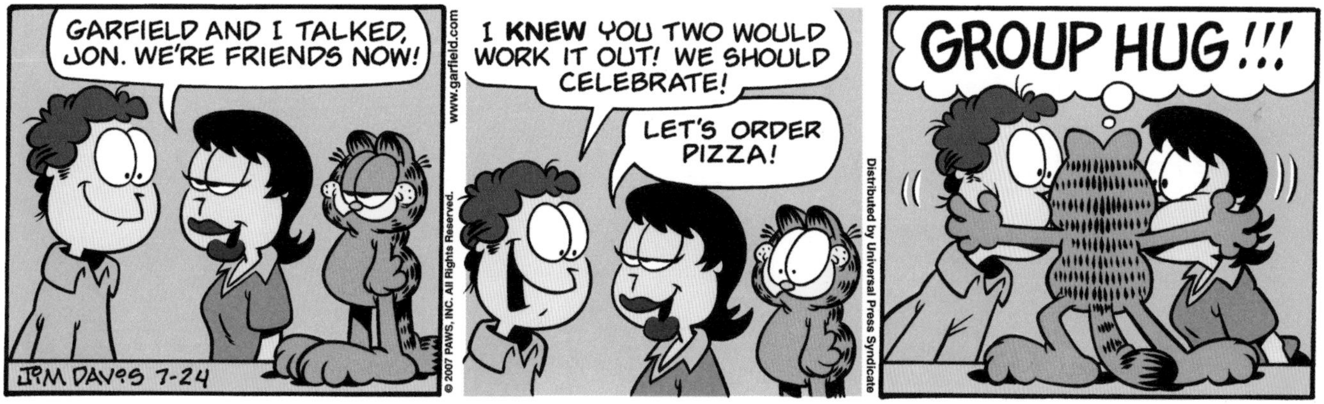
GARFIELD AND I TALKED, JON. WE'RE FRIENDS NOW!
7-24
© 2007 PAWS, INC. All Rights Reserved. www.garfield.com
I KNEW YOU TWO WOULD WORK IT OUT! WE SHOULD CELEBRATE!
LET'S ORDER PIZZA!
Distributed by Universal Press Syndicate
GROUP HUG!!!

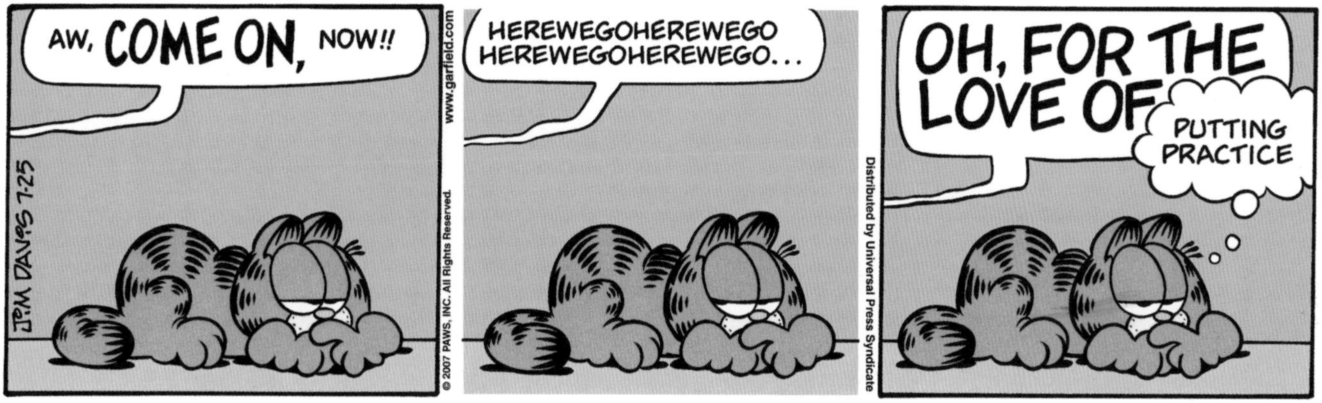
AW, COME ON, NOW!!
7-25
© 2007 PAWS, INC. All Rights Reserved. www.garfield.com
HEREWEGOHEREWEGO HEREWEGOHEREWEGO...
Distributed by Universal Press Syndicate
OH, FOR THE LOVE OF
PUTTING PRACTICE

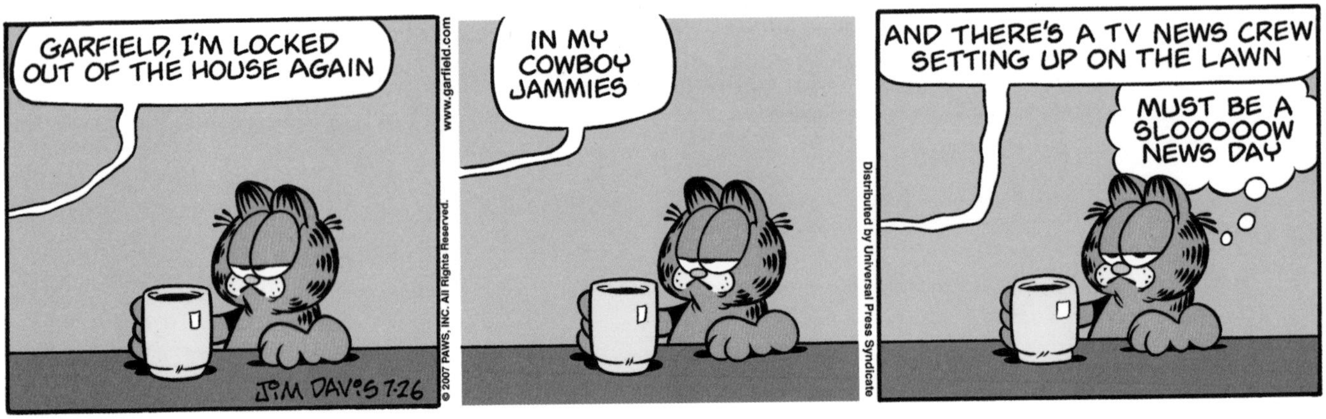
GARFIELD, I'M LOCKED OUT OF THE HOUSE AGAIN
JIM DAVIS 7-26
© 2007 PAWS, INC. All Rights Reserved.
www.garfield.com
IN MY COWBOY JAMMIES
Distributed by Universal Press Syndicate
AND THERE'S A TV NEWS CREW SETTING UP ON THE LAWN
MUST BE A SLOOOOOW NEWS DAY

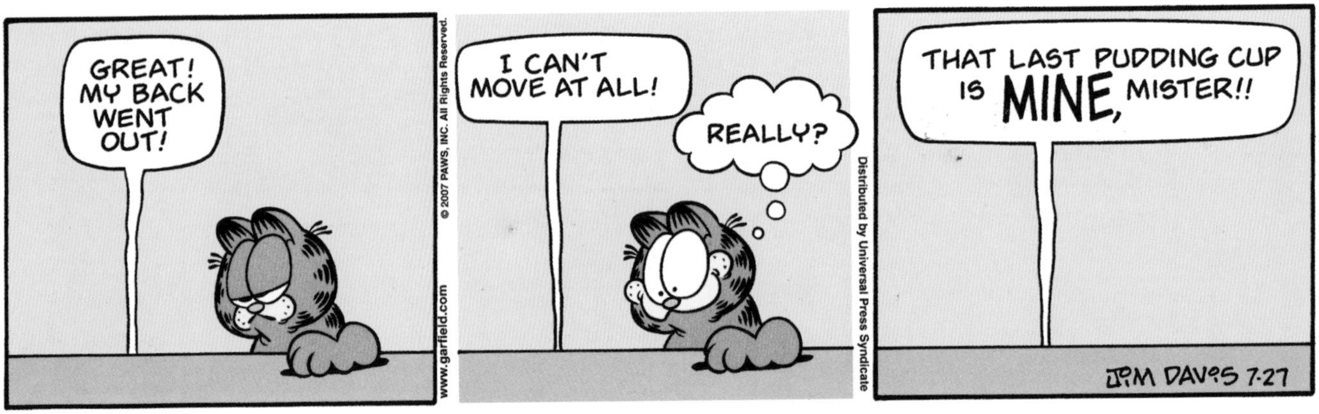
GREAT! MY BACK WENT OUT!
www.garfield.com
© 2007 PAWS, INC. All Rights Reserved.
I CAN'T MOVE AT ALL!
REALLY?
Distributed by Universal Press Syndicate
THAT LAST PUDDING CUP IS MINE, MISTER!!
JIM DAVIS 7-27

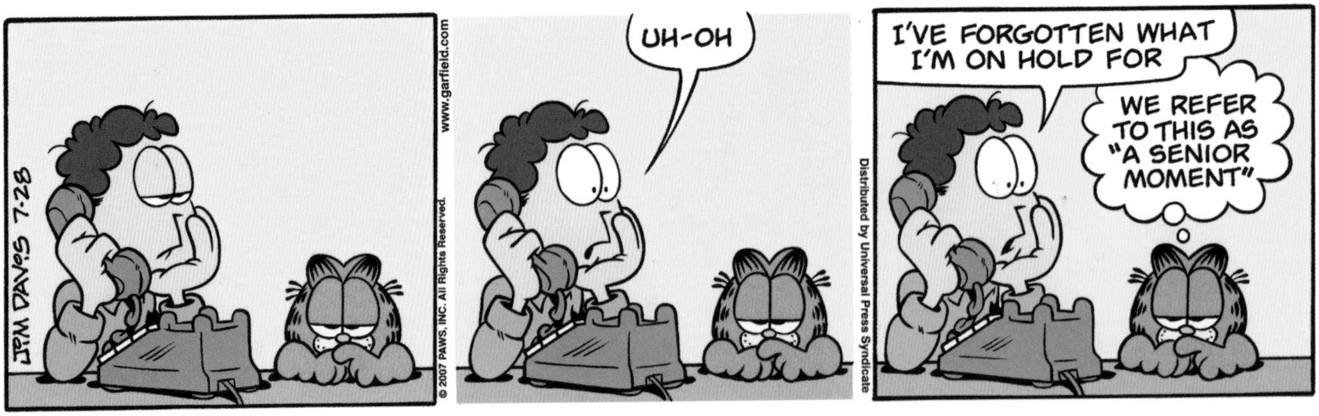
JIM DAVIS 7-28
© 2007 PAWS, INC. All Rights Reserved.
www.garfield.com
UH-OH
Distributed by Universal Press Syndicate
I'VE FORGOTTEN WHAT I'M ON HOLD FOR
WE REFER TO THIS AS "A SENIOR MOMENT"

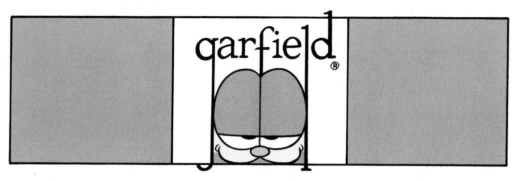

GET OUT OF MY POOL!

© 2007 PAWS, INC. All Rights Reserved.

Distributed by Universal Press Syndicate

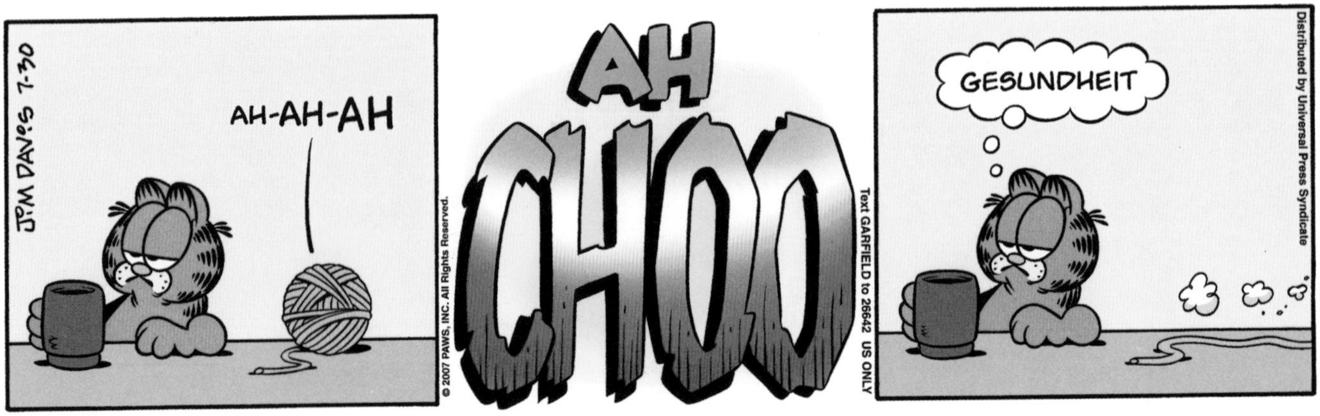
JIM DAVIS 7-30
AH-AH-AH
© 2007 PAWS, INC. All Rights Reserved.
AH CHOO
Text GARFIELD to 26642 US ONLY
GESUNDHEIT
Distributed by Universal Press Syndicate

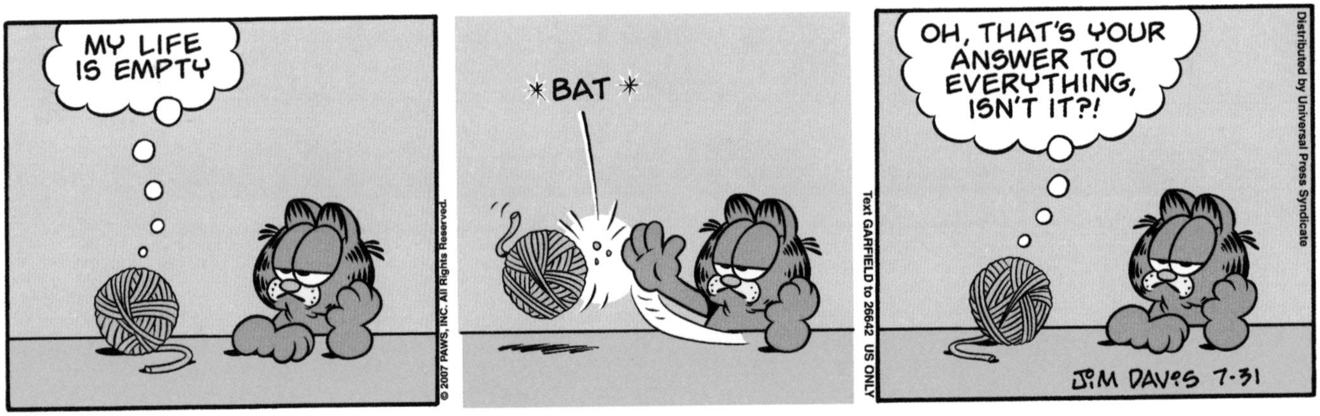
MY LIFE IS EMPTY
© 2007 PAWS, INC. All Rights Reserved.
BAT
Text GARFIELD to 26642 US ONLY
OH, THAT'S YOUR ANSWER TO EVERYTHING, ISN'T IT?!
JIM DAVIS 7-31
Distributed by Universal Press Syndicate

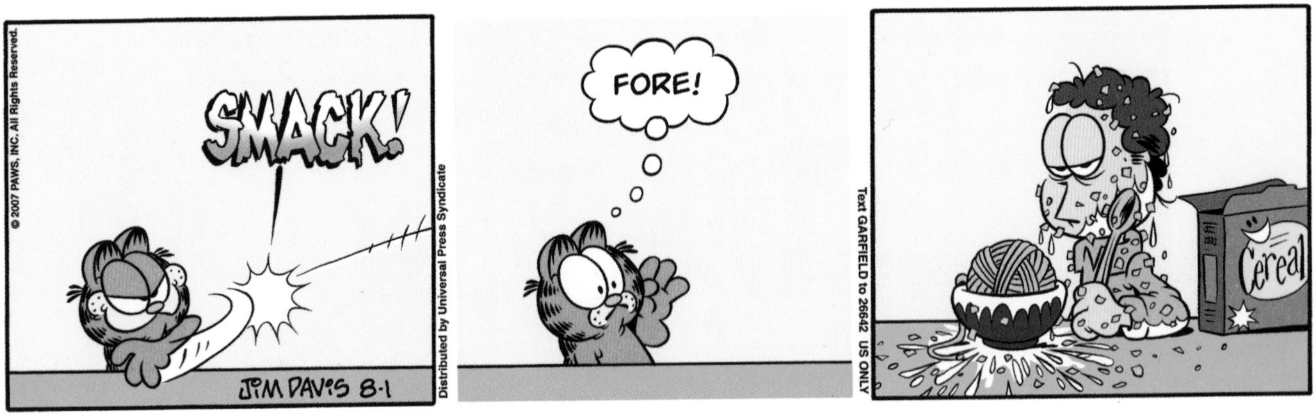
© 2007 PAWS, INC. All Rights Reserved.
SMACK!
JIM DAVIS 8-1
Distributed by Universal Press Syndicate
FORE!
Text GARFIELD to 26642 US ONLY
Cereal

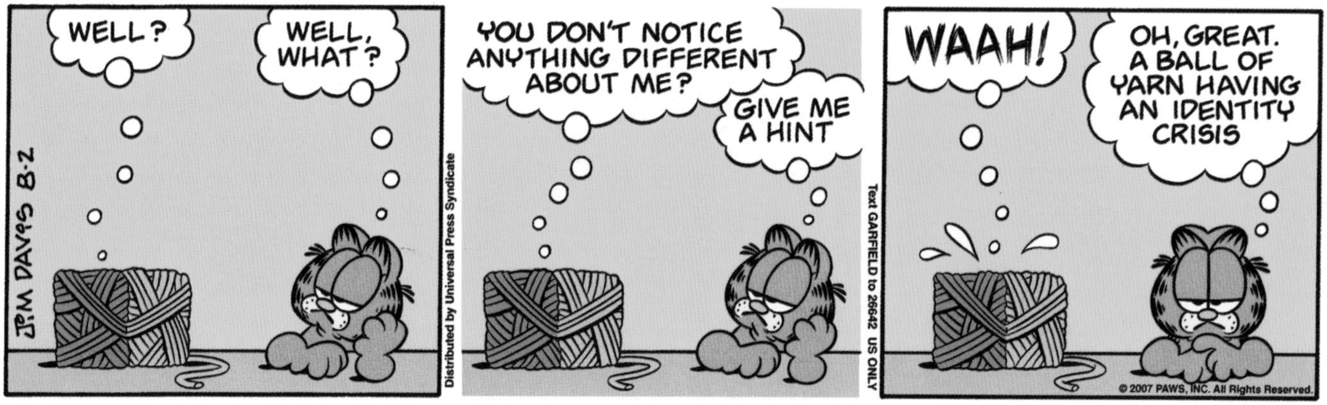
JIM DAVIS 8-2
WELL?
WELL, WHAT?
Distributed by Universal Press Syndicate
YOU DON'T NOTICE ANYTHING DIFFERENT ABOUT ME?
GIVE ME A HINT
Text GARFIELD to 26642 US ONLY
WAAH!
OH, GREAT. A BALL OF YARN HAVING AN IDENTITY CRISIS
© 2007 PAWS, INC. All Rights Reserved.

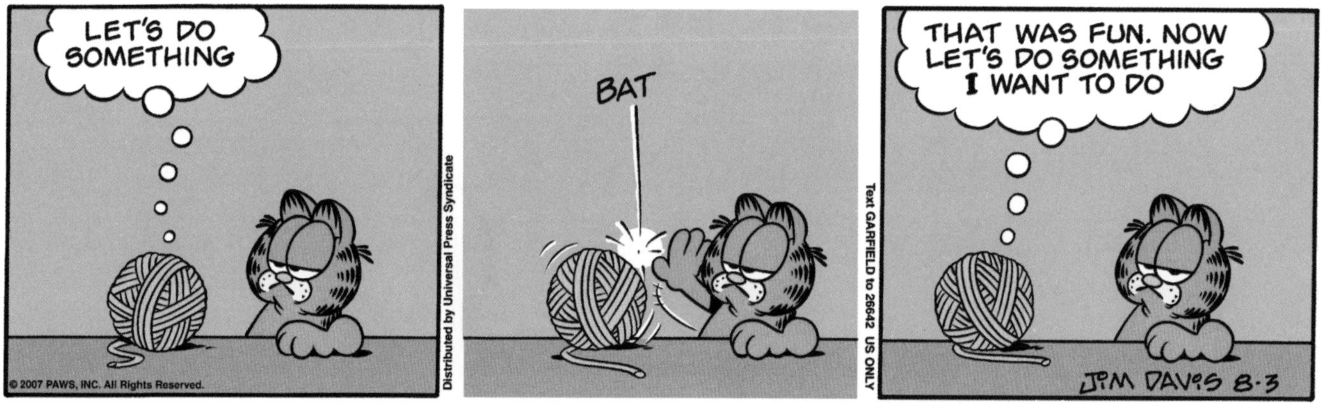
LET'S DO SOMETHING
© 2007 PAWS, INC. All Rights Reserved.
Distributed by Universal Press Syndicate
BAT
Text GARFIELD to 26642 US ONLY
THAT WAS FUN. NOW LET'S DO SOMETHING I WANT TO DO
JIM DAVIS 8-3

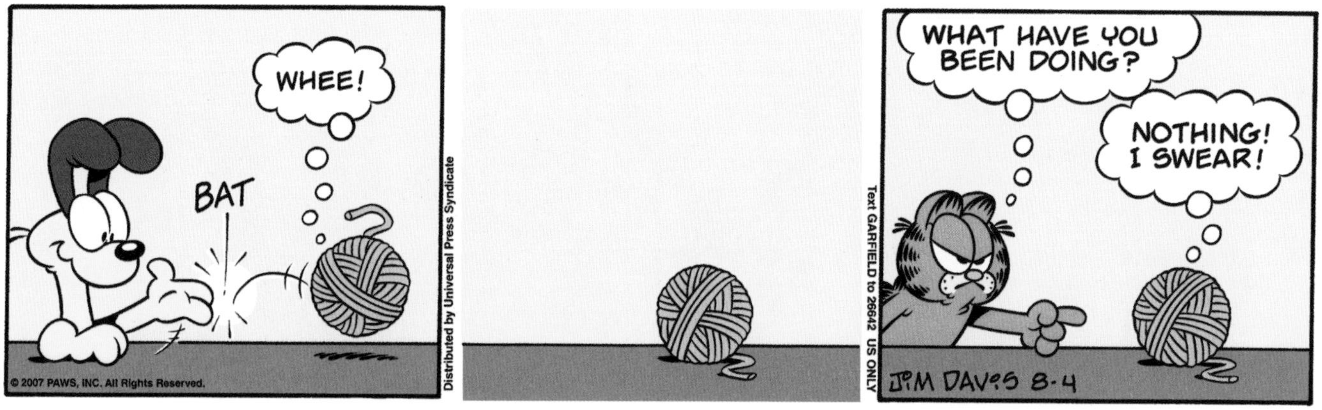
WHEE!
BAT
© 2007 PAWS, INC. All Rights Reserved.
Distributed by Universal Press Syndicate
Text GARFIELD to 26642 US ONLY
WHAT HAVE YOU BEEN DOING?
NOTHING! I SWEAR!
JIM DAVIS 8-4

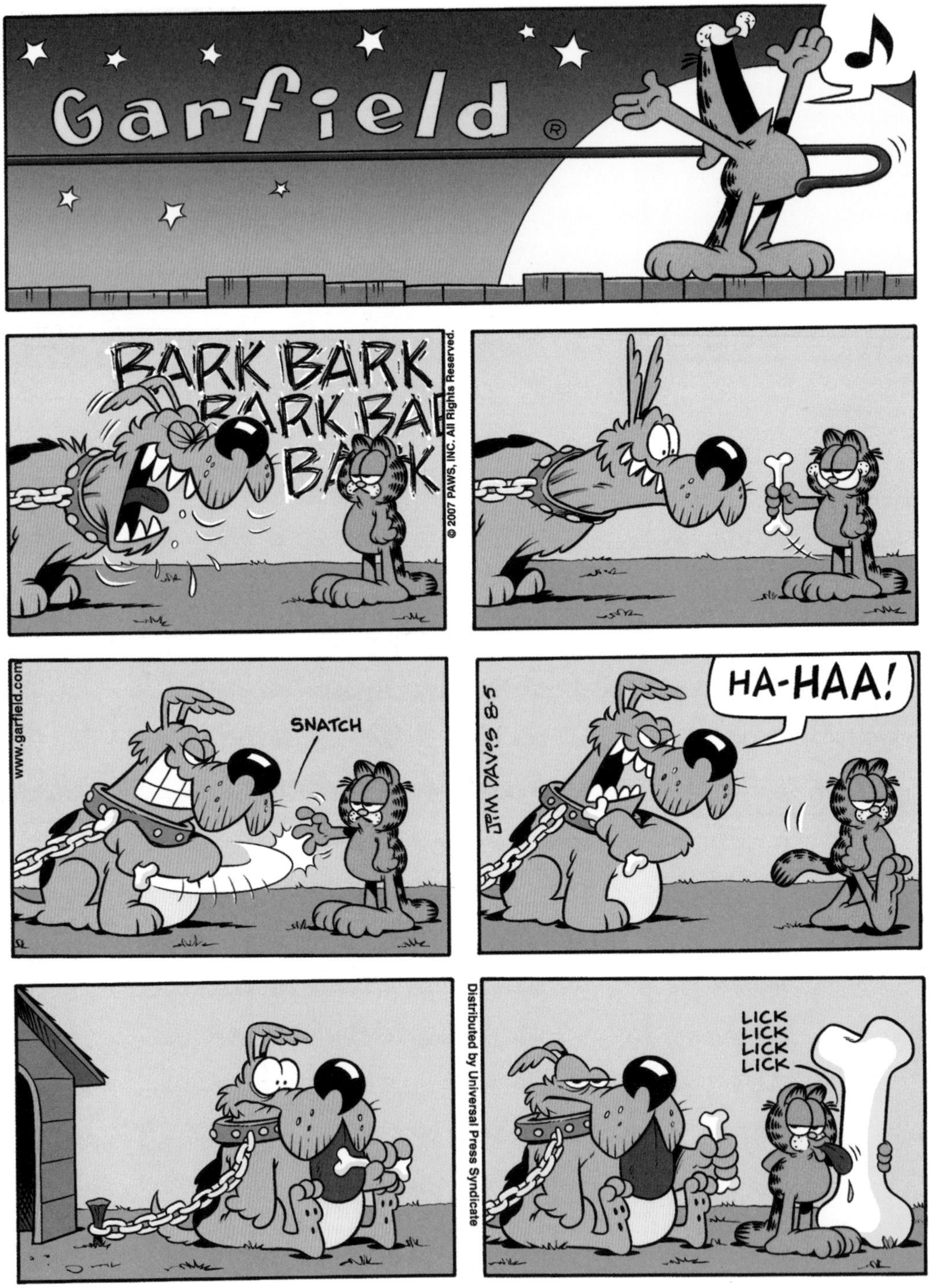
Garfield
BARK BARK
© 2007 PAWS, INC. All Rights Reserved.
www.garfield.com
SNATCH
HA-HAA!
Distributed by Universal Press Syndicate
LICK
LICK
LICK
LICK

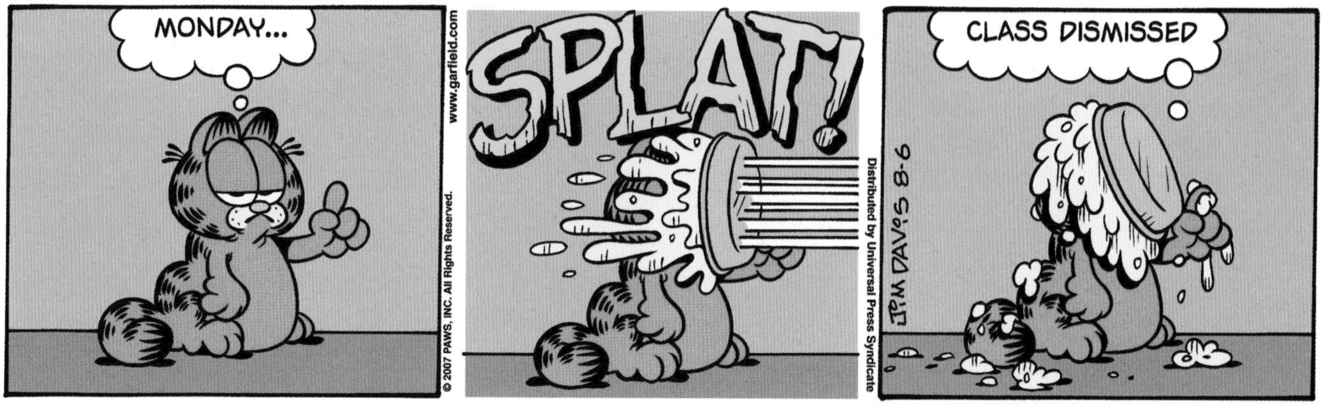
MONDAY...
SPLAT!
CLASS DISMISSED
© 2007 PAWS, INC. All Rights Reserved. www.garfield.com
Distributed by Universal Press Syndicate
JIM DAVIS 8-6

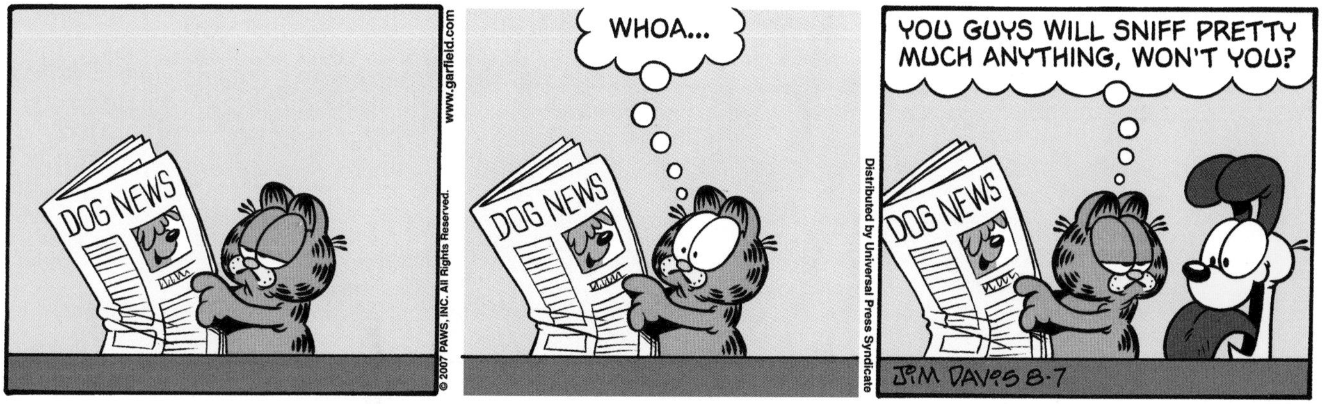
DOG NEWS
WHOA...
YOU GUYS WILL SNIFF PRETTY MUCH ANYTHING, WON'T YOU?
© 2007 PAWS, INC. All Rights Reserved. www.garfield.com
Distributed by Universal Press Syndicate
JIM DAVIS 8-7

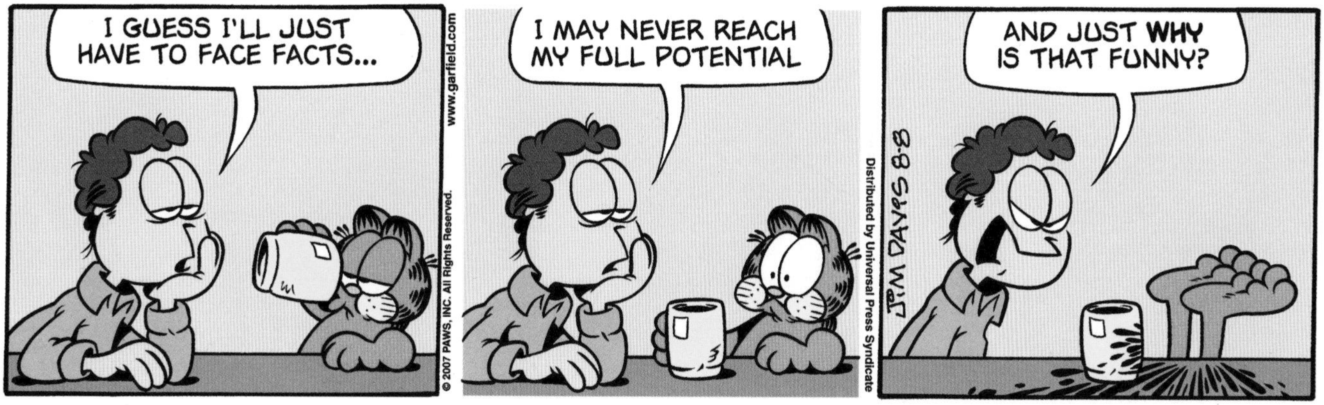
I GUESS I'LL JUST HAVE TO FACE FACTS...
I MAY NEVER REACH MY FULL POTENTIAL
AND JUST **WHY** IS THAT FUNNY?
© 2007 PAWS, INC. All Rights Reserved. www.garfield.com
Distributed by Universal Press Syndicate
JIM DAVIS 8-8

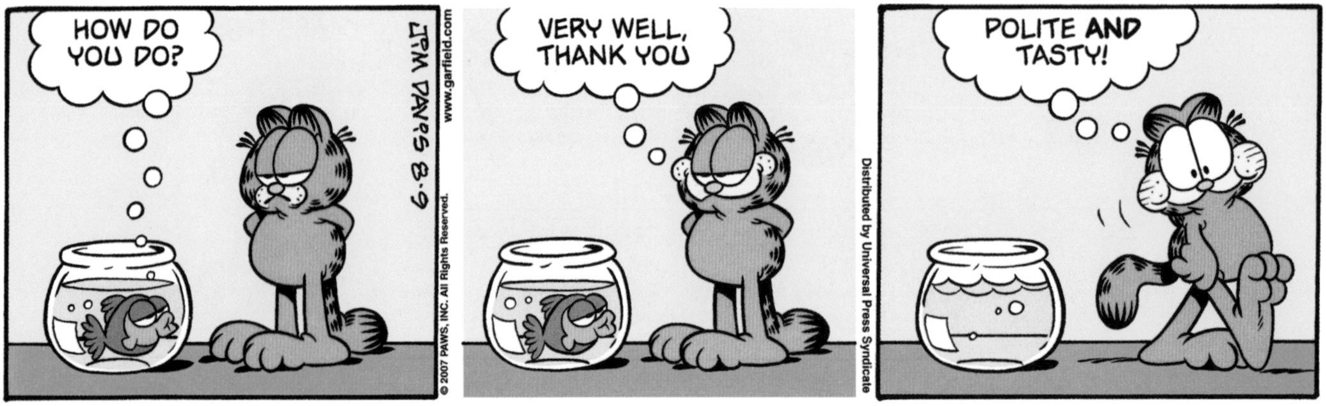
HOW DO YOU DO?
VERY WELL, THANK YOU
POLITE AND TASTY!

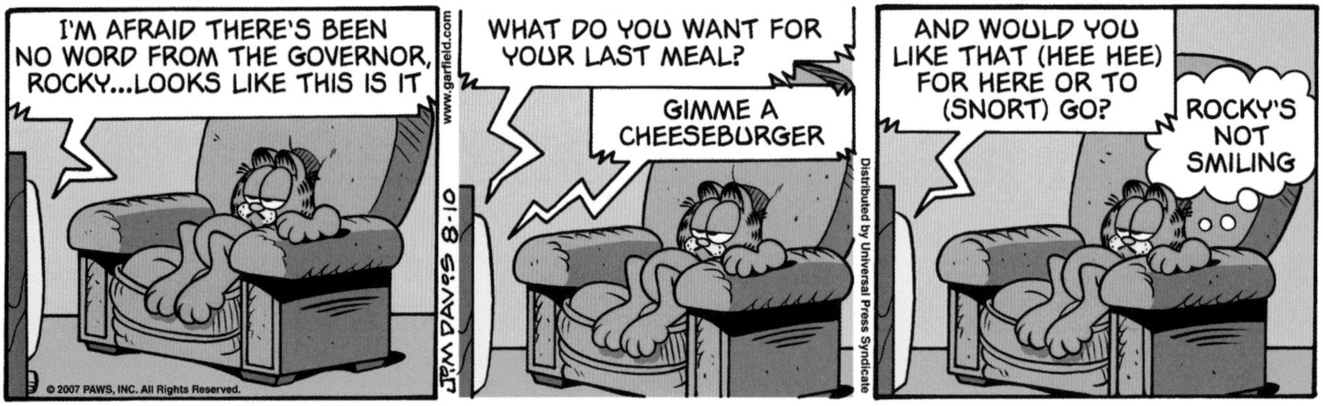
I'M AFRAID THERE'S BEEN NO WORD FROM THE GOVERNOR, ROCKY...LOOKS LIKE THIS IS IT
WHAT DO YOU WANT FOR YOUR LAST MEAL?
GIMME A CHEESEBURGER
AND WOULD YOU LIKE THAT (HEE HEE) FOR HERE OR TO (SNORT) GO?
ROCKY'S NOT SMILING

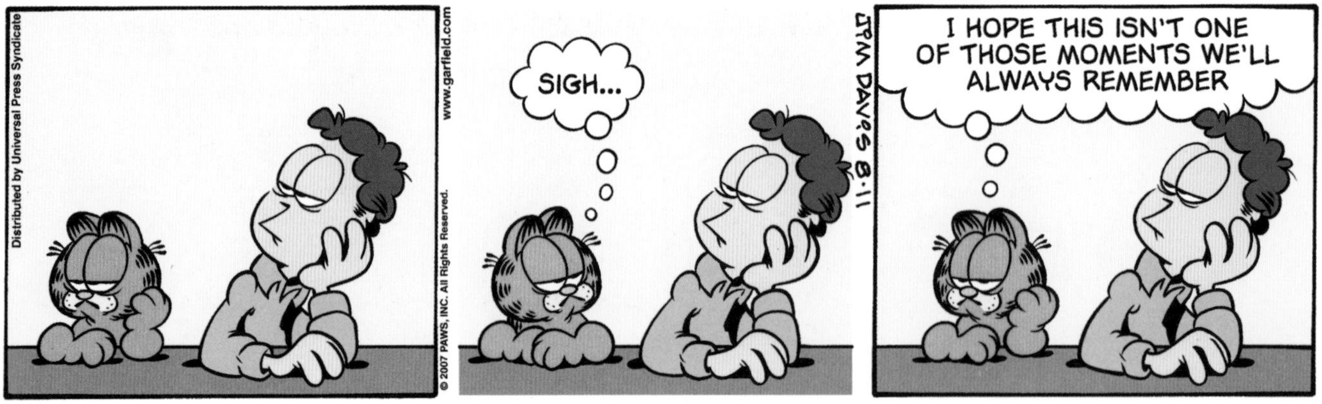
SIGH...
I HOPE THIS ISN'T ONE OF THOSE MOMENTS WE'LL ALWAYS REMEMBER

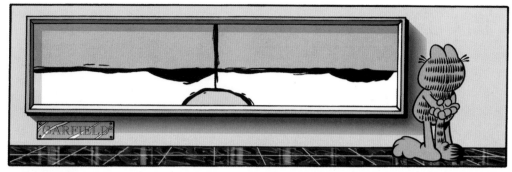

© 2007 PAWS, INC. All Rights Reserved.

Distributed by Universal Press Syndicate

I THINK I'LL CHANGE AGAIN AND GO FOR ANOTHER DIP IN OUR KIDDIE POOL

YEEE!

WOOOOOO WOO WOO WOO WOO

HEE-HOO HEE-HOO HEE-HOO

YAH-HA-HA-HA-HA-HA

YOU'VE GOTTA LOVE THE "COLD, WET SWIM TRUNKS DANCE"

YEE! YEE! HOOOOO HAAAH!!

HUBERT, CALL A COP!!

Text GARFIELD to 26642 US ONLY

JIM DAVIS 8-12

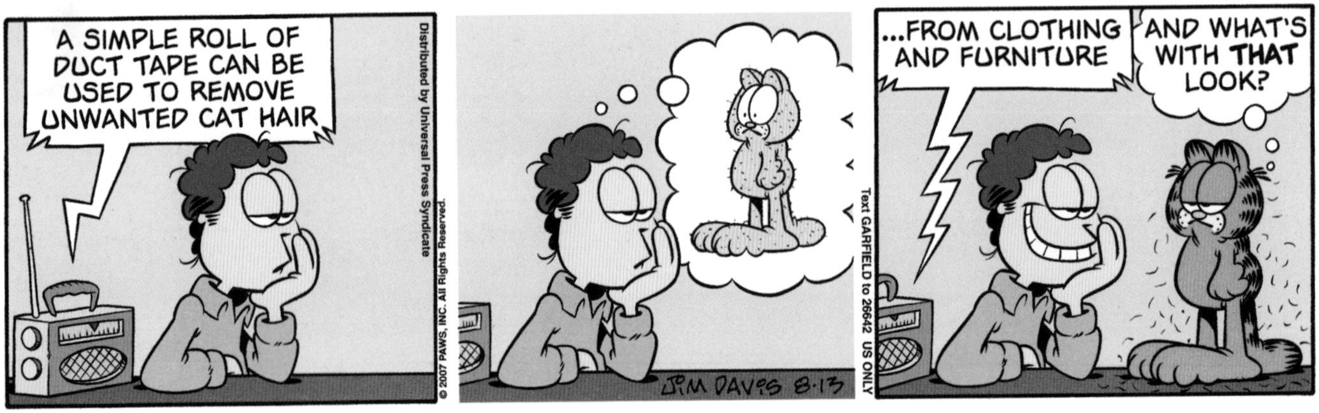
A SIMPLE ROLL OF DUCT TAPE CAN BE USED TO REMOVE UNWANTED CAT HAIR
Distributed by Universal Press Syndicate
© 2007 PAWS, INC. All Rights Reserved.
JIM DAVIS 8-13
Text GARFIELD to 26642 US ONLY
...FROM CLOTHING AND FURNITURE
AND WHAT'S WITH **THAT** LOOK?

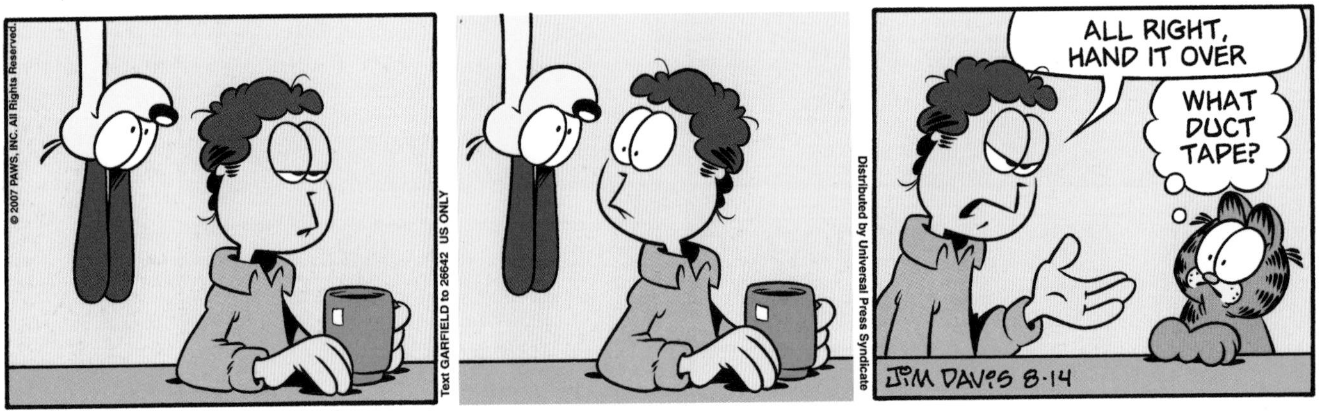
© 2007 PAWS, INC. All Rights Reserved.
Text GARFIELD to 26642 US ONLY
Distributed by Universal Press Syndicate
ALL RIGHT, HAND IT OVER
WHAT DUCT TAPE?
JIM DAVIS 8-14

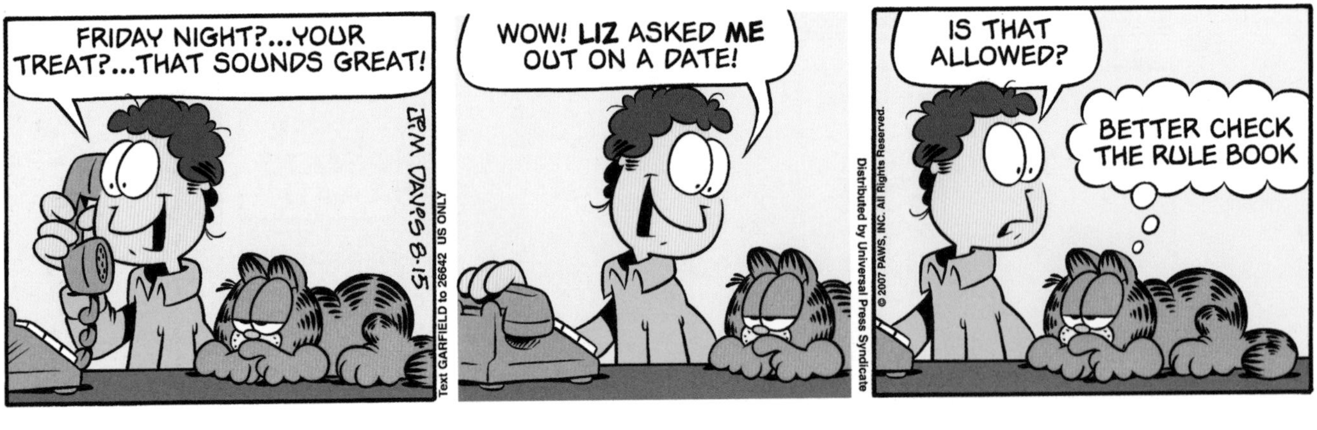
FRIDAY NIGHT?...YOUR TREAT?...THAT SOUNDS GREAT!
JIM DAVIS 8-15
Text GARFIELD to 26642 US ONLY
WOW! **LIZ** ASKED **ME** OUT ON A DATE!
Distributed by Universal Press Syndicate
© 2007 PAWS, INC. All Rights Reserved.
IS THAT ALLOWED?
BETTER CHECK THE RULE BOOK

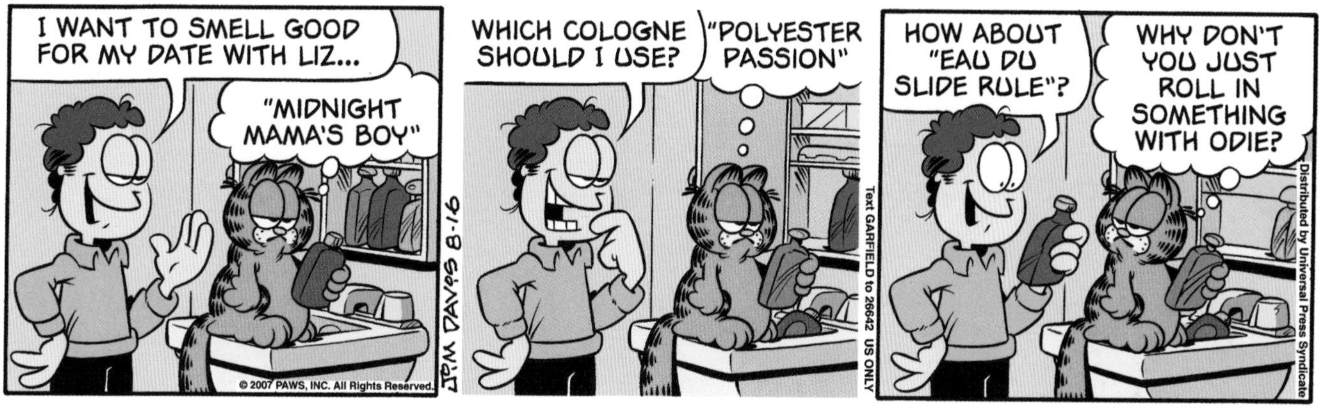
I WANT TO SMELL GOOD FOR MY DATE WITH LIZ...
"MIDNIGHT MAMA'S BOY"
© 2007 PAWS, INC. All Rights Reserved.
WHICH COLOGNE SHOULD I USE?
"POLYESTER PASSION"
Text GARFIELD to 26642 US ONLY
HOW ABOUT "EAU DU SLIDE RULE"?
WHY DON'T YOU JUST ROLL IN SOMETHING WITH ODIE?
Distributed by Universal Press Syndicate

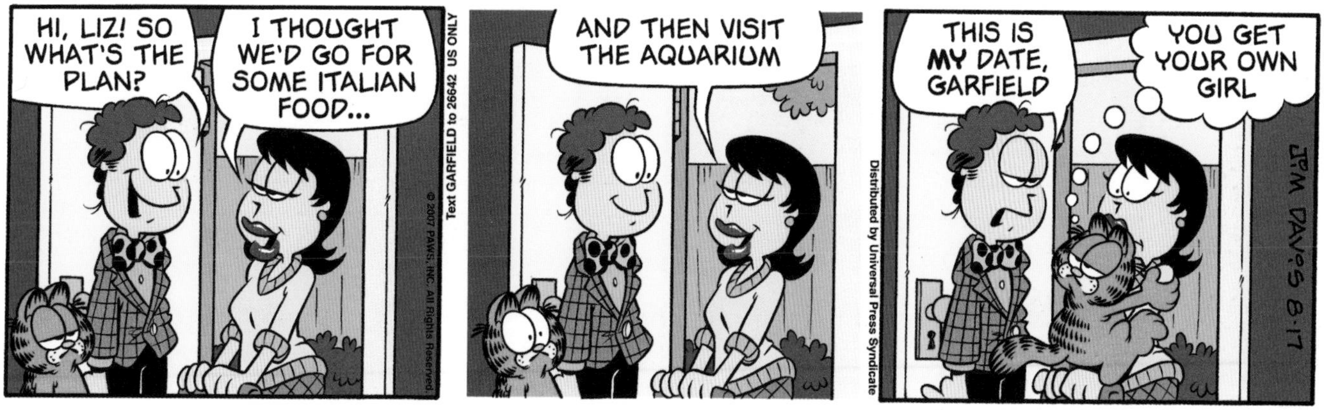
HI, LIZ! SO WHAT'S THE PLAN?
I THOUGHT WE'D GO FOR SOME ITALIAN FOOD...
© 2007 PAWS, INC. All Rights Reserved.
Text GARFIELD to 26642 US ONLY
AND THEN VISIT THE AQUARIUM
Distributed by Universal Press Syndicate
THIS IS MY DATE, GARFIELD
YOU GET YOUR OWN GIRL

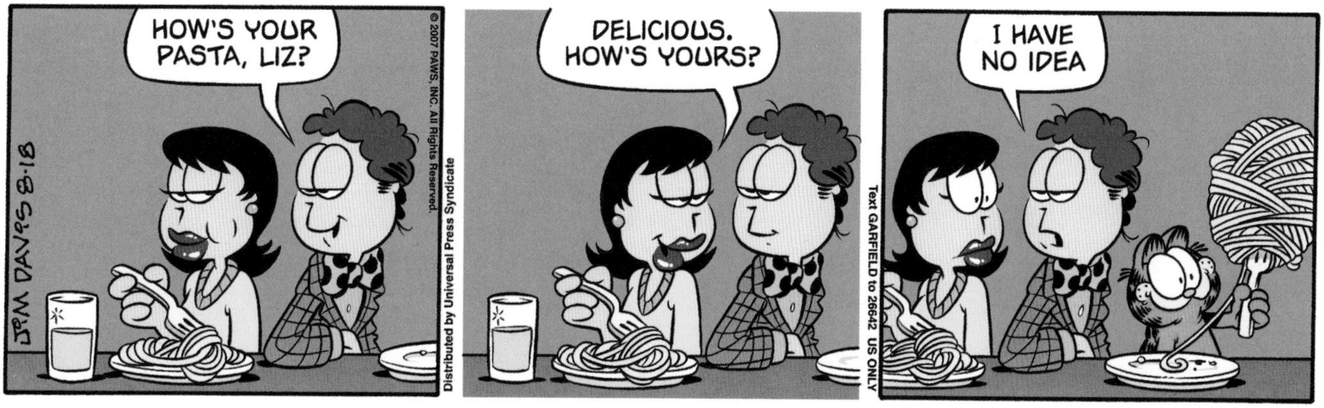
HOW'S YOUR PASTA, LIZ?
© 2007 PAWS, INC. All Rights Reserved.
Distributed by Universal Press Syndicate
DELICIOUS. HOW'S YOURS?
Text GARFIELD to 26642 US ONLY
I HAVE NO IDEA

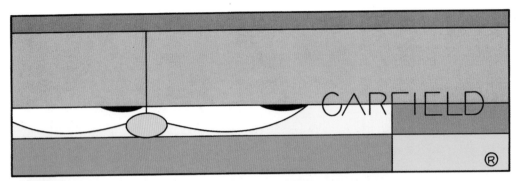

© 2007 PAWS, INC. All Rights Reserved.

GARFIELD, WE HAVEN'T EVEN ORDERED YET...

DON'T FILL UP ON BREAD!

JIM DAVIS 8-19

www.garfield.com

WHAT?!

Distributed by Universal Press Syndicate

GARFIELD? FILL UP?

GOOD POINT

KEEP 'EM COMING!

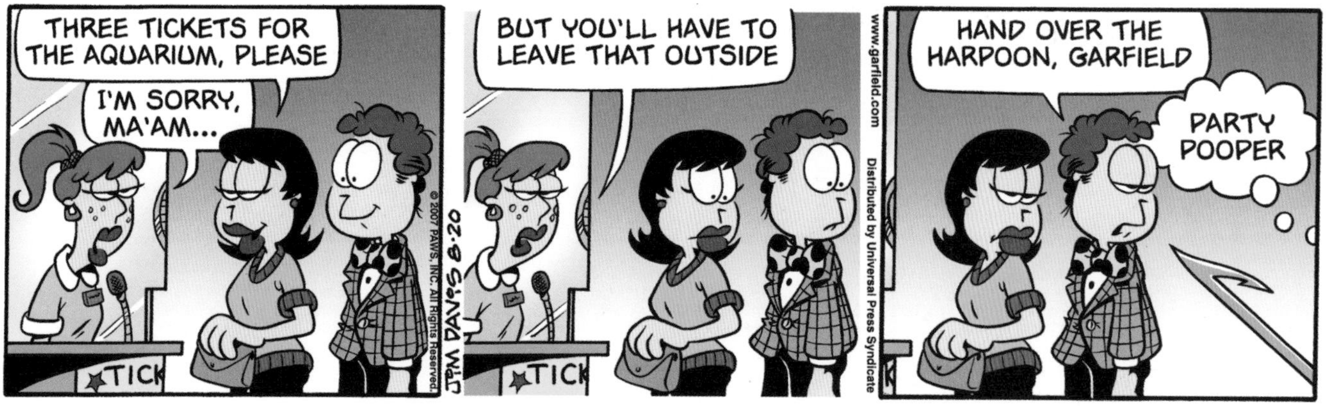
THREE TICKETS FOR THE AQUARIUM, PLEASE
I'M SORRY, MA'AM...
BUT YOU'LL HAVE TO LEAVE THAT OUTSIDE
HAND OVER THE HARPOON, GARFIELD
PARTY POOPER
JPM DAVIS 8·20
© 2007 PAWS, INC. All Rights Reserved.
www.garfield.com
Distributed by Universal Press Syndicate

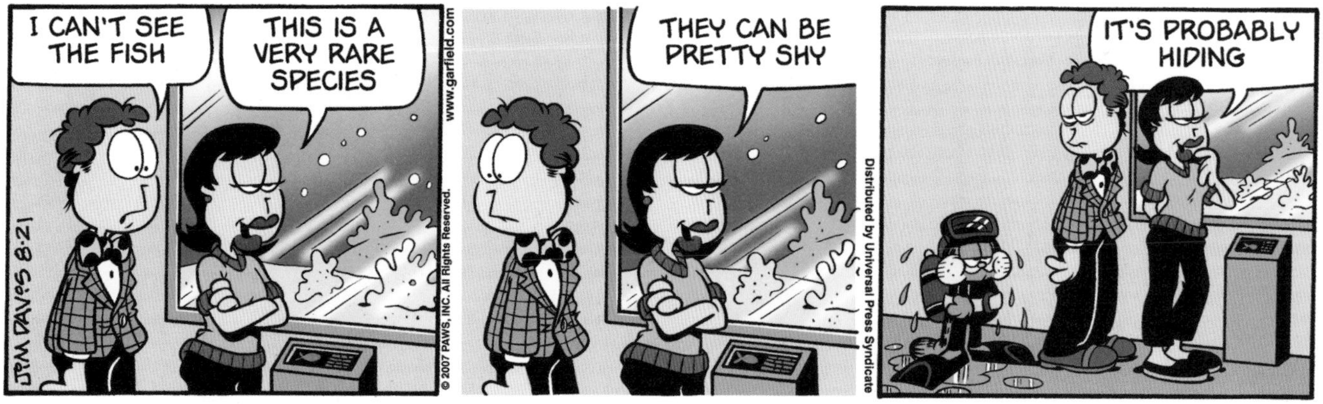
I CAN'T SEE THE FISH
THIS IS A VERY RARE SPECIES
THEY CAN BE PRETTY SHY
IT'S PROBABLY HIDING
JPM DAVIS 8·21
© 2007 PAWS, INC. All Rights Reserved.
www.garfield.com
Distributed by Universal Press Syndicate

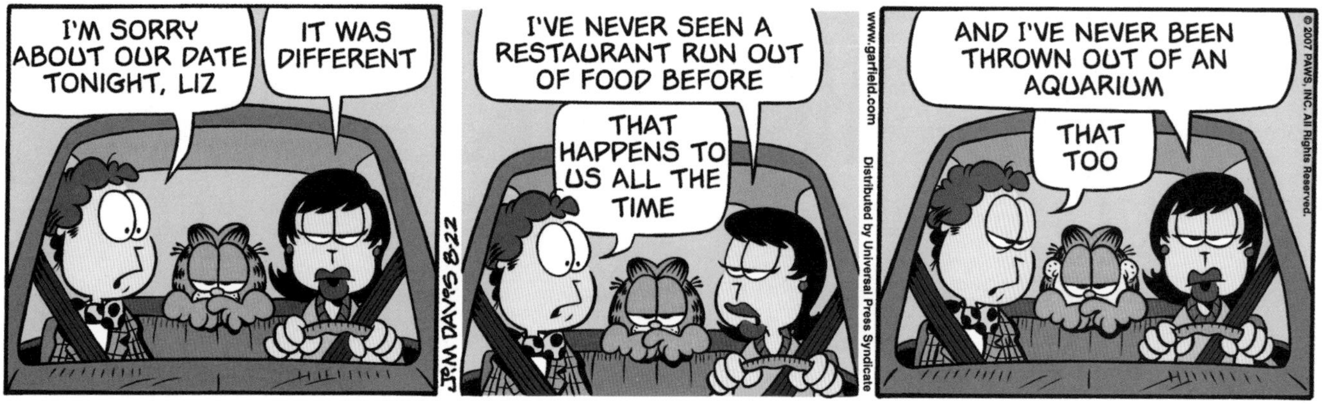
I'M SORRY ABOUT OUR DATE TONIGHT, LIZ
IT WAS DIFFERENT
I'VE NEVER SEEN A RESTAURANT RUN OUT OF FOOD BEFORE
THAT HAPPENS TO US ALL THE TIME
AND I'VE NEVER BEEN THROWN OUT OF AN AQUARIUM
THAT TOO
JPM DAVIS 8·22
www.garfield.com
Distributed by Universal Press Syndicate
© 2007 PAWS, INC. All Rights Reserved.

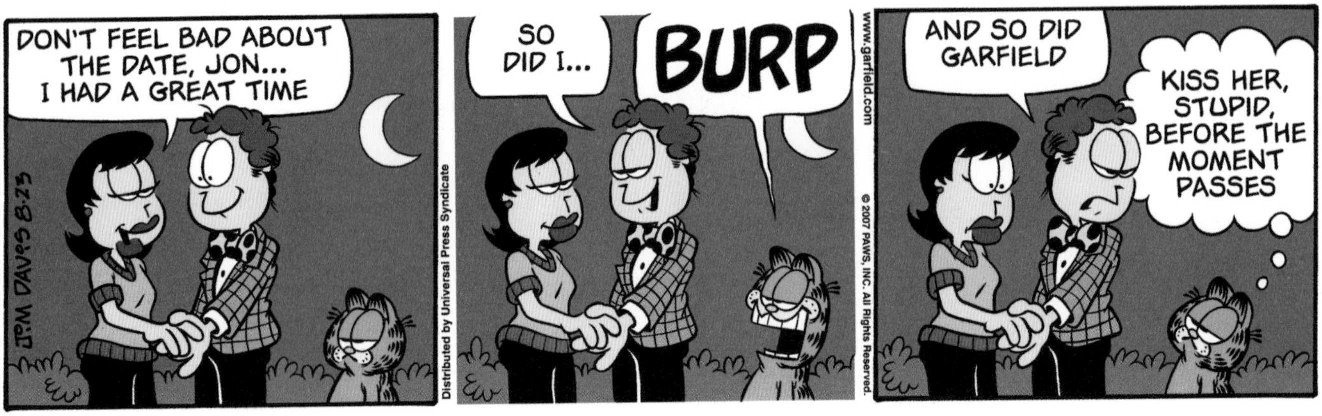
DON'T FEEL BAD ABOUT THE DATE, JON... I HAD A GREAT TIME
SO DID I...
BURP
AND SO DID GARFIELD
KISS HER, STUPID, BEFORE THE MOMENT PASSES

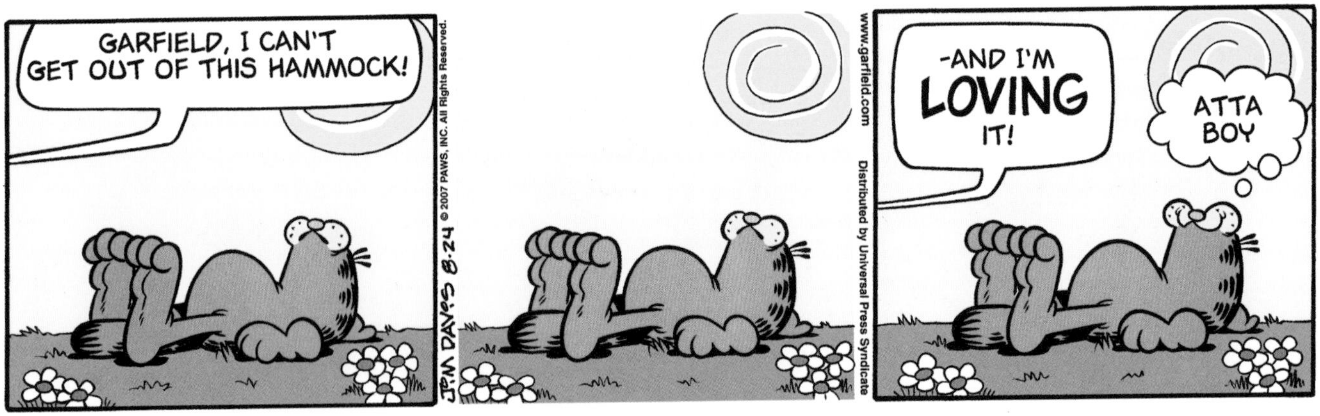
GARFIELD, I CAN'T GET OUT OF THIS HAMMOCK!
-AND I'M LOVING IT!
ATTA BOY

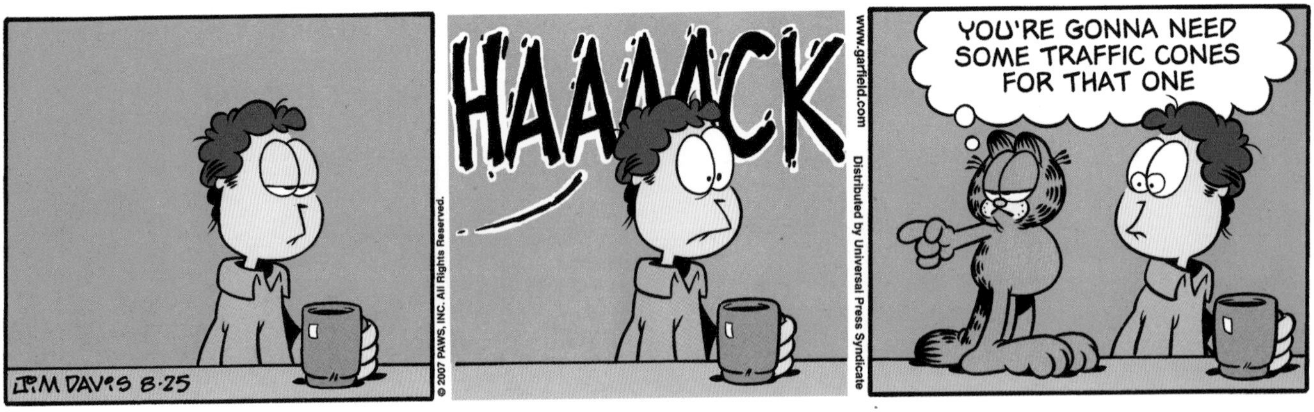
HAAAACK
YOU'RE GONNA NEED SOME TRAFFIC CONES FOR THAT ONE

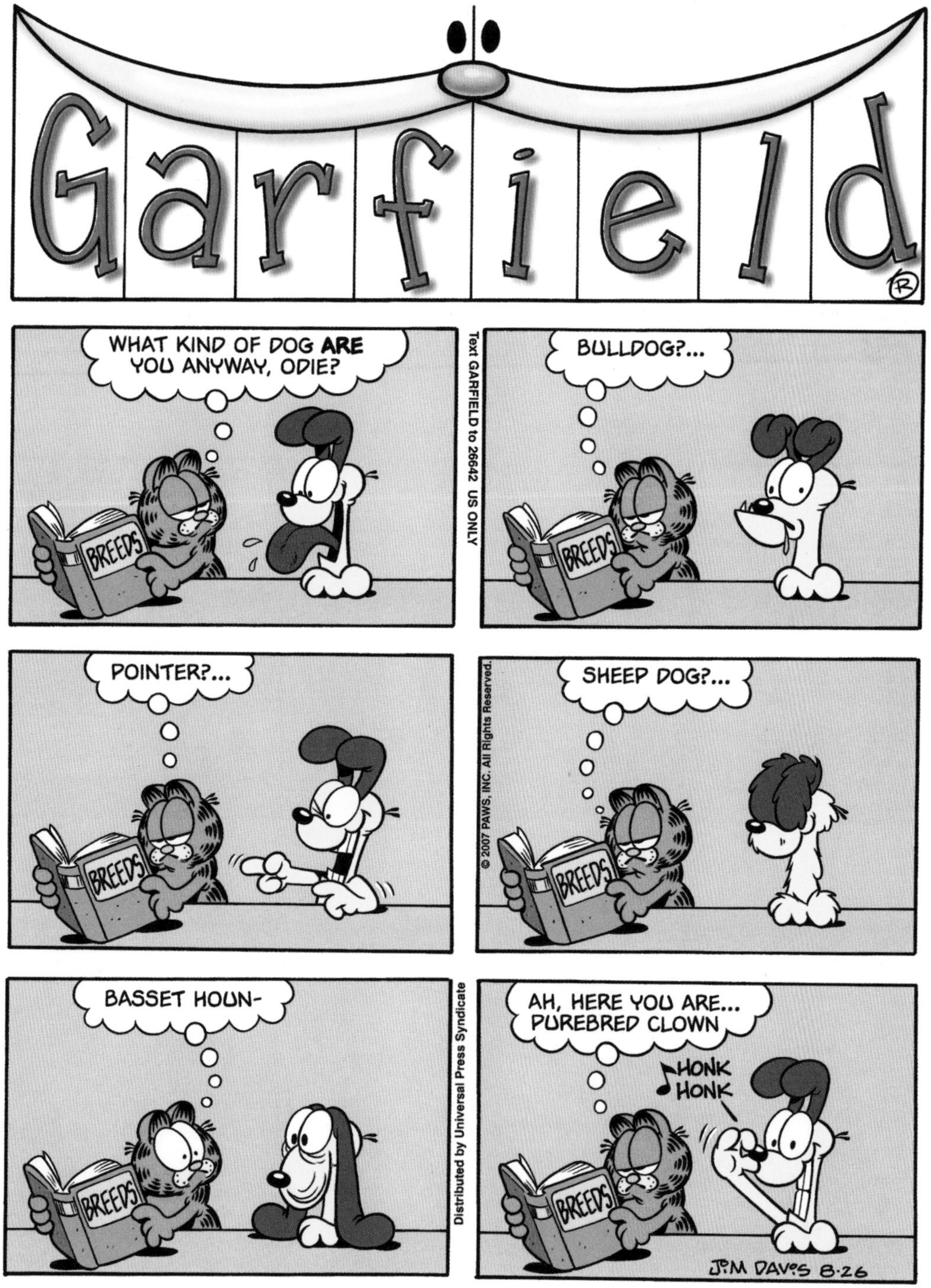
Garfield®
WHAT KIND OF DOG ARE YOU ANYWAY, ODIE?
BREEDS
Text GARFIELD to 26642 US ONLY
BULLDOG?...
POINTER?...
© 2007 PAWS, INC. All Rights Reserved.
SHEEP DOG?...
BASSET HOUN-
Distributed by Universal Press Syndicate
AH, HERE YOU ARE... PUREBRED CLOWN
HONK HONK
JIM DAVIS 8-26

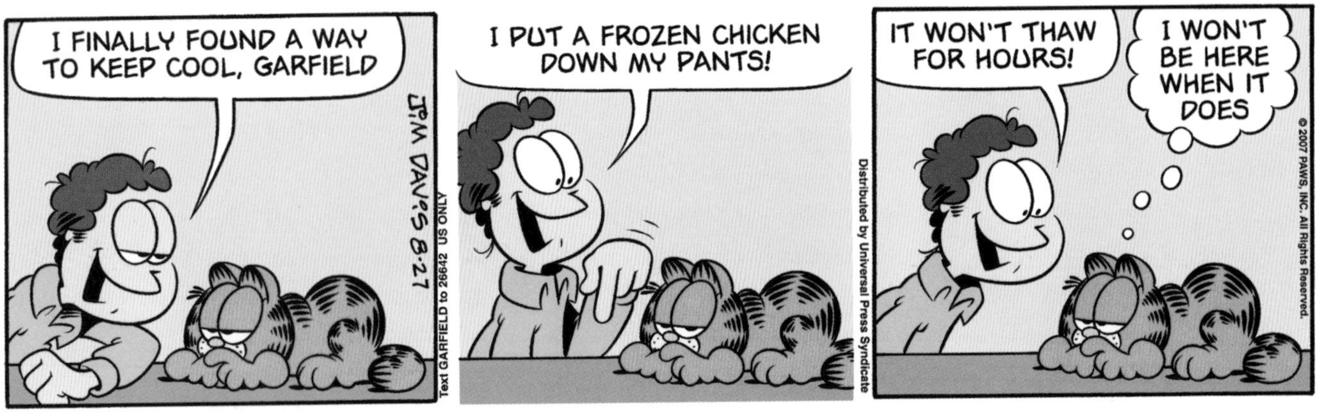
I FINALLY FOUND A WAY TO KEEP COOL, GARFIELD
JIM DAVIS 8·27
Text GARFIELD to 26642 US ONLY
I PUT A FROZEN CHICKEN DOWN MY PANTS!
Distributed by Universal Press Syndicate
IT WON'T THAW FOR HOURS!
I WON'T BE HERE WHEN IT DOES
© 2007 PAWS, INC. All Rights Reserved.

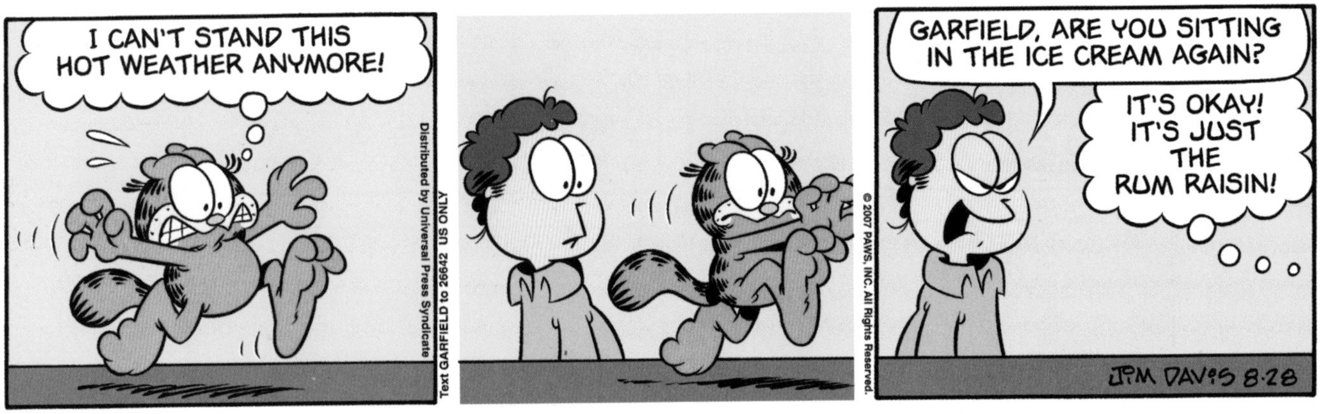
I CAN'T STAND THIS HOT WEATHER ANYMORE!
Distributed by Universal Press Syndicate
Text GARFIELD to 26642 US ONLY
© 2007 PAWS, INC. All Rights Reserved.
GARFIELD, ARE YOU SITTING IN THE ICE CREAM AGAIN?
IT'S OKAY! IT'S JUST THE RUM RAISIN!
JIM DAVIS 8·28

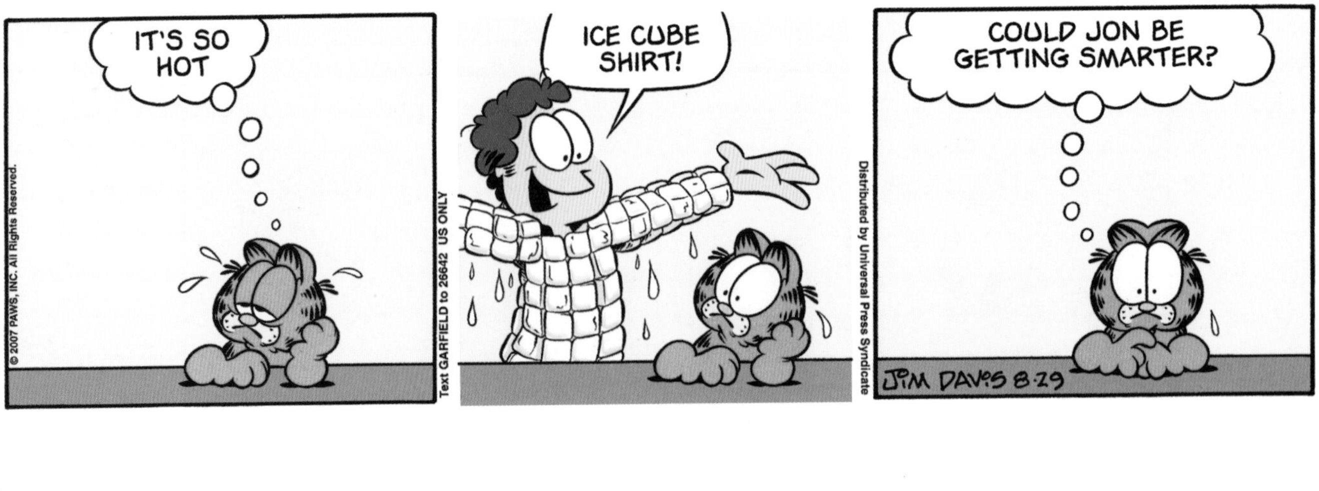
IT'S SO HOT
© 2007 PAWS, INC. All Rights Reserved.
Text GARFIELD to 26642 US ONLY
ICE CUBE SHIRT!
Distributed by Universal Press Syndicate
COULD JON BE GETTING SMARTER?
JIM DAVIS 8·29

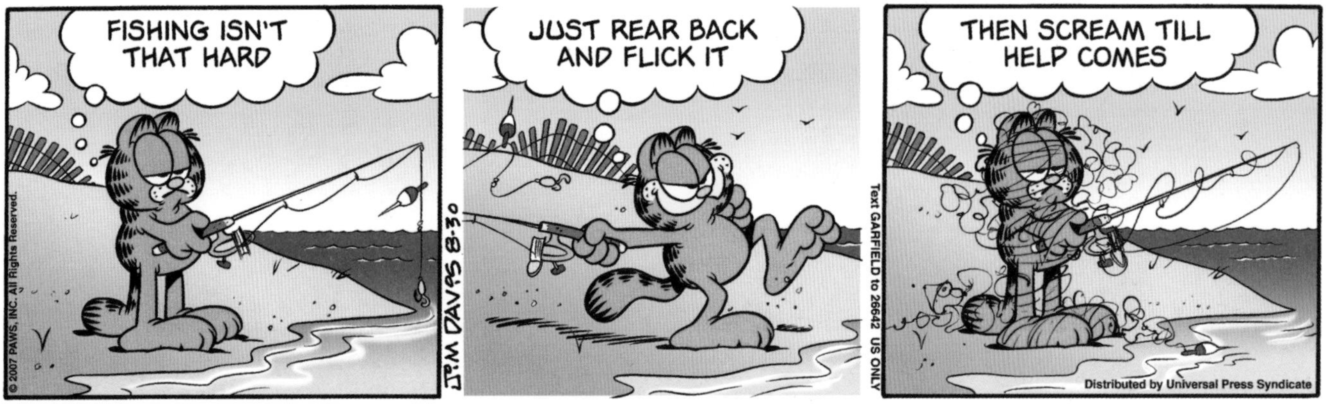
FISHING ISN'T THAT HARD
JUST REAR BACK AND FLICK IT
THEN SCREAM TILL HELP COMES
© 2007 PAWS, INC. All Rights Reserved.
Text GARFIELD to 26642 US ONLY
Distributed by Universal Press Syndicate

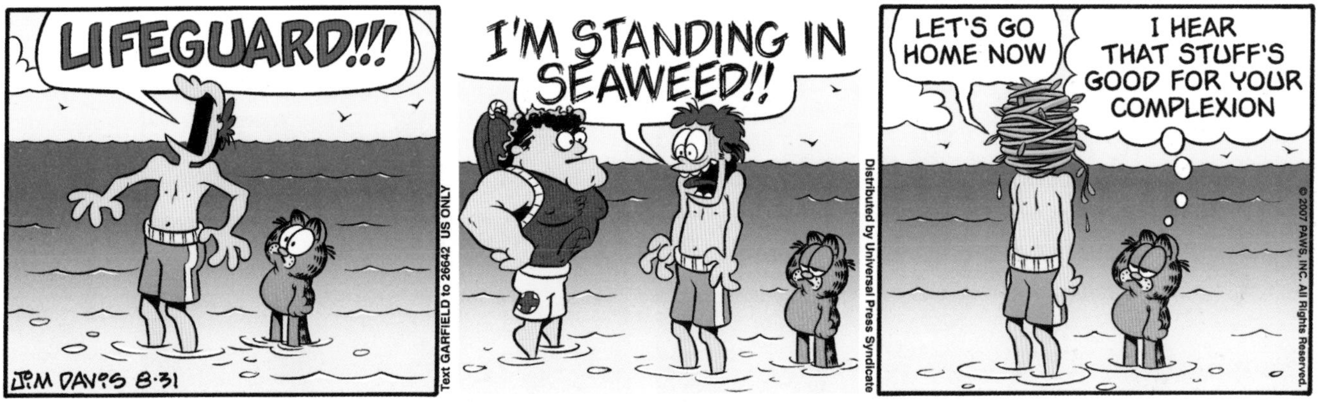
LIFEGUARD!!!
I'M STANDING IN SEAWEED!!
LET'S GO HOME NOW
I HEAR THAT STUFF'S GOOD FOR YOUR COMPLEXION
Text GARFIELD to 26642 US ONLY
Distributed by Universal Press Syndicate
© 2007 PAWS, INC. All Rights Reserved.

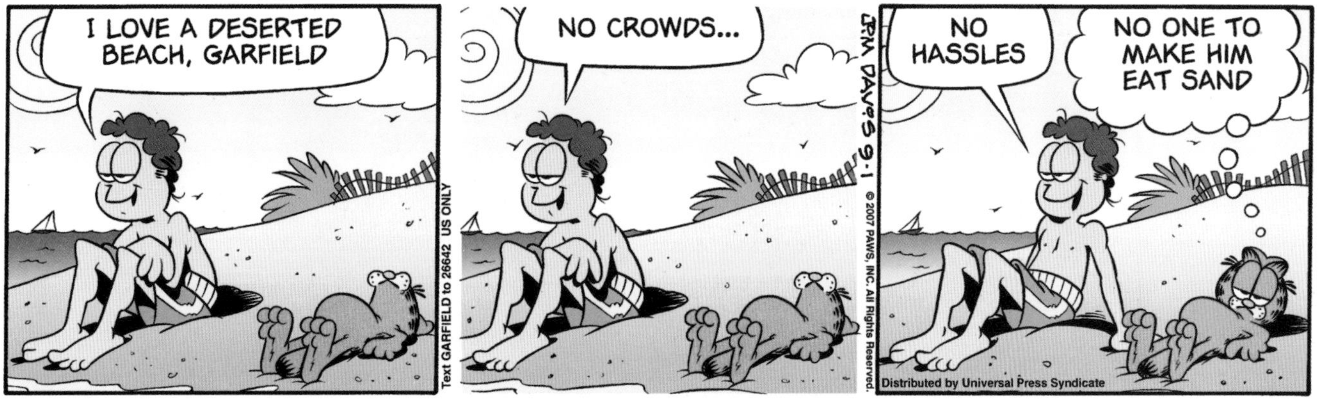
I LOVE A DESERTED BEACH, GARFIELD
NO CROWDS...
NO HASSLES
NO ONE TO MAKE HIM EAT SAND
Text GARFIELD to 26642 US ONLY
© 2007 PAWS, INC. All Rights Reserved.
Distributed by Universal Press Syndicate

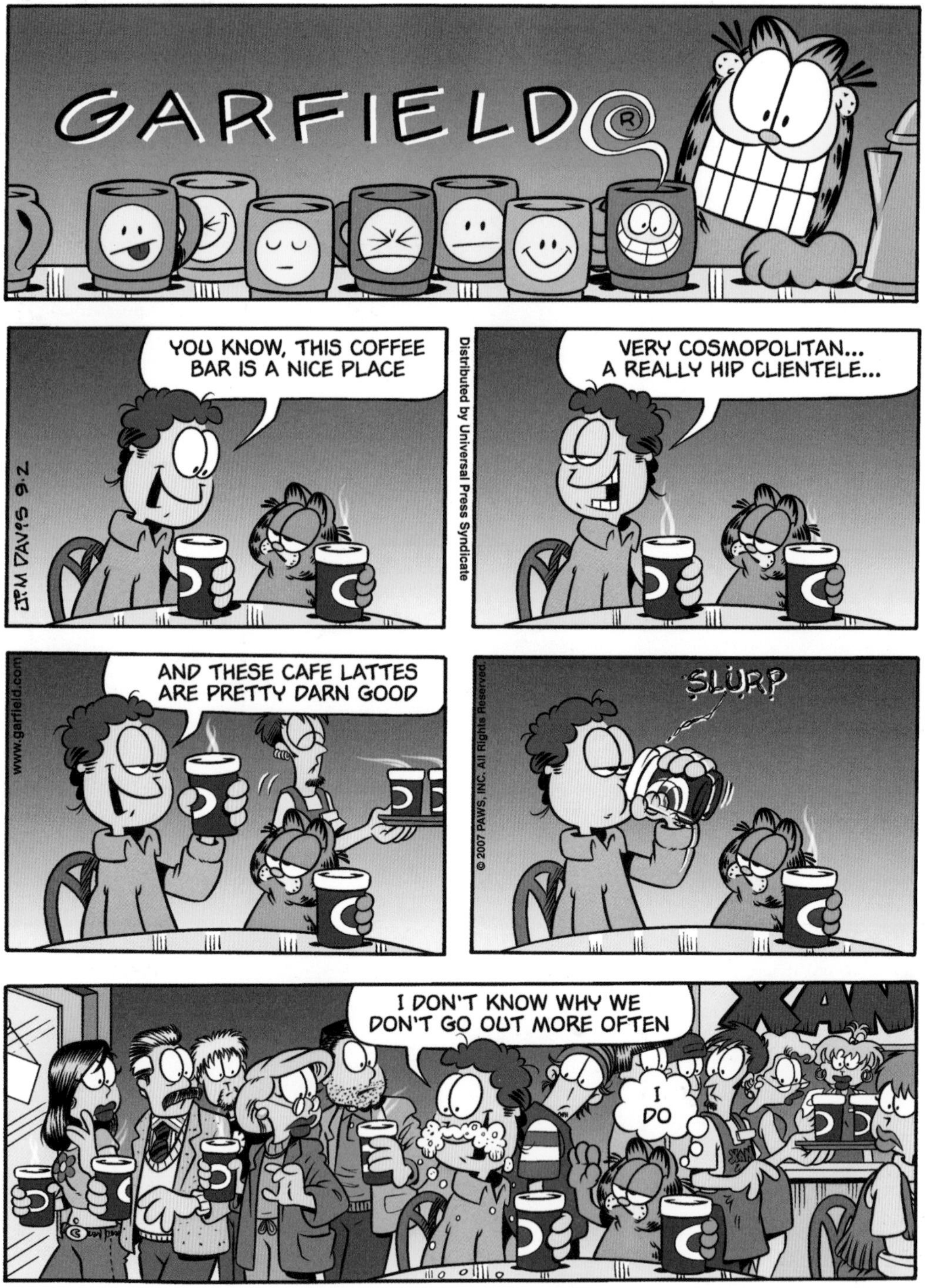
GARFIELD®
YOU KNOW, THIS COFFEE BAR IS A NICE PLACE
JIM DAVIS 9.2
Distributed by Universal Press Syndicate
VERY COSMOPOLITAN... A REALLY HIP CLIENTELE...
www.garfield.com
AND THESE CAFE LATTES ARE PRETTY DARN GOOD
© 2007 PAWS, INC. All Rights Reserved.
SLURP
I DON'T KNOW WHY WE DON'T GO OUT MORE OFTEN
I DO

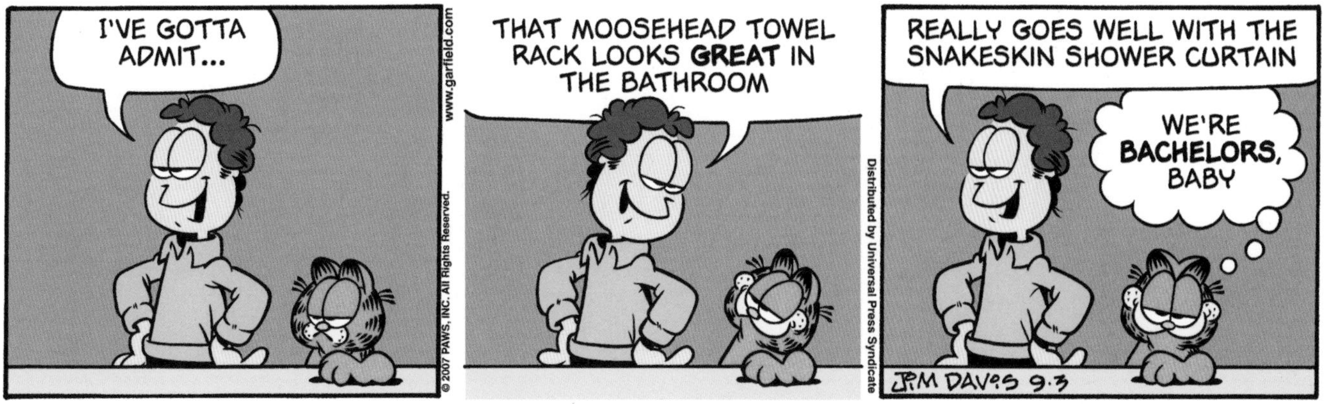
I'VE GOTTA ADMIT...
THAT MOOSEHEAD TOWEL RACK LOOKS GREAT IN THE BATHROOM
REALLY GOES WELL WITH THE SNAKESKIN SHOWER CURTAIN
WE'RE BACHELORS, BABY
JIM DAVIS 9-3

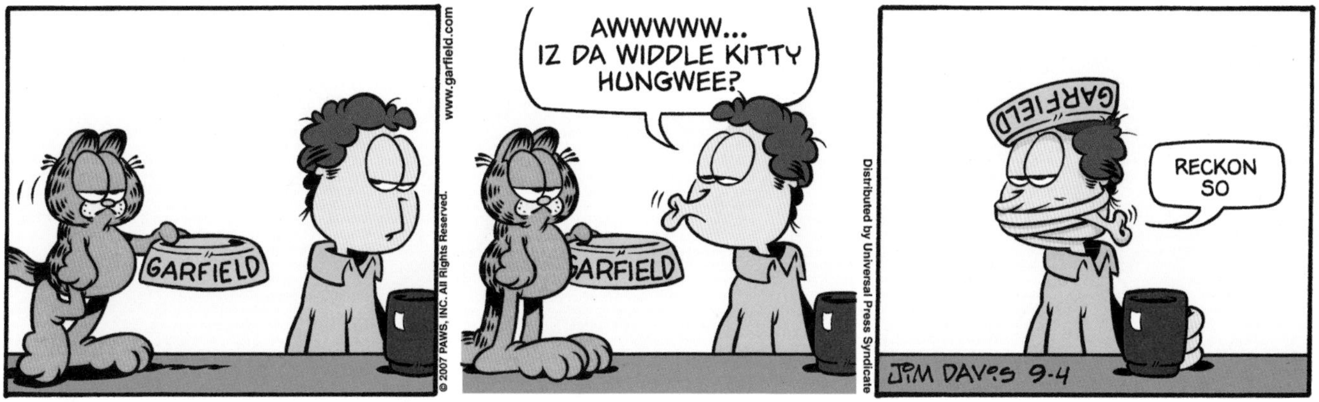
GARFIELD
AWWWWW... IZ DA WIDDLE KITTY HUNGWEE?
GARFIELD
GARFIELD
RECKON SO
JIM DAVIS 9-4

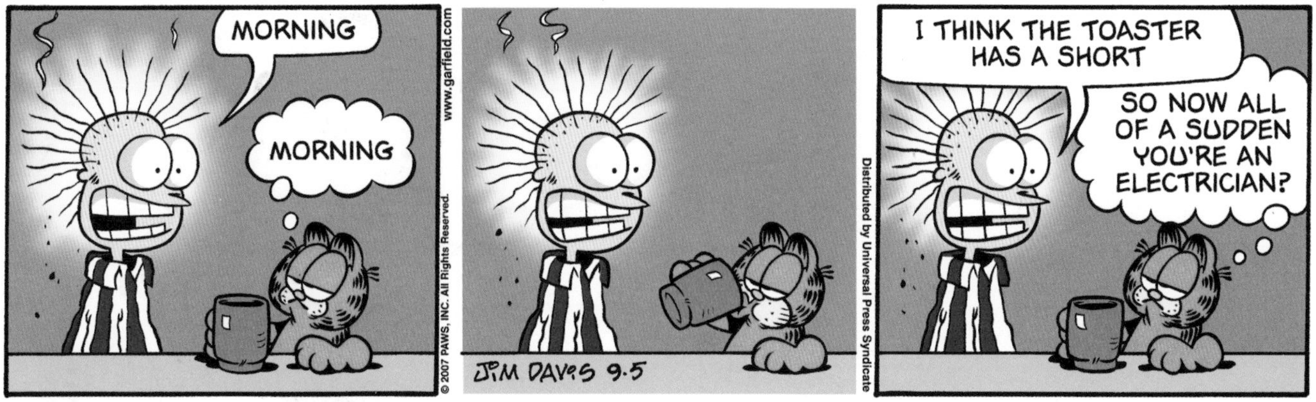
MORNING
MORNING
JIM DAVIS 9-5
I THINK THE TOASTER HAS A SHORT
SO NOW ALL OF A SUDDEN YOU'RE AN ELECTRICIAN?

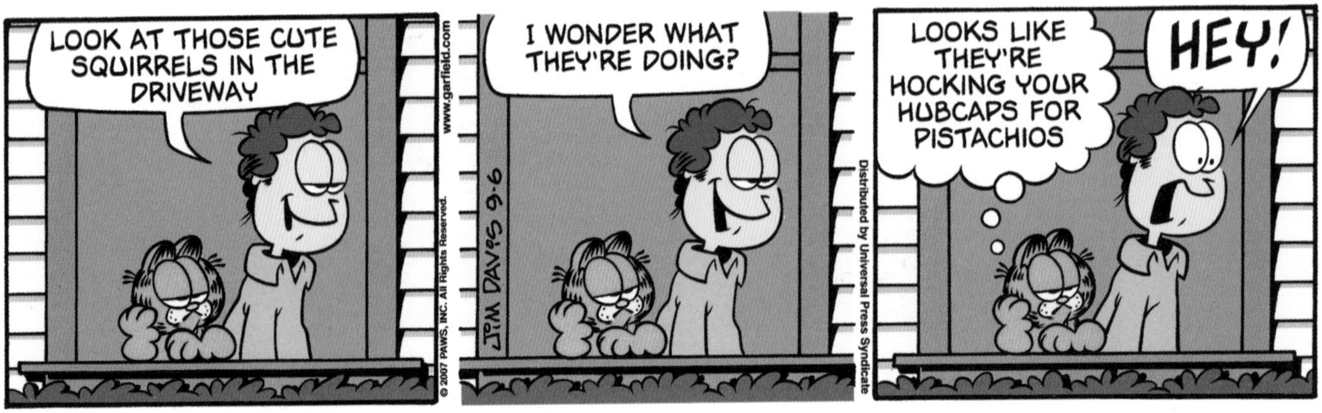
LOOK AT THOSE CUTE SQUIRRELS IN THE DRIVEWAY
© 2007 PAWS, INC. All Rights Reserved. www.garfield.com
I WONDER WHAT THEY'RE DOING?
JIM DAVIS 9-6
Distributed by Universal Press Syndicate
LOOKS LIKE THEY'RE HOCKING YOUR HUBCAPS FOR PISTACHIOS
HEY!

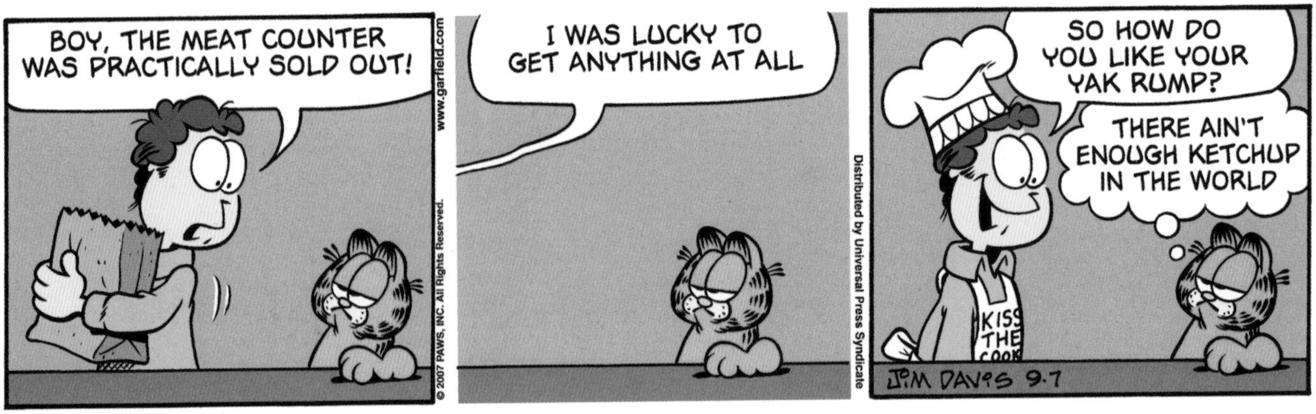
BOY, THE MEAT COUNTER WAS PRACTICALLY SOLD OUT!
© 2007 PAWS, INC. All Rights Reserved. www.garfield.com
I WAS LUCKY TO GET ANYTHING AT ALL
Distributed by Universal Press Syndicate
SO HOW DO YOU LIKE YOUR YAK RUMP?
THERE AIN'T ENOUGH KETCHUP IN THE WORLD
KISS THE COOK
JIM DAVIS 9-7

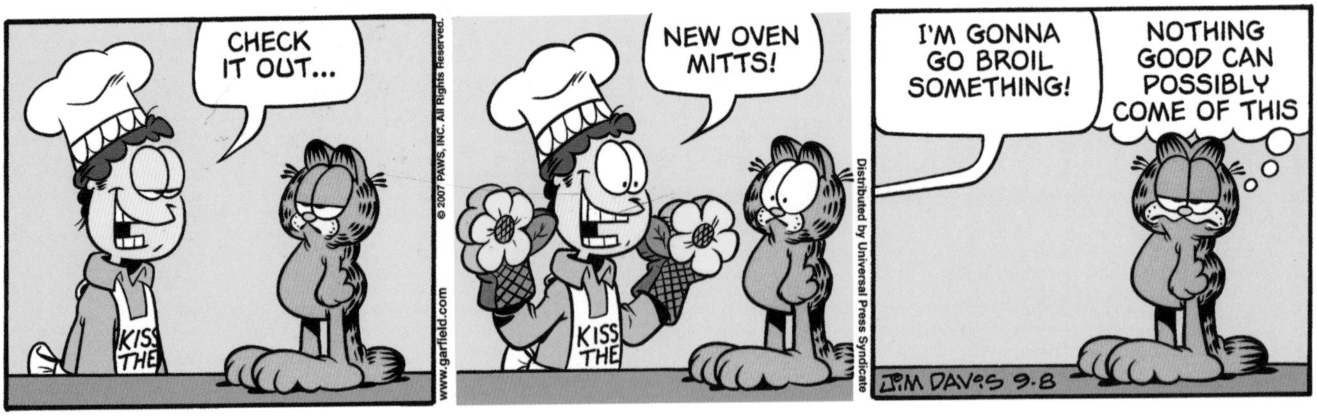
CHECK IT OUT...
KISS THE
© 2007 PAWS, INC. All Rights Reserved. www.garfield.com
NEW OVEN MITTS!
KISS THE
Distributed by Universal Press Syndicate
I'M GONNA GO BROIL SOMETHING!
NOTHING GOOD CAN POSSIBLY COME OF THIS
JIM DAVIS 9-8

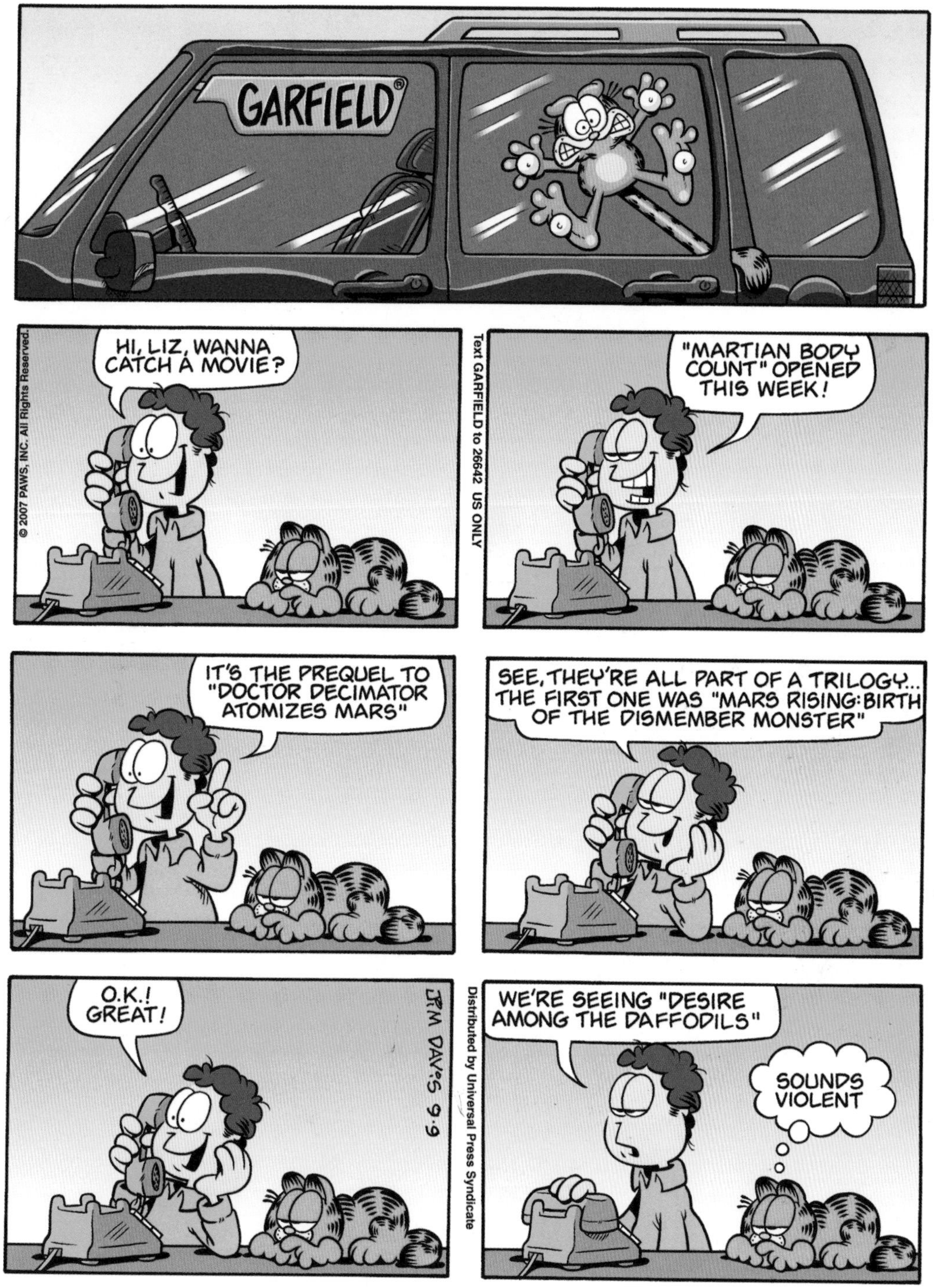
GARFIELD®
© 2007 PAWS, INC. All Rights Reserved.
HI, LIZ, WANNA CATCH A MOVIE?
Text GARFIELD to 26642 US ONLY
"MARTIAN BODY COUNT" OPENED THIS WEEK!
IT'S THE PREQUEL TO "DOCTOR DECIMATOR ATOMIZES MARS"
SEE, THEY'RE ALL PART OF A TRILOGY... THE FIRST ONE WAS "MARS RISING: BIRTH OF THE DISMEMBER MONSTER"
O.K.! GREAT!
JIM DAVIS 9-9
Distributed by Universal Press Syndicate
WE'RE SEEING "DESIRE AMONG THE DAFFODILS"
SOUNDS VIOLENT

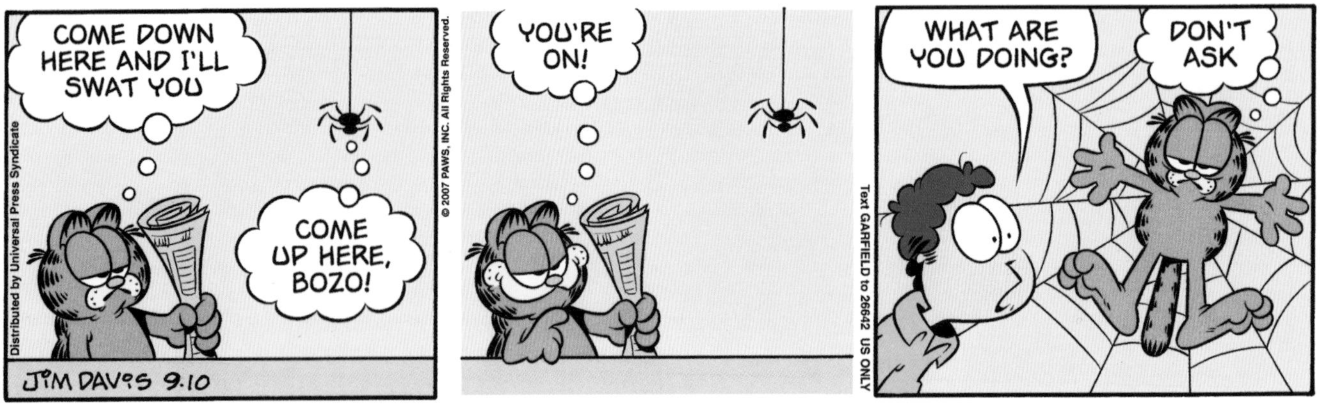
COME DOWN HERE AND I'LL SWAT YOU
COME UP HERE, BOZO!
JIM DAVIS 9.10
Distributed by Universal Press Syndicate
© 2007 PAWS, INC. All Rights Reserved.
YOU'RE ON!
Text GARFIELD to 26642 US ONLY
WHAT ARE YOU DOING?
DON'T ASK

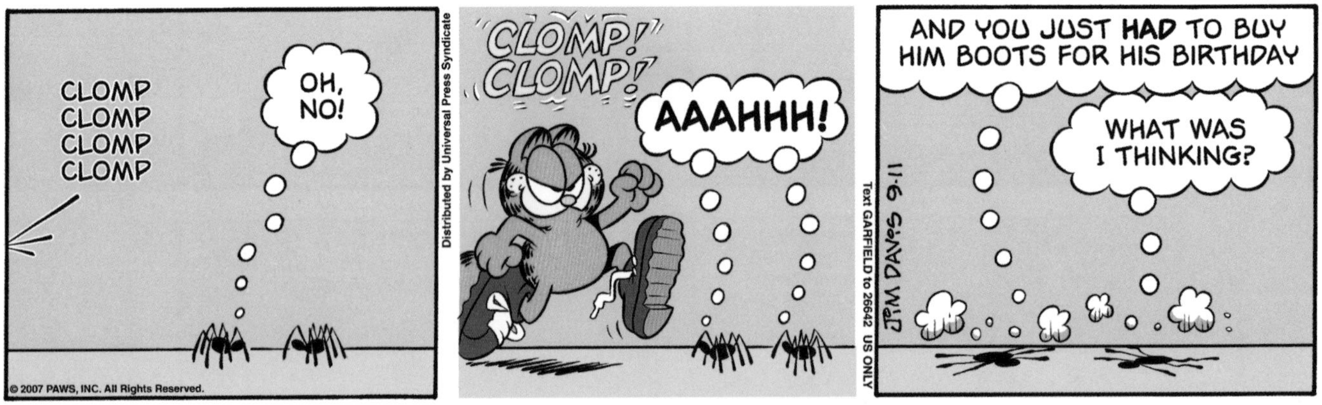
CLOMP
CLOMP
CLOMP
CLOMP
OH, NO!
© 2007 PAWS, INC. All Rights Reserved.
Distributed by Universal Press Syndicate
CLOMP! CLOMP!
AAAHHH!
Text GARFIELD to 26642 US ONLY
JIM DAVIS 9.11
AND YOU JUST **HAD** TO BUY HIM BOOTS FOR HIS BIRTHDAY
WHAT WAS I THINKING?

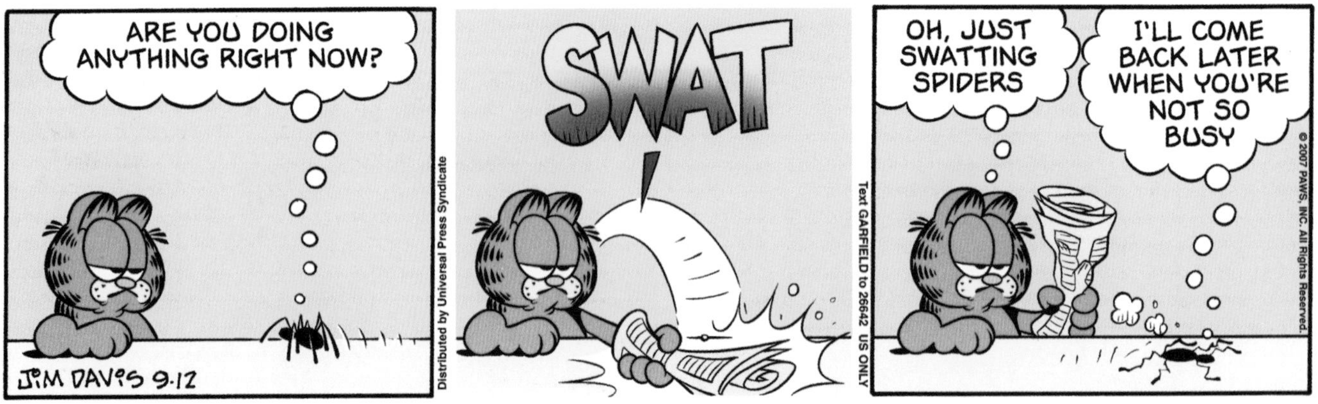
ARE YOU DOING ANYTHING RIGHT NOW?
JIM DAVIS 9.12
Distributed by Universal Press Syndicate
SWAT
Text GARFIELD to 26642 US ONLY
OH, JUST SWATTING SPIDERS
I'LL COME BACK LATER WHEN YOU'RE NOT SO BUSY
© 2007 PAWS, INC. All Rights Reserved.

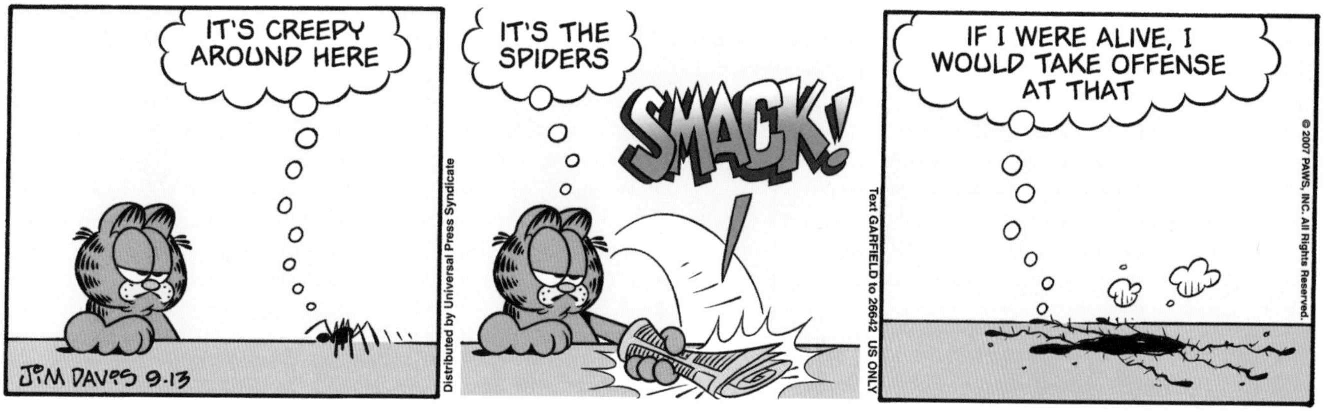
IT'S CREEPY AROUND HERE
JIM DAVIS 9.13
Distributed by Universal Press Syndicate
IT'S THE SPIDERS
SMACK!
Text GARFIELD to 26642 US ONLY
IF I WERE ALIVE, I WOULD TAKE OFFENSE AT THAT
© 2007 PAWS, INC. All Rights Reserved.

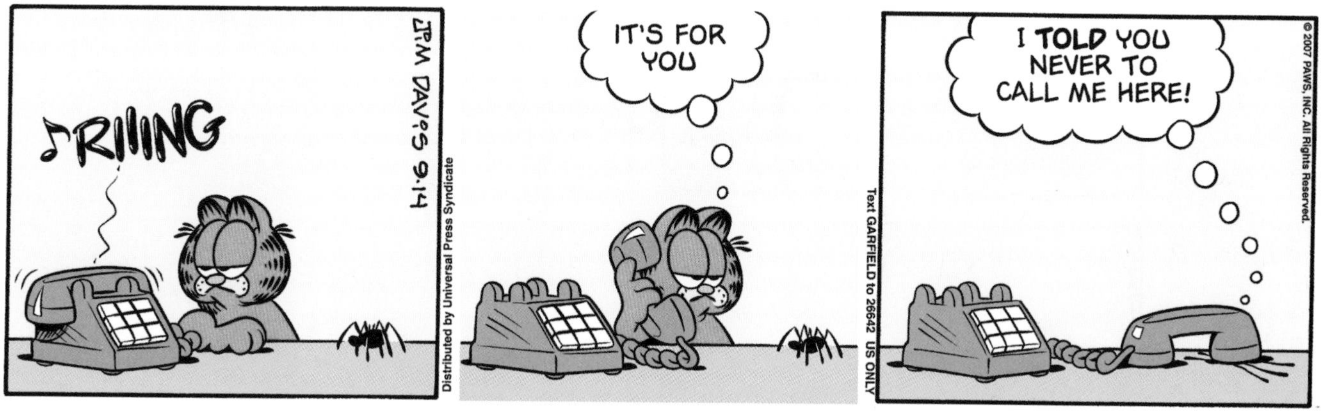
♪RIIING
JIM DAVIS 9.14
Distributed by Universal Press Syndicate
IT'S FOR YOU
Text GARFIELD to 26642 US ONLY
I **TOLD** YOU NEVER TO CALL ME HERE!
© 2007 PAWS, INC. All Rights Reserved.

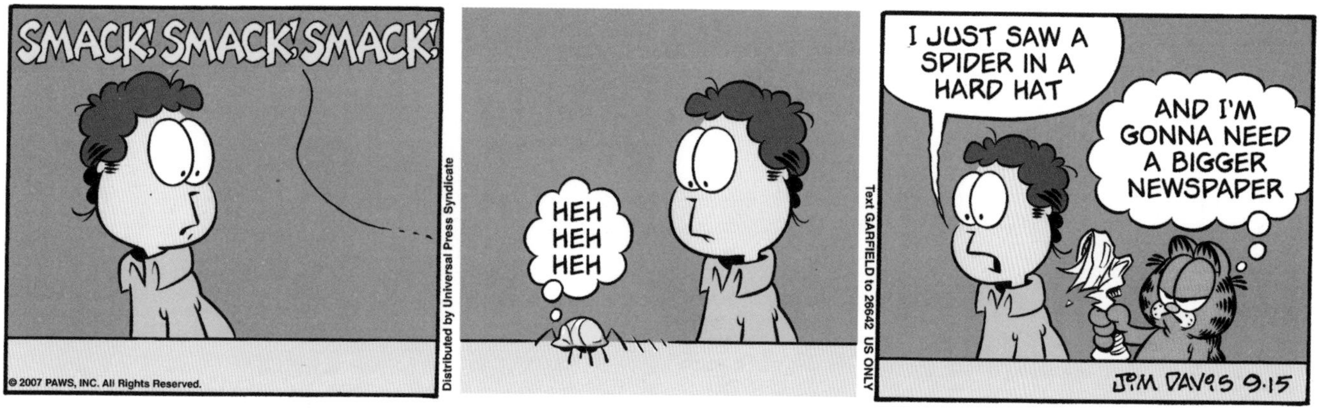
SMACK! SMACK! SMACK!
© 2007 PAWS, INC. All Rights Reserved.
Distributed by Universal Press Syndicate
HEH HEH HEH
Text GARFIELD to 26642 US ONLY
I JUST SAW A SPIDER IN A HARD HAT
AND I'M GONNA NEED A BIGGER NEWSPAPER
JIM DAVIS 9.15

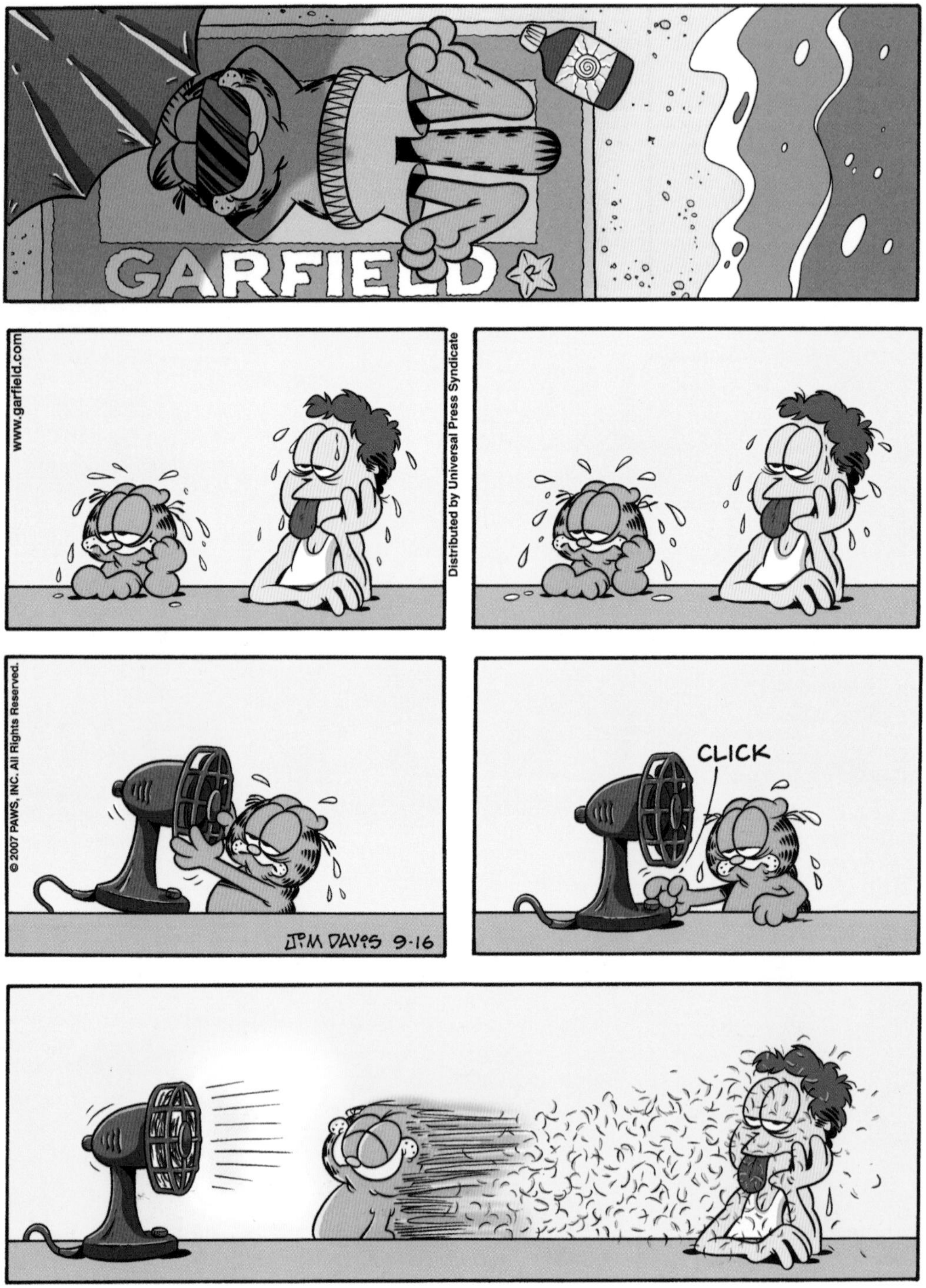
GARFIELD
www.garfield.com
Distributed by Universal Press Syndicate
© 2007 PAWS, INC. All Rights Reserved.
CLICK
JIM DAVIS 9-16

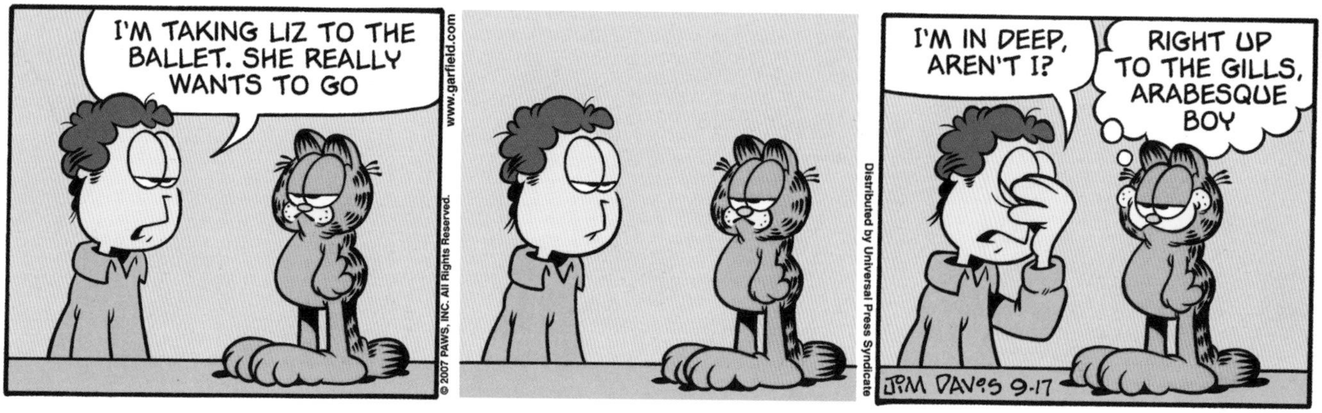
I'M TAKING LIZ TO THE BALLET. SHE REALLY WANTS TO GO
I'M IN DEEP, AREN'T I?
RIGHT UP TO THE GILLS, ARABESQUE BOY
JIM DAVIS 9-17
© 2007 PAWS, INC. All Rights Reserved.
www.garfield.com
Distributed by Universal Press Syndicate

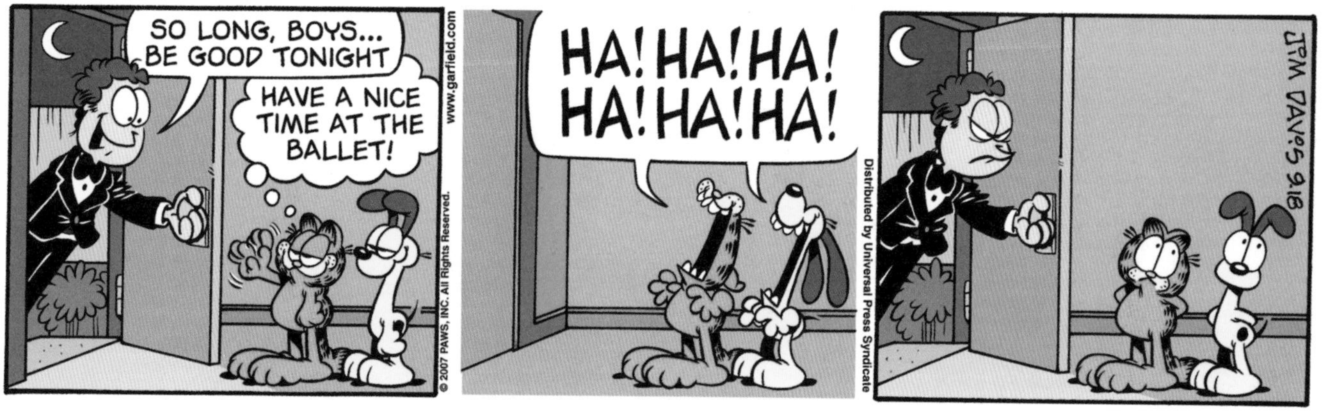
SO LONG, BOYS... BE GOOD TONIGHT
HAVE A NICE TIME AT THE BALLET!
HA! HA! HA! HA! HA! HA!
JIM DAVIS 9-18
© 2007 PAWS, INC. All Rights Reserved.
www.garfield.com
Distributed by Universal Press Syndicate

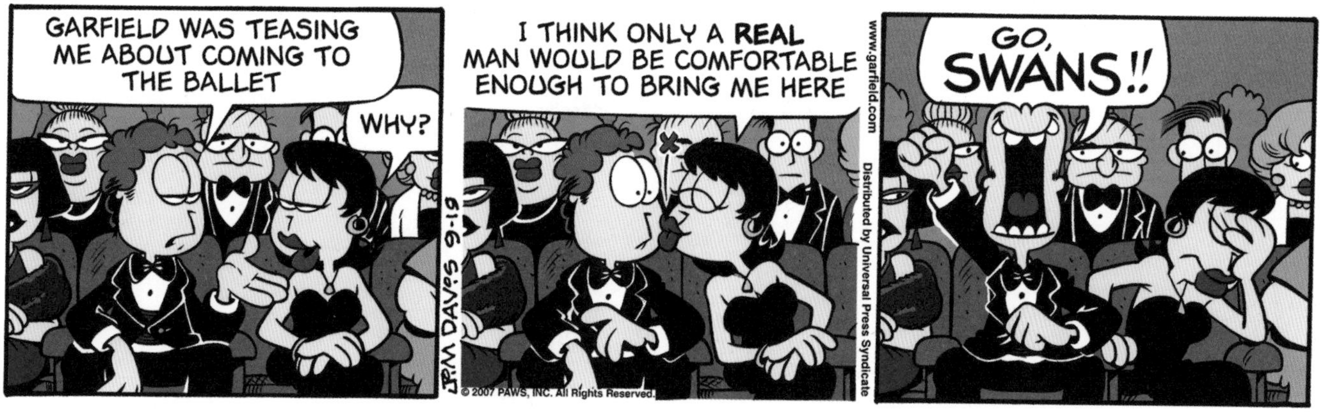
GARFIELD WAS TEASING ME ABOUT COMING TO THE BALLET
WHY?
I THINK ONLY A REAL MAN WOULD BE COMFORTABLE ENOUGH TO BRING ME HERE
GO, SWANS!!
JIM DAVIS 9-19
© 2007 PAWS, INC. All Rights Reserved.
www.garfield.com
Distributed by Universal Press Syndicate

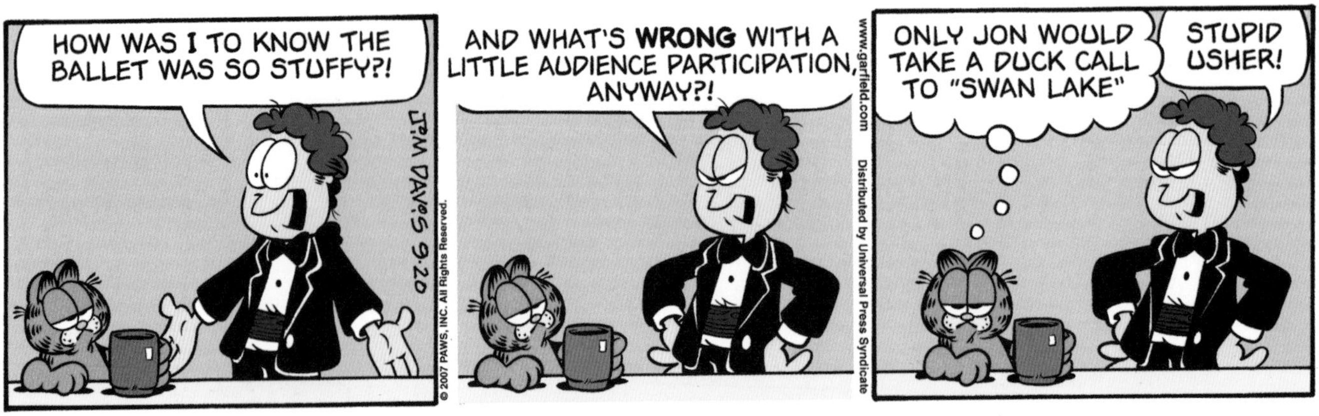
HOW WAS I TO KNOW THE BALLET WAS SO STUFFY?!
JIM DAVIS 9.20
© 2007 PAWS, INC. All Rights Reserved.
AND WHAT'S **WRONG** WITH A LITTLE AUDIENCE PARTICIPATION, ANYWAY?!
www.garfield.com Distributed by Universal Press Syndicate
ONLY JON WOULD TAKE A DUCK CALL TO "SWAN LAKE"
STUPID USHER!

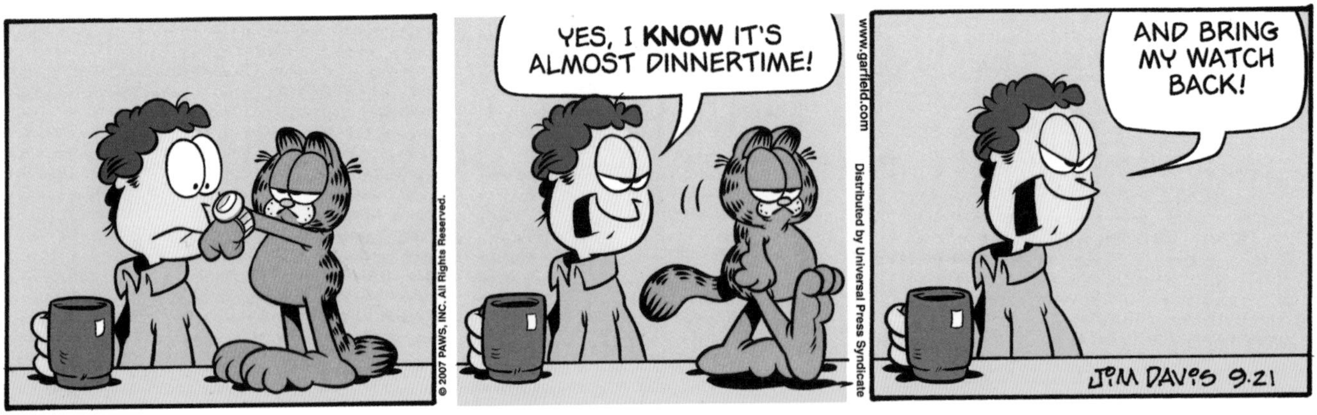
© 2007 PAWS, INC. All Rights Reserved.
YES, I **KNOW** IT'S ALMOST DINNERTIME!
www.garfield.com Distributed by Universal Press Syndicate
AND BRING MY WATCH BACK!
JIM DAVIS 9.21

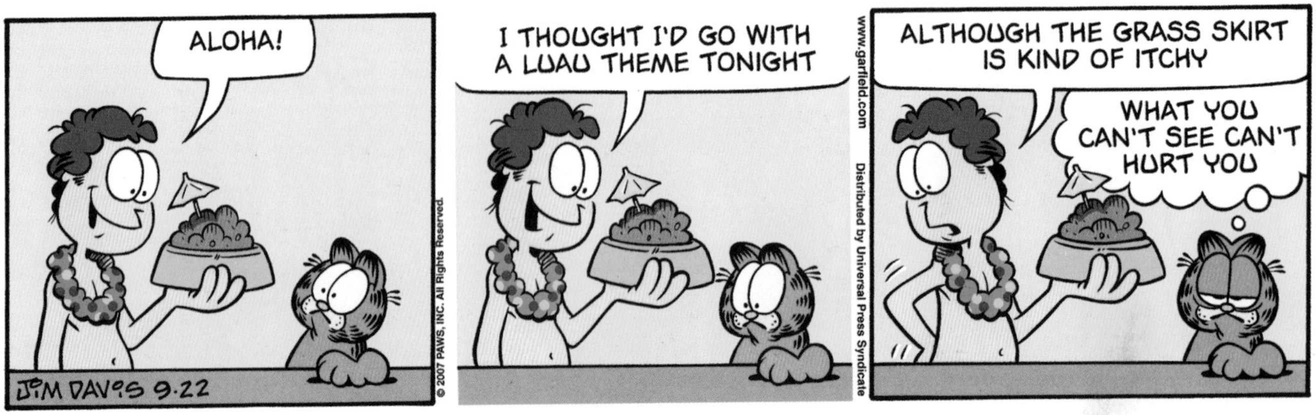
ALOHA!
JIM DAVIS 9.22
© 2007 PAWS, INC. All Rights Reserved.
I THOUGHT I'D GO WITH A LUAU THEME TONIGHT
www.garfield.com Distributed by Universal Press Syndicate
ALTHOUGH THE GRASS SKIRT IS KIND OF ITCHY
WHAT YOU CAN'T SEE CAN'T HURT YOU

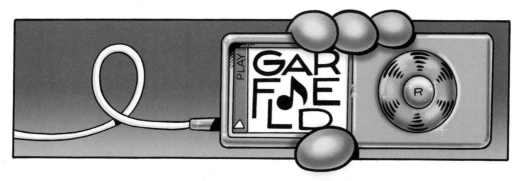

HEY! THAT SQUIRREL IS STEALING SEEDS FROM OUR BIRD FEEDER AGAIN!

SLAM!

Text GARFIELD to 26642 US ONLY

© 2001 PAWS, INC. All Rights Reserved.

SHOO! SHOO, YOU STUPID SQUIRREL!

SLAM!

JIM DAVIS 9-23

Distributed by Universal Press Syndicate

HEY! WHERE'S MY HAMBURGER?

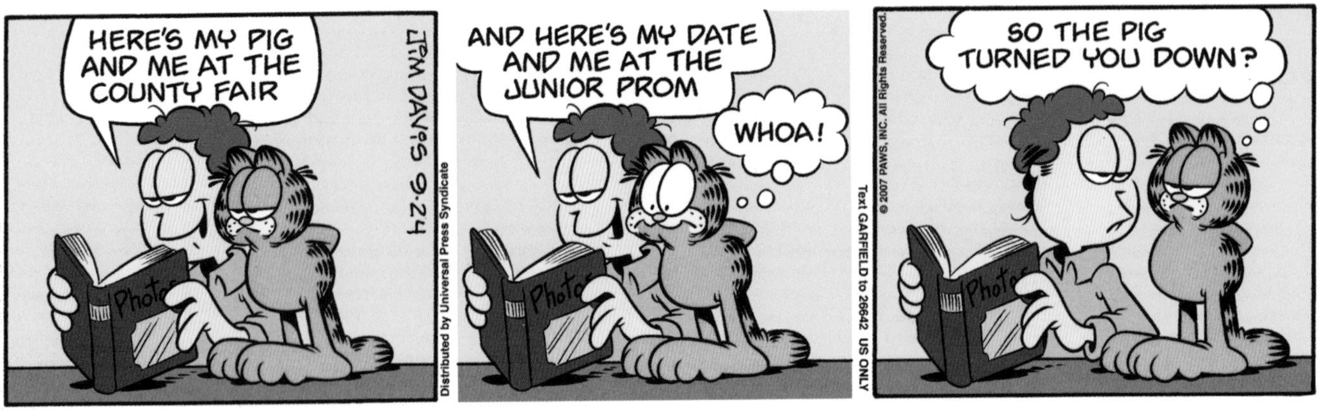
HERE'S MY PIG AND ME AT THE COUNTY FAIR
JIM DAVIS 9·24
Distributed by Universal Press Syndicate
AND HERE'S MY DATE AND ME AT THE JUNIOR PROM
WHOA!
Text GARFIELD to 26642 US ONLY
© 2007 PAWS, INC. All Rights Reserved.
SO THE PIG TURNED YOU DOWN?

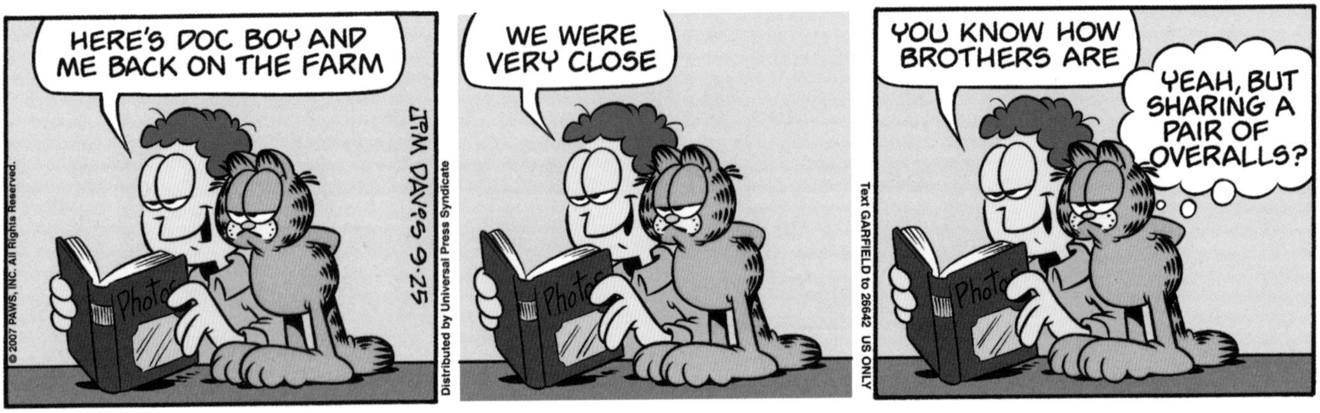
© 2007 PAWS, INC. All Rights Reserved.
HERE'S DOC BOY AND ME BACK ON THE FARM
JIM DAVIS 9·25
Distributed by Universal Press Syndicate
WE WERE VERY CLOSE
Text GARFIELD to 26642 US ONLY
YOU KNOW HOW BROTHERS ARE
YEAH, BUT SHARING A PAIR OF OVERALLS?

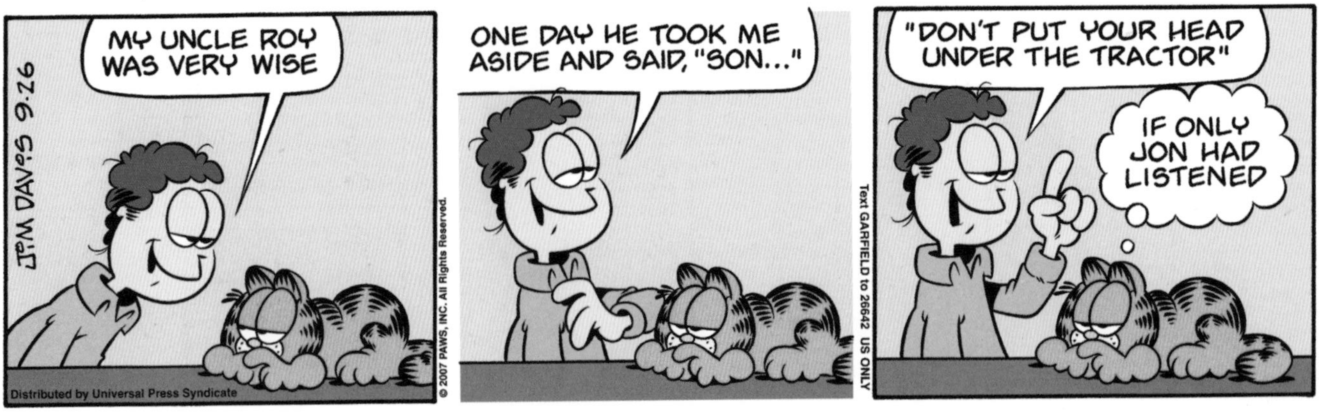
JIM DAVIS 9·26
MY UNCLE ROY WAS VERY WISE
Distributed by Universal Press Syndicate
© 2007 PAWS, INC. All Rights Reserved.
ONE DAY HE TOOK ME ASIDE AND SAID, "SON..."
Text GARFIELD to 26642 US ONLY
"DON'T PUT YOUR HEAD UNDER THE TRACTOR"
IF ONLY JON HAD LISTENED

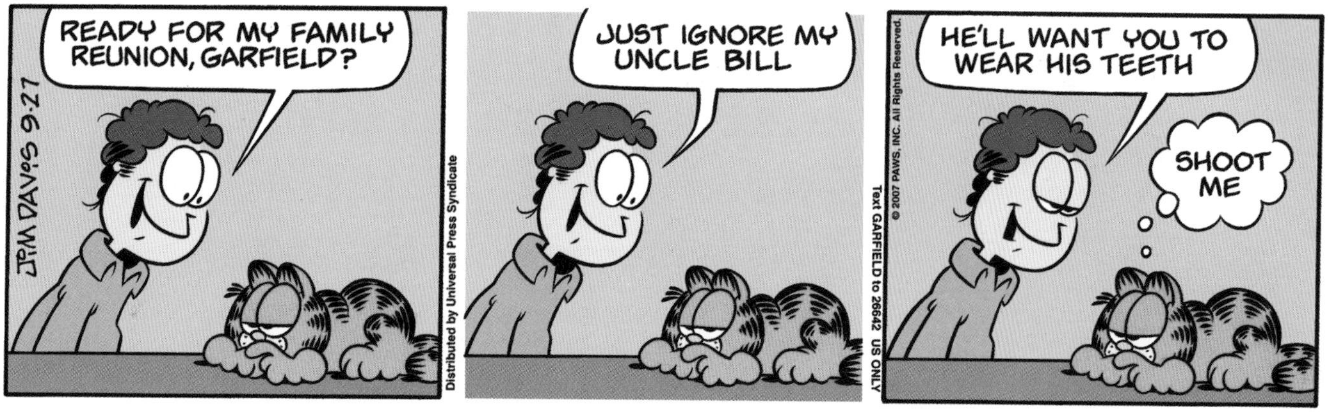
JPM DAVPS 9·27
READY FOR MY FAMILY REUNION, GARFIELD?
JUST IGNORE MY UNCLE BILL
HE'LL WANT YOU TO WEAR HIS TEETH
SHOOT ME
Distributed by Universal Press Syndicate
© 2007 PAWS, INC. All Rights Reserved.
Text GARFIELD to 26642 US ONLY

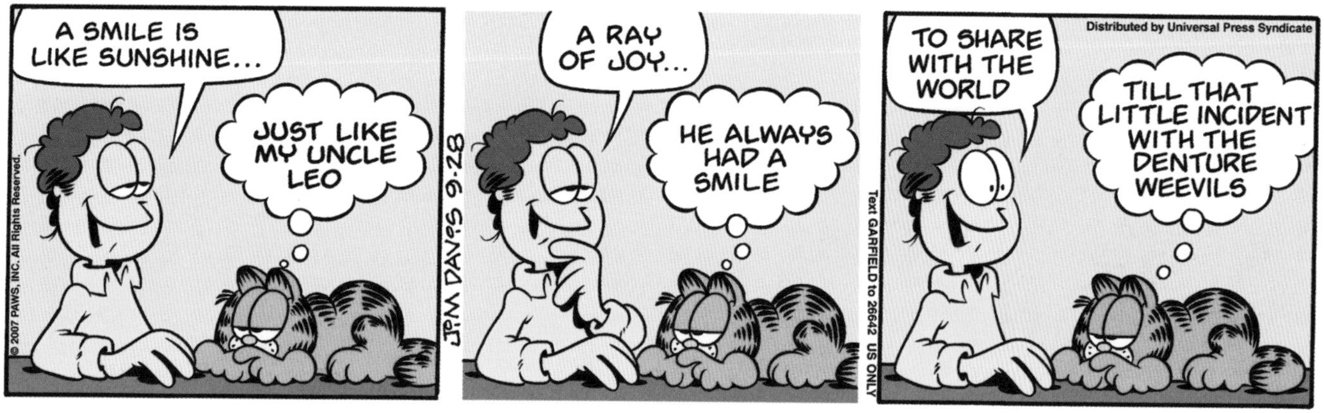
A SMILE IS LIKE SUNSHINE...
JUST LIKE MY UNCLE LEO
A RAY OF JOY...
HE ALWAYS HAD A SMILE
JPM DAVPS 9·28
TO SHARE WITH THE WORLD
TILL THAT LITTLE INCIDENT WITH THE DENTURE WEEVILS
© 2007 PAWS, INC. All Rights Reserved.
Text GARFIELD to 26642 US ONLY
Distributed by Universal Press Syndicate

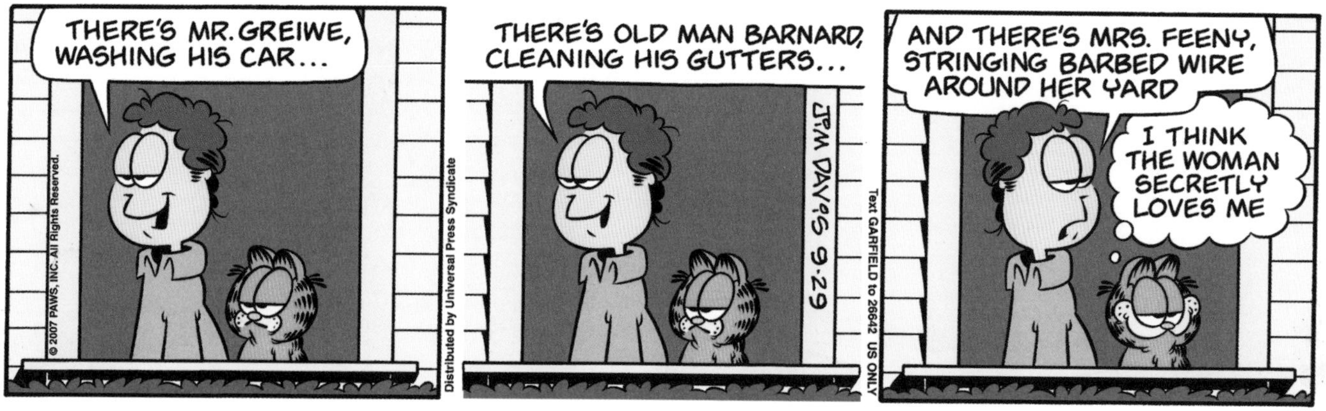
THERE'S MR. GREIWE, WASHING HIS CAR...
THERE'S OLD MAN BARNARD, CLEANING HIS GUTTERS...
JPM DAVPS 9·29
AND THERE'S MRS. FEENY, STRINGING BARBED WIRE AROUND HER YARD
I THINK THE WOMAN SECRETLY LOVES ME
© 2007 PAWS, INC. All Rights Reserved.
Distributed by Universal Press Syndicate
Text GARFIELD to 26642 US ONLY

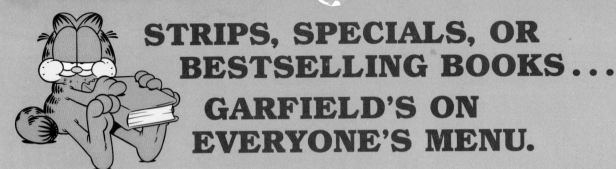

STRIPS, SPECIALS, OR BESTSELLING BOOKS . . . GARFIELD'S ON EVERYONE'S MENU.

Don't miss even one episode in the Tubby Tabby's hilarious series!

- GARFIELD AT LARGE ....(#1) 978-0-345-44382-3
- GARFIELD GAINS WEIGHT ....(#2) 978-0-345-44975-7
- GARFIELD BIGGER THAN LIFE ....(#3) 978-0-345-45027-2
- GARFIELD WEIGHS IN ....(#4) 978-0-345-45205-4
- GARFIELD TAKES THE CAKE ....(#5) 978-0-345-44978-8
- GARFIELD EATS HIS HEART OUT ....(#6) 978-0-345-46459-0
- GARFIELD SITS AROUND THE HOUSE ....(#7) 978-0-345-46463-7
- GARFIELD TIPS THE SCALES ....(#8) 978-0-345-46909-0
- GARFIELD LOSES HIS FEET ....(#9) 978-0-345-46467-5
- GARFIELD MAKES IT BIG ....(#10) 978-0-345-46468-2
- GARFIELD ROLLS ON ....(#11) 978-0-345-47561-9
- GARFIELD OUT TO LUNCH ....(#12) 978-0-345-47562-6
- GARFIELD FOOD FOR THOUGHT ....(#13) 978-0-345-47563-3
- GARFIELD SWALLOWS HIS PRIDE ....(#14) 978-0-345-91386-9
- GARFIELD WORLDWIDE ....(#15) 978-0-345-91754-6
- GARFIELD ROUNDS OUT ....(#16) 978-0-345-49169-5
- GARFIELD CHEWS THE FAT ....(#17) 978-0-345-49170-1
- GARFIELD GOES TO WAIST ....(#18) 978-0-345-49173-2
- GARFIELD HANGS OUT ....(#19) 978-0-345-49174-9
- GARFIELD TAKES UP SPACE ....(#20) 978-0-345-49178-7
- GARFIELD SAYS A MOUTHFUL ....(#21) 978-0-345-49179-4
- GARFIELD BY THE POUND ....(#22) 978-0-345-37579-7
- GARFIELD KEEPS HIS CHINS UP ....(#23) 978-0-345-37959-7
- GARFIELD TAKES HIS LICKS ....(#24) 978-0-345-38170-5
- GARFIELD HITS THE BIG TIME ....(#25) 978-0-345-38332-7
- GARFIELD PULLS HIS WEIGHT ....(#26) 978-0-345-38666-3
- GARFIELD DISHES IT OUT ....(#27) 978-0-345-39287-9
- GARFIELD LIFE IN THE FAT LANE ....(#28) 978-0-345-39776-8
- GARFIELD TONS OF FUN ....(#29) 978-0-345-40386-5
- GARFIELD BIGGER AND BETTER ....(#30) 978-0-345-40770-2
- GARFIELD HAMS IT UP ....(#31) 978-0-345-41241-6
- GARFIELD THINKS BIG ....(#32) 978-0-345-41671-1
- GARFIELD THROWS HIS WEIGHT AROUND ....(#33) 978-0-345-42749-6
- GARFIELD LIFE TO THE FULLEST ....(#34) 978-0-345-43239-1
- GARFIELD FEEDS THE KITTY ....(#35) 978-0-345-43673-3
- GARFIELD HOGS THE SPOTLIGHT ....(#36) 978-0-345-43922-2
- GARFIELD BEEFS UP ....(#37) 978-0-345-44109-6
- GARFIELD GETS COOKIN' ....(#38) 978-0-345-44582-7
- GARFIELD EATS CROW ....(#39) 978-0-345-45201-6
- GARFIELD SURVIVAL OF THE FATTEST ....(#40) 978-0-345-46458-3
- GARFIELD OLDER AND WIDER ....(#41) 978-0-345-46462-0
- GARFIELD PIGS OUT ....(#42) 978-0-345-46466-8
- GARFIELD BLOTS OUT THE SUN ....(#43) 978-0-345-46615-0
- GARFIELD GOES BANANAS ....(#44) 978-0-345-91346-3
- GARFIELD LARGE & IN CHARGE ....(#45) 978-0-345-49172-5
- GARFIELD SPILLS THE BEANS ....(#46) 978-0-345-49177-0
- GARFIELD GETS HIS JUST DESSERTS ....(#47) 978-0-345-91387-6
- GARFIELD WILL EAT FOR FOOD ....(#48) 978-0-345-49176-3
- GARFIELD WEIGHS HIS OPTIONS ....(#49) 978-0-345-49181-7

DVD TIE-INS

- GARFIELD AS HIMSELF 978-0-345-47805-4
- GARFIELD HOLIDAY CELEBRATIONS 978-0-345-47930-3
- GARFIELD TRAVEL ADVENTURES 978-0-345-48087-3

AND DON'T MISS...

- GARFIELD AT 25: IN DOG YEARS I'D BE DEAD 978-0-345-45204-7
- GARFIELD'S JOKE ZONE/INSULTS 978-0-345-46263-3
- GARFIELD FAT CAT 3-PACK/ VOL. 1 978-0-345-46455-2
- GARFIELD FAT CAT 3-PACK/ VOL. 2 978-0-345-46465-1
- GARFIELD FAT CAT 3-PACK/ VOL. 3 978-0-345-48088-0
- GARFIELD FAT CAT 3-PACK/ VOL. 4 978-0-345-49171-8
- GARFIELD FAT CAT 3-PACK/ VOL. 5 978-0-345-49180-8
- GARFIELD FAT CAT 3-PACK/ VOL. 13 978-0-345-46460-6
- GARFIELD FAT CAT 3-PACK/ VOL. 14 978-0-345-49175-6
- SEASON'S EATINGS: A VERY MERRY GARFIELD CHRISTMAS 978-0-345-47560-2
- GARFIELD'S GUIDE TO EVERYTHING 978-0-345-46461-3
- ODIE UNLEASHED! 978-0-345-46464-4
- GARFIELD'S BOOK OF CAT NAMES 978-0-345-48516-8
- THE GARFIELD JOURNAL 978-0-345-46469-9
- LIGHTS, CAMERA, HAIRBALLS!: GARFIELD AT THE MOVIES 978-0-345-49134-3
- 30 YEARS OF LAUGHS AND LASAGNA 978-0-345-50379-4
- GARFIELD MINUS GARFIELD 978-0-345-51387-8
- GARFIELD FROM THE TRASH BIN 978-0-345-51881-1

New larger, full-color format! (titles #1–#21)